CONFLICT
IN THE
CRIMEA

CONFLICT
IN THE
CRIMEA

British Redcoats on the soil of Russia

by

D. S. Richards

Pen & Sword
MILITARY

First published in Great Britain in 2006 by
Pen & Sword Military
an imprint of
Pen & Sword Books Ltd
47 Church Street
Barnsley
South Yorkshire
S70 2AS

Copyright © D.S. Richards, 2006
ISBN 1 84415 343 6

Typeset in Sabon by Mac Style, Nafferton, E. Yorkshire
Printed and bound in England by CPI UK.

For a complete list of Pen & Sword titles please contact
PEN & SWORD BOOKS LIMITED
47 Church Street, Barnsley, South Yorkshire, S70 2AS, England
E-mail: enquiries@pen-and-sword.co.uk
Website: www.pen-and-sword.co.uk

CONTENTS

To Walter Richards

DRAMATIS PERSONAE

Sister Mary Aloysius	Volunteer Nurse
Lady Alicia Blackwood	Volunteer Nurse
Lieutenant W.A. Braybrooke	95 Regiment of Foot
Lieutenant Hon. Somerset J.G. Calthorpe	Headquarters Staff
Lieutenant George Carmichael	95 Regiment of Foot
Lieutenant Hon. Henry Hugh Clifford	1st Battalion Rifle Brigade
Cornet George Clowes	8 Hussars
Lieutenant F. Curtis	46 Regiment of Foot
Lieutenant George Frederick Dallas	46 Regiment of Foot
Mrs Henry Duberly	Wife of an officer in the 8 Hussars
Captain Nicholas Dunscombe	46 Regiment of Foot
Captain Arthur Maxwell Earle	57 Regiment of Foot
Trumpeter Robert Stuart Farquharson	4 Queen's Own Light Dragoons
Mr Roger Fenton	War Photographer
Sergeant Major Henry Franks	5 Dragoon Guards
Lieutenant Richard Temple Godman	5 Dragoon Guards
Sergeant Major Timothy Gowing	7 Royal Fusiliers
Captain Bruce Hamley	Royal Artillery
Captain Robert Hodasevich	2 Chasseur Brigade
Captain John Hume	55 Regiment of Foot
Lieutenant Colonel Atwell Lake	ADC to General Williams
Sergeant Albert Mitchell	13 Hussars
Mr A. Money	Non Combatant
Lieutenant Frederick Morgan	1st Battalion Rifle Brigade
Major Reynell Pack	7 Royal Fusiliers
Lieutenant George Shuldham Peard	20 Regiment of Foot

vii

PREFACE

Waterloo had been the last act in the Napoleonic War and for the next forty years peace reigned in Europe, but on 28 March 1854 Britain found herself once again involved in conflict with a powerful European nation.

A petty dispute over the custody of the various churches and shrines in Jerusalem and Bethlehem grew into a major political crisis when on 3 May 1853, Prince Menschikoff presented an ultimatum on behalf of the Tsar, to the Sultan of Turkey demanding the acceptance of a Russian protectorate over all Greek subjects in the Ottoman Empire. Britain and France felt bound to lend their support to the Ottomans in order to preserve the balance of power, with Britain in particular, concerned that communication with India might be under threat should the Russians gain entry to the eastern Mediterranean for their Black Sea Fleet. From that point war was inevitable and for the first time in as many years as most people could remember, Britons and Frenchmen found themselves standing side by side as allies against a common enemy. A move which was greeted with enthusiasm on both sides of the Channel.

The first eight months of the war, in spite of two major victories, proved to be something of a testing period to the military and political bodies of Victorian Britain. Encouraged by cheap and efficient postal services, uncensored letters from serving soldiers in the field soon made the general public aware that with the collapse of the commissariat and the inefficiency of the General Staff, the troops were suffering appalling hardships exposed as they were to a Russian winter in barely adequate clothing and only the shelter of a canvas tent. The introduction of the new electric telegraph had made it easy for newspaper correspondents such as William Howard Russell to furnish reports, highly critical of the authorities, to their readers in a

ix

matter of hours. The outrage and growing concern of the public was eventually to bring about the collapse of the Aberdeen government and lead to a much improved hospital system and better conditions for the rank and file.

As in previous works it has been my practice to make extensive use of the comments and experiences of the men and women engaged in the conflict in the belief that the contents of their letters and diaries not only add to the interest of the narrative, but serve to illustrate the horror of nineteenth century warfare in a far more effective way. The fact that victory was ultimately achieved, albeit in large measure by the French, was due to the bravery and perseverance of the junior officers and men, rather than the skills of the generals. This is readily apparent from the observations made in those very same letters.

In acknowledging the assistance I have received from many sources, I would particularly like to thank Major C.D. Robins OBE, FRHistS for permission to include a number of observations made by Captain Dunscombe, in the book *Captain Dunscombe's Diary* published by Withycut House in 2003, and Mr Henry Alban Davies for his permission to include a number of comments made by Captain Dallas in the book *Eyewitness in the Crimea* published by Greenhill Books in 2001 – both excellent publications which graphically record the discomfort and danger faced by the combatants in the campaigns of that war.

I should also like to express my thanks for the help afforded me by the staff of the National Army Museum at Chelsea, without whose excellent records and research facilities, this work would never have been completed. My thanks also for their permission to include the illustrations and maps so essential to a military history. I would also like to express my appreciation to Susan Econicoff for her assistance in preparing this work for publication.

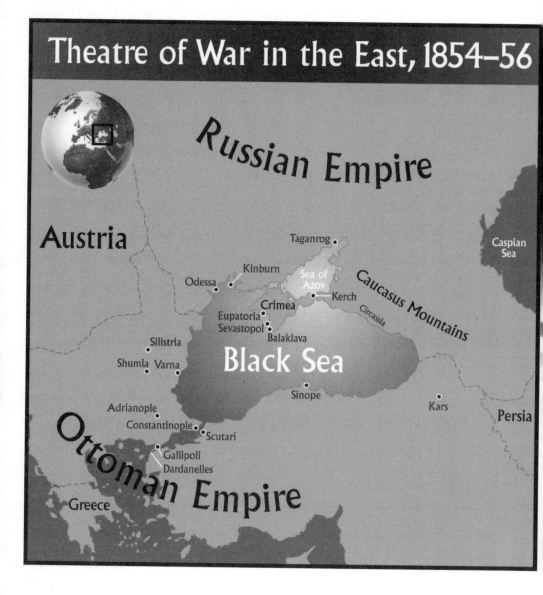

Theatre of War in the East, 1854–56

Russian Empire

Austria

Caspian Sea

Taganrog

Kinburn

Odessa

Sea of Azov

Kerch

Caucasus Mountains

Crimea

Eupatoria

Sevastopol

Balaklava

Circassia

Silistria

Shumla   Varna

Black Sea

Sinope

Kars

Persia

Adrianople

Constantinople

Scutari

Gallipoli

Dardanelles

Ottoman Empire

Greece

Chapter One

THE DRIFT TO WAR

Following the overthrow of Napoleon Bonaparte, the people of Europe and Asia had enjoyed several decades of peaceful coexistence, but that tranquil period was about to come to an end when, in November 1853, Russia sought to expand its empire by applying pressure on Turkey, a nation thought by Tsar Nicholas too feeble to resist his demands for a protectorate over all Greek Orthodox subjects in what had become a rapidly shrinking Ottoman Empire which included the Balkans, most of Hungary and, at one time, part of the Ukraine.

Twenty-five years earlier, Russia had gained territory in the Caucasus and the mouth of the Danube from the Turks after supporting the Orthodox Greeks in their battle for independence from Turkish control, and Tsar Nicholas was confident that further pressure on Turkey would result in Russia gaining control of the Dardanelle Straits and with it, maritime access to the Mediterranean for its Black Sea fleet.

Like many similar disputes, that between Russia and Turkey had its beginnings in a long standing religious controversy. In 1453 when Constantinople or Byzantium as it was then known, fell to the Turks, the Moslem religion was in the ascendancy and the position of the Christians in territories controlled by the Turks, became difficult if not hazardous. In later years as Ottoman power declined, increasing numbers of Christians began to visit the Holy Places in Palestine including the Sepulchre in Jerusalem, the care of which was shared between the Roman Catholic Church and the Greek Orthodox Church.

1

In 1740, a treaty signed between the French government and the Sultan of Turkey gave the Catholic Church 'sovereign authority' over the Holy Land and in recognition, a silver star, embellished with the royal arms of France, was erected over the alleged site of Christ's birthplace in Bethlehem by the Franciscan friars who considered themselves the rightful custodians of the shrine. It mattered not that Catholics living in the area were very much in the minority, greatly outnumbered by worshipers of the Coptic and Orthodox churches.

In 1852 Napoleon III created outrage among the rival Christian churches when he won a concession from the Sultan which allowed him to deliver the keys of the Church of the Nativity in Bethlehem into the custody of the French clergy. Matters came to a head the following year with the arrival in Constantinople of the Tsar's envoy, Prince Alexander Menschikoff, to demand of the Sultan that all concessions to the Catholic Church be withdrawn, and that a Russian protectorate be recognized over all the Orthodox subjects in the Ottoman Empire. In return, the envoy was authorized to make the offer of a defensive treaty should the Sultan feel threatened by the French for meeting Russia's demands. The Sultan Abdul Mejid however, believing he had the support of the British and French governments, refused to acknowledge what amounted to an ultimatum from St Petersburg, and on 18 May the Russian embassy was evacuated and Menschikoff set sail for Odessa three days later.

On 2 July Tsar Nicholas ordered his Southern army Corps to cross the River Proth in the Danube plain and occupy the two former Turkish territories of Wallachia and Moldavia; a move which greatly alarmed a British government already nervous of the growing power of the Black Sea Fleet and the threat which Russian access to the Mediterranean would pose to the sea route to India. The Foreign Secretary Lord Clarendon reacted immediately by authorizing the dispatch of a squadron of six warships to Besika Bay at the mouth of the Dardanelles. Alarm bells were also sounded in France and Austria who, like Britain, were opposed to any expansion of Russia's influence in the Balkans.

On 9 October the Porte – the Imperial Court in Constantinople – emboldened by the knowledge that ships of the Royal Navy were already in Turkish waters, notified St Petersburg that unless

Russian forces vacated Wallachia and Moldavia within fourteen days, a state of war would exist between Turkey and Russia. No such assurance was given and twenty days later the Sultan's troops crossed the Danube into Wallachia to begin a series of skirmishes which ended with the Russian forces withdrawing in the direction of Bucharest.

Britain was reluctant to intervene but Napoleon III saw it as an opportunity to regain the international influence his country had lost after Waterloo. A Russian suspicion that the West was actively seeking a confrontation was well founded, for on 27 November Britain and France concluded a defensive alliance with Turkey. Three days later, Russia's Black Sea Fleet effectively demonstrated its strength by achieving a stunning victory at Sinope, a harbour on the Turkish Black Sea coast less than 200 miles from the main Russian naval base of Sevastopol. In an engagement lasting less than two hours, a flotilla of seven frigates, three corvettes, two screw driven steamers and a number of transports were totally destroyed by the Russians resulting in the deaths of almost 4,000 Turkish sailors. The action, whilst of short duration, had ended in disaster for the Turks for the fires from the burning transports had quickly spread to the harbour buildings and the damage to the port was devastating. One British registered ship was sunk together with the entire Turkish fleet. The only vessel left untouched was a Turkish man-of-war in the process of completion on the stocks. A year later, Doctor Humphrey Sandwith on his way from Constantinople to Kars, called at Sinope, and was not impressed. In his opinion it was 'a miserable little sea port where the wrecks of burned and sunken vessels were still visible'.

The Tsar ordered a public celebration but news of this Turkish naval disaster led to outrage in Paris and London, motivated perhaps by feelings of humiliation that their ships in the Dardanelles had been too late to prevent it. At a Cabinet meeting on 22 December, Lord Aberdeen the Prime Minister, was persuaded that war with Russia was now inevitable and Queen Victoria who, days before, had doubted whether Turkish independence was worth going to war for, now agreed with the view put forward by Lord Palmerston the Home Secretary, that Sinope 'was a stain on British honour and that something had to be done'. Little attention was given to the fact that Russia was at war and had every reason to regard the Turkish ships as legitimate targets, since the transports were about to sail for the Caucasian Front with troops and war material.

Diplomatic relations between Russia and Britain and France, and to a lesser degree, Austria and Prussia, had been strained almost to breaking point, but hope of a solution to the crisis was not abandoned despite the threat to Russia of an allied naval force in the eastern Mediterranean. The decision of the Admiralty to detach a squadron commanded by Admiral Dundas to prevent Russian warships from entering the Black Sea was undoubtedly a provocation but the Admiralty considered it unlikely that the Russians would risk a naval engagement and both the British and French admirals were instructed to open fire only as a last resort. The British ambassador in St Petersburg however, was dismayed by the move. According to Sir George Hamilton Seymour: 'Britain and France are in no position to dispatch troops to the Principalities without Prussian and Austrian support. Furthermore, it was a provocation which might pressure Nicholas into a declaration of war.'

On 12 January 1854, Admiral Dundas received his orders. His squadron was to sail into the Black Sea and ensure that any Russian naval vessel found there returned to Sevastopol.

It was a move which reinforced St Petersburg's belief that Britain and France were determined to safeguard the passage of Turkish ships supplying men and material to the Caucasus, but naval strength alone was not enough to contain events in the Balkans, and Britain's small army was woefully unprepared for an outbreak of hostilities with Russia. There were less than 45,000 troops available in Britain for service overseas and that army, small as it was, had no appreciable logistical support or effective commissariat.

It had been many years since Wellington's superb Peninsula army had been employed against the French and recruitment now relied mainly upon social misfits, the ranks of the unemployed and, to some extent, the criminal element of society. Drink was certainly a major problem, although, as Lieutenant Henry Clifford was at pains to point out, some allowance should be made in the case of the private soldier. 'You must not look upon the soldier as a responsible agent, for he is not able to take care of himself. Give him one farthing more than he really wants, and he gives way to his brutal propensities and immediately gets drunk.'

4

These deficiencies were not restricted to the suitability of volunteers, for the neglect and mismanagement of the army which followed the end of the Napoleonic years could be attributed to government economies and the Secretary of War, who was responsible for all things pertaining to the army. The Commissariat responsible for feeding the troops abroad, was directed by the Treasury, whilst all other aspects of military equipment including weapons, was accountable to a politician known as the Master General of Ordnance.

Flogging was still a punishment meted out at the discretion of the commanding officer and although the maximum number of strokes had been reduced to fifty in 1846, it was not until 1881 that flogging would be abolished. The life of an ordinary soldier, even without the danger and discomfort associated with campaigning, was miserable in the extreme. He enlisted for twenty-one years at the end of which, assuming that he was still alive, he would be rewarded with a small pension dependent on his record of behaviour, of a shilling a day. His daily ration of one pound of bread and three-quarters of a pound of meat, boiled in one of the two large cooking pots provided to each company, was occasionally changed to salt pork of dubious quality, and the pay of one shilling a day subject to deductions for various items, was hardly an inducement to enlist. The main source of recruitment, as in previous years, rested with the Irish, the agricultural labourer and to a lesser extent, the petty criminal.

The War Office policy of allowing gentlemen to purchase commissions had not changed since Wellington's time, consequently junior officers were almost exclusively the younger sons of families with wealth and influence, whose main interest tended to focus on riding to hounds rather than with regimental affairs. Field Marshal Viscount Wolseley as he then was, in drawing attention to the difficulties the army found itself in, wrote: 'Almost all our officers at that time were uneducated as soldiers, and many of those placed upon the staff at the beginning of the war were absolutely unfit for the position they had secured through family or political interest. There were of course, a few brilliant exceptions, but they made the incompetence of the many all the more remarkable.'

The injustices of the purchase system had been raised in the Commons by Sir de Lacy Evans in what he labelled: '... a most oppressive usury, and in its essence such a game of chance as should long before have brought it under the purlieus of the Gaming Acts. For to all intents and purpose an officer invested a sum of money for the privilege of serving the King.' The practice was too deep rooted however for his protest to gain the support of fellow members, but it was certainly an expensive investment for the would be purchaser. The rank of lieutenant colonel could cost as much as £4,400 and would yield no more than £365 per annum, subject to tax and regimental expenses. Even the rank of lieutenant could not be bought for less than £1,000 with a return of just £114 p.a. Only by selling his commission would the officer be able to recoup his investment and then without interest. Should he die on the battlefield, the entire sum would be forfeit, for the next in line would step into what was termed the 'death vacancy'. It was to be 1871 before the abuses of the purchase system were remedied.

It was no easy task for the War Office to select experienced officers young enough for the demanding duty of divisional command, and only one was of a suitable age. The leadership qualities of the thirty-five year-old Duke of Cambridge, a cousin of the Queen, who was to be given the 1st Division, had yet to be tested under the stress of battle, but he was popular and had the reputation of being industrious. Lord Lucan, fifty-four years of age, who had been on half pay since leaving the army in 1837, was given overall command of the Cavalry Division despite being unfamiliar with modern drill and the words of command. But he was conscientious and hard working, and a further point in his favour was the fact that he was familiar with the geography of the Balkans, an advantage since the few maps possessed by the army were rudimentary to say the least. His brother-in-law, the Earl of Cardigan, commanded the Light Brigade, and great was the animosity which existed between them.

Among the more able and experienced of the divisional generals selected, was the Irish born sixty-seven year-old commander of the 2nd Division, Sir George de Lacy Evans who had fought in the Peninsula, India and America. He also had been on half pay, since 1818. Commanding the 3rd Division was the lesser known figure of Sir Richard England, born in Canada in 1793. He had seen service in the Walcheren campaign, in Afghanistan and had fought in the Kaffir Wars. The 4th Division was given to sixty year-old

Sir George Cathcart, whose father had once been the British ambassador in St Petersburg. Sir George's career had been militaristic, if undistinguished, from the age of fifteen when his father had bought him a cornetcy in the Life Guards. Nevertheless he now found himself in the position of overall command in the event of the death of the Commander-in-Chief.

Finally, command of the Light Division was given to perhaps the most unpopular man in the British army, Sir George Brown – 'an old imbecile bully' one of his junior officers called him. That he was a martinet could not be denied. He was a firm advocate of flogging and a convinced opponent of all who supported army reform. He had, however, distinguished himself at Corunna and his courage was never in question.

As the year 1854 drew near, political circles on both sides of the Channel became convinced that a Russian spring offensive would be launched across the Danube which would overwhelm the Turkish army, leading to much thought being given as to what assistance could be given to the Turks in the defence of Constantinople and the Dardanelle Straits.

The main base for the Russian Black Sea fleet was Sevastopol and the Admiralty was well aware that, to ensure the Royal Navy's command of the Black Sea, it would be necessary for the military to take it at an early stage in the war. On 6 January, the 28-gun screw driven frigate *Retribution* commanded by Captain Drummond, steamed into Sevastopol Bay with orders to evacuate the Consul and take the vessel as close to the Black Sea port as he dared with the object of surveying the port's defences. The Consul had already departed but that did not prevent Drummond from carrying out his other duty despite being fired on from the fort.

On his return, his report to the Admiralty was far from encouraging. He considered Sevastopol to be impregnable to any attack from the sea, defended as it was by some 300 shore based guns and the possibility of broadsides from three lines of warships. In his opinion the only form of attack which was at all feasible, lay in a ground based operation from north of the citadel, with an army at least equal in strength to that of the Russians, with the addition of numerous batteries of large calibre artillery.

Despite exhaustive diplomatic activity, particularly by Austria, to resolve the problem of Russia's designs on the Ottoman Empire, it was becoming increasingly difficult to halt the drift to war. St Petersburg did little to conceal its rage at the deployment of the Royal Navy in the Black Sea, an act which it regarded as a direct provocation to its own fleet. In spite of a threat from Prince Menschikoff to break off diplomatic relations, Britain remained steadfast in the face of repeated demands for the withdrawal of Admiral Dundas's squadron, the refusal of which resulted in the Russian ambassador in London being ordered home on 6 February followed, shortly afterwards, by the French and British ambassadors in St Petersburg.

With the suspension of diplomatic relations, and the threat of war, steps were taken to appoint a commander for the expeditionary force now preparing for the Dardanelles. The choice was limited, but it ultimately fell upon sixty-six year-old Lord Raglan, who had served as Wellington's aide in the Peninsula some forty years before, but he was reputed to be a sound tactician with the added ability to speak fluent French. On 21 February his appointment was confirmed and a decision was taken, in the build up of the expeditionary force, to transfer 10,000 troops to Malta.

Across the Channel similar moves were afoot although there was some controversy over the appointment of Leroy de Saint Arnaud whose reputation rested solely upon his experience with the Foreign Legion in Algeria. He was later found to be suffering from terminal cancer and it was suspected that his promotion had been due to political manoeuvring.

Until the ice broke up in the Baltic, ships of the Royal Navy were unable to operate and for that reason there had been, as yet, no formal declaration of war, but on 27 February 1854 Lord Clarendon, the Foreign Secretary, sent an unequivocal message to his Russian opposite number, that unless Russian forces were withdrawn from the Principalities by the end of April, a state of war would exist between the two countries. It was closely followed by a similar ultimatum from the French. Tsar Nicholas chose not to reply. From that moment on the die was cast, there could now be no turning back from the brink.

Conscious of the need to raise revenue to meet the inevitable expense of a war in Europe, Gladstone increased income tax from 7d to 1s 2d in the pound on 6 March, explaining to the House that, '... the expenses of War are a moral check, which it has pleased the Almighty to impose upon the ambition and

8

lust of conquest that are inherent in so many nations'. Despite his justification for the increase, it came as no surprise to find that it was less than popular with the majority of the British public.

Six days later, an alliance was signed between Britain, France and the Turks, to be followed on 27 March by a declaration of war on Russia by Britain and France. Preparations for an expeditionary force had been under way for some time and as early as 14 February crowds had cheered the 1st Battalion Coldstream Guards as they left their barracks in Trafalgar Square for Waterloo station, en route to the transports waiting in Southampton Water. They were joined later by other Guards regiments, the 3rd Battalion Grenadiers and the 1st Battalion Scots Guards marching to the accompaniment of fife and drum which greatly affected the jubilant crowds lining the route.

'The men appeared to be in the highest of spirits,' reported *The Times*, 'and marched cheerfully along to the familiar air of "The Girl I Left Behind Me".' A week later they were on the high seas bound for Malta to be followed by the Scots Fusiliers and the 2nd Battalion of the Rifle Brigade. Eventually the Eastern Mediterranean was to see a massive build up of both French and British troops including the Cavalry Division and Field Artillery.

The war saw a remarkable change of attitude in the public's view of the British army. Four generations of peace had bred a general contempt for the ordinary redcoat. Timothy Gowing wrote: '... they were looked upon as being useless and expensive ornaments. But suddenly a change came over the people, and every sight of the Queen's uniform called forth emotions of enthusiasm from all conditions of men.'

But as he, in company with the Royal Fusiliers, marched through the streets to the dockyard at Portsmouth, Gowing expressed an opinion which at the time, may not have been widely shared by his comrades or the general public: 'We were going out to defend a rotten cause, a race that almost every Christian despises. However, as soldiers we had nothing to do with politics.'

For many of the redcoats making their first sea voyage to the Mediterranean it was hardly a memorable one. Whilst the officers' and senior NCOs' accommodation was reasonably comfortable, the same could not be said for that of the ordinary soldier. As Sergeant Major Henry Franks pointed out: '... as for the privates, well, I am afraid I must admit that the accommodation was not all that could be desired. About half of the men were supposed to be 'on Guard' each night, and the remainder got themselves stowed away in various places, but they seemed quite contented and made no complaint ...' Their time at sea varied according to whether the ship was steam driven or relied upon the wind. The slower sailing vessels took up to two months to reach Turkey and, in the often turbulent seas, the cavalry regiments suffered the greatest hardships. Cornet George Clowes writing to his father on 15 May described his passage through the Bay of Biscay as the most miserable he had ever experienced: 'Everybody was dreadfully sick in all directions, obliged to stay below with the horses who could not keep their legs and were down on the ground in heaps, lashing out at each other mad with fright and screaming like children.' Overall, it was estimated that more than 150 horses were lost to the cavalry. A crippling blow to regiments already desperately short of mounts.

The notification that Britain and France were at war with Russia did not reach Rear Admiral Sir James Dundas until 9 April, whilst the French Admiral Hamelin waited a further eight days before receiving notice of his country's decision. Eventually six British, and three French vessels left the straits near Varna for Odessa, a city of 100,000 situated between the Dnieper and the Dricestar, dropping anchor in the bay on 21 April. The purpose was to seek the release of all British and French ships in the port and failing this, to destroy the Imperial Mole but to avoid firing on the town or the mass of neutral shipping adjacent to the Quarantine Mole – a sarcastic reference to the practice of the port authorities in refusing foreign crews to disembark even though their vessels might spend many weeks at anchor.

That afternoon, the first shots in the war were fired when HMS *Furious* was engaged by the shore batteries following a refusal of the city's governor to comply with the demand to release allied shipping. Retaliation was both swift and effective. Two screw vessels from each of the British and French squadrons followed each other around in a wide circle of the bay as their guns opened fire on the Russian ships in the harbour and the buildings along the mole. Four other ships, *Furious*, *Terrible*, *Retribution*, and *Mogoden* then joined in the exchange of gunfire and at the end of the action twelve hours later, several Russian warships had been sunk and a magazine on the Imperial Mole destroyed by rockets in an explosion which was heard several miles away. The allied fleet, satisfied with the damage they had inflicted, then left that part of the coast for Sevastopol. The defences there however were far stronger than those of Odessa, and when the Russian ships could not be tempted out of the harbour, it was not thought a wise move to risk vessels in what was, in all probability, a fruitless exercise.

Other coastal bombardments followed at intervals but little damage was inflicted and when Admiral Dundas was ordered by the Admiralty to enforce a blockade of the Black Sea, that too was unsuccessful since Dundas did not possess enough ships for anything like an effective naval blockade. The early months of 1854 had been notable only for minor naval engagements such as these, and Aberdeen's government was being subjected to increasing demands from prominent parliamentarians such as Viscount Palmerston and Lord John Russell, to increase the pressure on Russia's land forces. A plan of campaign had yet to be decided however, for Lord Raglan was having difficulty in selecting experienced senior officers for his staff. Lord de Ros, who combined the duties of Quartermaster General and Chief of Staff, proved to be unsuited to fill both positions and at the end of August was replaced by General Sir Richard Airey, who unwittingly caused a sensation when he attended his first staff meeting wearing a red flannel suit. To complete the staff appointments, Brigadier General James Escourt was given the post of Adjutant General. An efficient administrator, he nevertheless laboured under the disadvantage of never having gone to war or having disciplined an army.

The sixty-six year-old Lord Raglan himself, was not without critics, for there were those such as the Duke of Newcastle, who questioned his suitability as C.-in-C. of the British army not having previously commanded so much as a battalion in the field. The one point in his favour was the fact that he had served as an aide-de-camp under the guidance of the Duke of Wellington and had lost his right arm at Waterloo. Within three weeks of war being declared, Raglan found himself sailing for Turkey in command of the only army Britain possessed.

Intelligence from the Balkans suggested that the anticipated Russian spring offensive along the Danube, with Silistria and

11

Shumla being the principal objectives in an attempt to prevent the Black Sea port of Varna from being used by the British and French forces, could only be a matter of weeks away. Lord Raglan was concerned enough to consult his French counterpart on the action to be taken, but time was running out and, in the last week of March, Russian infantry crossed the Danube and by 5 April, Silistria was under siege.

Conscious of the urgent necessity for protecting Constantinople, the French acted promptly by sending two divisions to Gallipoli under the command of Generals Canrobert and Bosquet. British troops were not due to arrive until mid-April led by another veteran of the Peninsula War, with a low opinion of the French. Lieutenant General Sir George Brown was a recalcitrant Scot, loathed by his junior officers, but trusted by Lord Raglan and he was to prove his worth in the battles to come.

By the middle of May a substantial part of the British and French expeditionary force was assembled at Gallipoli and around the Dardanelles, and on the 18th at a meeting attended by Omar Pasha, Lord Raglan and the French Commander Leroy de Saint Arnaud, a decision was taken to deploy British and French troops along the lower Danube to aid the Turkish troops fighting in the Principalities. This agreement was soon broken however, for when the allied commanders returned to Scutari, the French General began to doubt the wisdom of the decision he had taken, protesting to Raglan that he lacked the cavalry and artillery he felt necessary for an adequate protection of the Turkish army's flanks.

To his credit, Lord Raglan was determined to honour his promise to Omar Pasha and to that end troops were even then sailing towards Varna. The British commander's resolve had the unexpected result of changing Saint Arnaud's mind, for on 10 June Colonel Hugh Rose, as chargé d'affaires, crossed the Bosporus bearing the welcome news that the French had decided in favour of concentrating the main body of their army in Bulgaria.

The Russians meanwhile, were experiencing difficulties of their own. They were becoming increasingly concerned at their lengthening lines of communication and Field Marshal Count Paskevitch, who was then conducting the siege of Silistria, was beset by fears that should he press his advance against the Danubian provinces too hard, Austria and even Prussia, might intervene on the side of Turkey.

The Tsar suffered from no such qualms, believing that the Austrian Emperor had not forgotten the support Russia had given him in 1849 to entertain such views, and he urged Paskevitch to maintain the siege come what may. 'If the Austrians treacherously attack us, you have only to engage them with 4 Corps and the Dragoons,' he told the Field Marshal, 'that will be quite enough for them.'

In spite of the Tsar's confidence, it was not going to be that easy, for Silistria in itself was a formidable obstacle to the Russian advance. Although under siege, its garrison of 12,000 was still able to bring in supplies and extra troops and Prince Mikhail Gorchakoff's artillery, when it opened a bombardment from the high ground to the south-west of the town, proved to be less than effective. Not only were the earthworks difficult to destroy, but the defences were manned by steadfast Turkish and Albanian troops commanded by two experienced British officers on secondment and, despite a major infantry assault at the end of May, the defenders refused to be dislodged. On 10 June, a shell from a Turkish gun exploded near Paskevitch and a group of staff officers, resulting in the Russian Field Marshal being carried from the field with a severe wound which eventually caused him to return to Warsaw. Command passed to Prince Gorchakoff and, led by him, the Russian forces became involved in a series of savage hand to hand encounters resulting in heavy casualties to each side. Nine days after Paskevitch had handed over command, a mine containing 8,000 pounds of explosives erupted under the main defensive works. The Ottoman defenders waited in expectation of a major assault but apart from artillery activity no other enemy action occurred. On the 22nd Gorchakoff received orders from the Tsar to lift the siege and cross the Danube. Leo Tolstoy who was there, noted that '...as soon as we left the various Bulgar villages that we were occupying, the Turks moved in and, except for the women young enough for a harem, massacred everyone they found there'. In fact the unexpected had occurred to cause the Russians to retire. The Austrian ambassador to St Petersburg had unwittingly saved Silistria by demanding that Russian forces withdraw from south of the Danube, and with the knowledge that Franz Joseph had ordered his army to the Transylvanian border, a furious Tsar Nicholas was left with little alternative but to comply. The Austrians, following behind the retreating Russians were careful not to make contact and it was to be 22 August before they entered Wallachia.

The British troops who had left their homeland to sail for Turkey, after three weeks at sea, found themselves in the totally different environment of the Dardanelles with Gallipoli 'filthy in the extreme'. Lord Raglan who had reached Varna on 24 April, spent no more than a day there before sailing up the Bosporus for Constantinople, which prompted Lieutenant Jocelyn Strange, when writing to his father, to comment: 'Lord Raglan of course does not let out anything to anyone as to future movements, so I dare say you know more about them at home than we do ...'

William Howard Russell, correspondent of *The Times*, was full of admiration for the French, who were the first to land:

> The French came first, and like all first comers, they were the best served. They, understand things much better than we do. The way in which they have provided for the soldiers is wonderful. They seem to have thought of everything, they have even brought a machine for roasting the coffee and grinding it ...

Lieutenant Braybrooke who had journeyed from Ceylon to join the British troops in Turkey, and who had arrived in Varna in August, was less than impressed by the appearance of the port: 'In all my life I never saw such a dusty, filthy, tumble-down place as Varna. Most of the villages and all of the pattahs of the towns of Ceylon, though dirty enough, are beautifully clean in comparison with this filthy hole.' It was a view shared by Captain John Hume, who looked upon Varna: '... as being a wretched place with very few shops. The French as their usual custom was, had appropriated the best part of the town ...'

The British and French troops bivouacked in the countryside were in good spirits for they had quickly discovered that fruit and vegetables were freely available, and the wooded hills provided plenty of game and kindling for their cooking pots. 'Never were tents pitched in a more lovely spot,' wrote the correspondent of *The Times*. 'When the morning sun had risen it was scarcely possible to imagine one so far from England.'

The cavalry regiments, after a tiresome fifteen mile trek, found themselves in an equally enchanting landscape which more than compensated Mrs Duberly for the discomfort of spending eight hours in the saddle: 'The heat was intense, the fatigue overwhelming; but the country – anything more beautiful I never saw. Vast plains, verdant hills covered with shrubs and flowers; a noble lake; and a road which was merely a cart track, winding through a luxuriant woodland country, across plains and through deep bosquets of brushwood.' Equally impressed was Lieutenant Braybrooke. 'I cannot say how much I admired the country between Varna and Kostenjie (seventeen miles from Varna), the scenery is very beautiful,' he wrote, 'extensive plains surrounded by gracefully formed mountains, which are covered with verdue to their very summits.'

Despite enjoying the scenery and the fruit to be obtained, the British troops around Varna, unlike the French, spent the first few nights without adequate protection from the weather due to the Commissariat lacking the necessary horses, mules and carts to transport tents and baggage from the ships across the bay. Left to their own devices many soldiers took advantage of the cheap local wine with the inevitable result that drunkenness became widespread, leading to outbreaks of ill discipline, with some excuse, thought Major Sterling of the Highland Brigade: 'Drink is the only Christian vice we have much chance of indulging in here, gluttony is out of the question; and there is not a woman visible, I suppose, nearer than Bucharest.' Unlike Major Sterling, William Russell, a correspondent of *The Times*, was horrified by what he saw:

The conduct of many of the men, French and English, seemed characterized by a recklessness verging on insanity. They might be seen lying drunk in the kennels, or in the ditches beside the roadside, under the blazing rays of the sun, covered with swarms of flies. Three or four of them would make a happy bargain with a Greek for a large basket of apricots, scarlet pumpkins, watermelons, greengages, and plums. They ate the luscious fruit until nought remained but a heap of peel, rind and stones, they then diluted the mess with raki or peach brandy, and would stagger home or to sleep as best they could. It was no wonder indeed that cholera throve and fattened among us.

Major Sterling had obviously not seen as much of the opposite sex as Lieutenant Henry Clifford, who was pleased to comment: 'I am afraid that the old Pashas with their 100 young wives are not over pleased with the appearance of so many young officers. The fact is the Turkish ladies are quite as fond of admiration as English or any other women, and like to be looked at better by a dashing handsome young officer with a fine uniform, than by an old gentleman with one foot in the grave.' Nigel Kingscote noted: 'How pretty the opposite sex were was difficult for the young officer to determine. The women all wear a white veil over their faces, and their loose gown is all one colour, generally a bright one, and yellow slippers; very picturesque indeed, though they all shuffle along as if their legs were tied.'

The allied ground forces had yet to be engaged but though there was widespread disappointment that the Russians no longer posed a threat to Constantinople, there was never a suggestion that the troops should be brought home from the Black Sea region. *The Times* led the clamour for a decisive blow to be struck against Russia in order to ensure what the paper termed 'a permanent peace'. And on 18 July the government made known its policy through a statement by Lord Clarendon. 'We are still of the opinion that the Crimea should be our objective and that we shall have done nothing until it is achieved.'

The humidity of the Bulgarian summer, combined with poor hygiene and a profound ignorance of the causes of those twin scourges of Victorian armies – cholera and dysentery – now threatened to make serious inroads in the strength of the allied regiments encamped around Varna, which was rapidly losing its attraction for many British soldiers. Henry Clifford wrote:

> The town is much the same kind of place as Gallipoli. Houses made of wood – the streets paved with stone and slanting to the centre, which forms a sort of large drain, into which is emptied all sorts of filth. In trying to get out of the way of a dead dog the other day, I found my foot on a dead rat. The streets are never cleaned in any way, so the stench beats anything I have ever smelt.

It was with a heartfelt sigh of relief that on 5 September the troops received an order to vacate the unhealthy valley for a new destination in the Crimea. Major Anthony Sterling informed his father:

> The order to the army to invade the Crimea is out. The fleet and transports rendezvous at Balchick Bay, some fifteen miles north of Varna from whence 900 sail of ships, great and small, will start in

a body for an unknown point of disembarkation. The infantry will land by Divisions, first the Light Division, and then the 1st, 2nd, 3rd and 4th. It is evident from the orders given that our leaders expect to land without any opposition.

Among those who bid a thankful farewell to Varna on the 7th, was Lieutenant Braybrooke. 'The wind is fair and the weather propitious, the vessels gliding along quietly and in good order look beautiful,' he wrote. Nine days later British and French troops made an unopposed landing on the beaches of Calamita Bay near the small town of Eupatoria some distance from Sevastopol. An explanation for disembarking the troops so far from the principal objective, was forthcoming from *The Times* correspondent:

> The one draw back to a successful landing on Russian soil was the fact that the High Command had no idea of the terrain or even where to disembark. After a reconnaissance of the Crimean coast it was decided that Eupatoria, 40 miles from Sebastopol, would in all probability be the best spot for a landing.

Before disembarking, the troops were reminded of the punishment associated with plundering. 'Our troops had very strict orders not to loot, but to pay for everything they took,' Captain Hume confirmed. 'The French, I heard, were not so particular, and I have no doubt we get credit for their plundering.'

In a letter to his father, Lieutenant the Hon. Jocelyn Strange, wrote:

> We were all thankful to leave that horrid place, Varna, but leave behind many poor fellows. You may imagine what we have suffered from our sickness when I tell you that we land on the Crimea and go into action 642 bayonets out of 4,000 men we brought from England. The Coldstreams have been still more unfortunate, and they go into action without a single captain, and with only two ensigns.

The huge number of ships which eventually anchored off the coast may have astonished the local population, but the fact that the landing was uneventful was small comfort to the redcoats. Strange's letter continued:

We landed without opposition the day before yesterday (14 September) with nothing but what we carry on our backs. The first night it rained tremendously and we bivouacked on a ploughed field. It was my first experience of real hardship and it was not pleasant ... I have not washed or had my clothes off for three days, as we have only just water enough for drinking.

This view was echoed by William Russell:

Few of those who were with the expedition will forget the night of the 14th September. No tents had been sent on shore. Towards night the sky looked very black and lowering, the wind rose, and the rain fell in torrents. The showers increased about midnight, and early in the morning fell in drenching sheets which pierced through the blankets and greatcoats of the homeless and tent-less soldiers – no fire to cheer them, no hot grog, and the prospect of no breakfast.

Not all the troops suffered so, as Corporal Gowing noted when landing with the French at Old Fort:

The first night in the Crimea was a night long to be remembered by those who were there. It came on to rain in torrents, while the wind blew a perfect hurricane, and all from the commanders down to the drummer boys, had to stand and take it as it came. And the rain did fall, only as it does in the tropics. We looked next morning like a lot of drowned rats. The French had their little tents with them, and so had the small detachment of Turks who were with us, but there was not a single tent for the English army. Thousands of Britain's sons, who had come to fight for Queen and Country, were thrown ashore, as it were, without shelter of any kind.

Now that the allied army was ashore and advancing inland, the troops soon discovered that the landscape differed markedly from the rich vegetation of the Bulgarian coast. It was barren and completely devoid of shelter. As the light drizzle of the afternoon changed to a steady downpour, soaking the troops in the open, adding to their misery was the total absence of dry tinder or brushwood to boil a kettle or cook a meal.

The next day saw an improvement in the weather and a chaotic array of tents, stores and munitions began to accumulate on the beach, awaiting the arrival of bullock wagons hired from the local community. Little thought was given to solving the problem of attending to the sick, many of whom were still weak from the effects of cholera and dysentery. William Russell, in his dispatch to *The Times*, made known to his readers the lack of adequate facilities available to the medical staff:

They have landed this army without any kind of hospital transport, litters or carts, or anything! Everything was ready at Varna! Now, with all this cholera and diarrhoea about, there are no means of taking the sick down to the boats.

Many of the victims Russell had seen, were to find an early grave, not on a battlefield, but at the bottom of a hill not far from their landing site.

The allies had completed the disembarkation by the 15th, but it was to be another three days before the British were ready for operations, which caused the French General Saint Arnaud to remark that '...the English have the unpleasant habit of always being late'. The complaint seems to have been fully justified by the fact that a march south towards Sevastopol was delayed until the 19th, five days after the initial landing. The British contingent when it eventually set off, amounted to five divisions, 26,000 infantry, 1,000 cavalry and an artillery strength of sixty cannon.

The French, having made the largest contribution to the expedition comprising some 30,000 troops and sixty-eight pieces of artillery, claimed the privilege of forming the right wing, which meant that their flanks were protected by the sea and the men-of-war on one side and the British infantry and cavalry on the other. In addition to the two main armies, the Ottoman Empire was represented by a contingent of 7,000 Turkish infantry, armed with muskets and bayonets. The only cavalry available for reconnoitring being provided by the 11 Hussars and the 14 Light Dragoons, under Lord Cardigan.

The march, for British troops weakened by the effects of a debilitating Bulgarian summer and a week's confinement aboard the cramped naval vessels, was exhausting enough without the discomfort of a heavy serge uniform and the encumbrance of greatcoat, haversack, rifle and ball ammunition. Lieutenant Peard, of the 20 Regiment, wrote: 'Many of our men fell down in the ranks, attacked by cholera, or from becoming faint and exhausted for want of water. If they recovered shortly, they followed us with the rearguard; but if not, they were left to the tender mercies of any passer by.' To ease the discomfort of marching, most regiments were headed by their bands playing popular tunes and with Colours uncased and streaming in the light breeze, while the stirring sound of the Highland pipes did something, perhaps, to raise the spirits of Scot and Englishman alike. But as the sun climbed higher in the sky, the heat and dust became increasingly oppressive to troops unused to route marching. Tunics were torn open and greatcoats and heavy bearskins cast aside with increasing frequency. At length even these measures were found to be insufficient to relieve the stress brought on by thirst and exhaustion and increasing numbers of stragglers began to fall by the wayside. 'Many sick men fell out, and were carried to the rear,' observed Russell. 'It was a painful sight – a sad contrast to the magnificent appearance of the army in front, to behold litter after litter borne past to the carts, with the poor sufferers who had dropped from illness and fatigue.' Bringing up the rear, Captain Paget was equally dismayed by the sight of the growing piles of discarded equipment and the increasing numbers of collapsed men. 'This went on gradually increasing until ere a mile or two was passed the stragglers were lying thick upon the ground,' he noted, 'and it is no exaggeration to say that the last two miles resembled a battlefield.'

In the late afternoon of 19 September, after just such a tiresome march, the River Bulganek was reached – at this time of the year quite shallow – and the columns of troops quickly broke ranks in a frantic rush to slake a pressing thirst from its brackish waters. Only in the Highland regiments did discipline prevail. Halted by Sir Colin Campbell before the stream was reached, the Scots were only allowed to proceed by company to fill canteens, thus avoiding the confusion and petty squabbles which accompanied the wild rush of less disciplined regiments.

That night the troops bivouacked beneath the leafy groves of olive and pomegranate trees to enjoy what rest they could before the sun rose on what was to prove an eventful day. After waiting for a reconnaissance to be made of the enemy's positions, the columns marched off in bright sunshine to where masses of the enemy could be seen three miles away across the River Alma.

Lieutenant Braybrooke reported:

About 4.30pm the Light and Second Divisions formed a splendid line on the side of a range of hills facing the Russians; the First Division supporting the Light Division, and the 3rd Division doing the same good office toward the Second; the Fourth Division in reserve. The sight is a glorious one. The men are in first-rate spirits, and will not disgrace their ancestors of the Peninsula and Waterloo.

Many of the senior officers had not fought a battle since Waterloo and for most of the rank and file it was to be a new experience that may well have induced in some, despite the confidence of Lieutenant Braybrooke, strong feelings of doubt as to whether their behaviour under fire would match that of their comrades, and for many, fears of sustaining a frightful wound. Considering that Raglan's men faced the prospect of advancing without cover, towards a position of considerable strength, such fears were perfectly understandable.

The Russian position was certainly one of great strength. A two mile long ridge of fragmented boulders formed the western slope of the Chatyrdagh mountain upon which Prince Menschikoff had chosen to conceal long lines of infantry behind a breastwork of trees felled to form a series of abattis, whilst deep trenches had been dug in its slopes. On the summit of Kourgane Hill 600 feet above the Alma and dominating the Sevastopol road, two fortified earthworks known as the Greater and Lesser Redoubts had been constructed, with batteries of cannon and 24-pound howitzers, whilst on the high ground to the west known as Telegraph Hill, three other batteries mounting a total of twenty-five cannon had been sited to dominate the ascent to the main redoubts. Two regiments of elite troops were entrenched on these upper slopes, whilst swarms of riflemen occupied the vineyards and deep ravines which proliferated the broken ground above the river.

Prince Menschikoff, with 33,000 troops available to him, could be excused for believing that he had the manpower and artillery to enable him to hold the heights of the Alma for at least three weeks, certainly enough time for the garrison to supplement and strengthen the defence works around Sevastopol.

Chapter Two

BATTLE OF THE ALMA

The Russian leader's confidence was undoubtedly shared by the citizens of Sevastopol for on Telegraph Hill were drawn up numerous carriages bearing an assortment of prominent officials and elegantly dressed ladies with parasols, picnic boxes and opera glasses, all in a flutter of anticipation to witness the soldiers of 'Holy Mother Russia' drive the 'Island curs' as they referred to the British, back across the river to their ships anchored in Calamita Bay.

They had every reason for feelings of optimism. The heights above the Alma afforded the Russians a strong natural defensive position, and Prince Menschikoff was unshaken in his belief that he could hold his ground while Sevastopol's defence works were made all but impregnable, but whether the majority of his troops shared their leader's confidence, was open to question. An anonymous Russian NCO expressed his doubts when he wrote; 'At the evening meal many of the soldiers ate little .... As we lay down to sleep, dressed in our field marching order, for the first time there arose a feeling of apprehension and uncertainty.' Captain Hodasevich, a Pole serving with the 2 Chasseur Brigade was also worried:

As it became dark we could see plainly enough the enemy's fires on the River Boulganak. I laid down in my hut of branches and tried to sleep, but in vain, not withstanding the fatigue of the previous day ... All was still and had little appearance of the coming strife. These were both armies lying, as it were, side by side. How many, or who would be sent to their last account, it would be impossible to say. The question involuntarily thrust itself upon me, should I be one of that number?

On the southern and far side of the Alma – opposite the British – the ground rose in a series of ridges and hollows, varying in height from sixty to 150 feet. The highest point before levelling out into a plateau on Telegraph Hill where the road to Sevastopol wound its way round Kourgane Hill, was recognized by Lord Raglan as being the key to the position. This was the highest escarpment above the river facing the British, and on a forward jutting slope the Russian General had chosen to position eighteen battalions and seventy guns behind a shallow ridge of earth known as the Great Redoubt, and shortly to become the scene of savage fighting. Further up the slope, several batteries of field guns were in a position inevitably to become known to the British as the Lesser Redoubt.

That evening the French Commander rode over to Raglan's headquarters to discuss the strategy to be adopted on the following day, 20 September. Marshal Saint Arnaud was all for making an attack near the coast early in the morning with the British sweeping round to roll up the Russian right wing. Raglan, who had no plan of his own, objected, stating that his cavalry were greatly outnumbered by the enemy and would be unable to protect the infantry's flanks.

Neither Raglan or Saint Arnaud had been able to obtain any information about conditions in the Crimea, so for their respective governments to expect unqualified success was, as Lieutenant Strange pointed out, '…demanding that it be done under the handicap of complete ignorance of the terrain over which it was to be achieved, the climate under which it was to be undertaken, and the strength of the enemy's forces'.

Eventually, it was agreed that the French, supported by the Turks, would engage the Russians on the right of the British line while Raglan's divisions launched a frontal assault against Kourgane Hill, despite having little knowledge of the enemy's strength on the other side of the Alma. Commented Russell:

It appears somewhat strange that no reconnaissance was made of the Russian position. They (the generals) even concerted their plan before they had seen the enemy at all, relying on the bravery of the troops not only to force the Russians from their lines but if necessary, to swim or ford a stream of unknown depth.

23

Menschikoff had, in fact, concentrated his entire strength of 33,000 between the two hills; 20,000 to combat the British advancing on Kourgane Hill, and 13,000 to face the French. His cavalry, amounting to some 3,600, he positioned on his right flank. As far as artillery was concerned, by far the largest concentration was ranged against the British; eighty-six guns, whilst just thirty-six cannon faced the French.

The morning dawned bright and clear with every prospect of becoming a hot sultry day. By 5.30 a.m. the French and Turkish troops were ready to advance in keeping with Saint Arnaud's plan, but Raglan's troops were by no means ready, it was to be 7.00 a.m. before many redcoats had recovered from a fitful sleep. Rations had yet to be distributed, and most officers were still engaged with their ablutions.

Following a five hour delay, the allied army at last began its advance on a front of four miles, the French and Turks on the coastal side, whilst the British divisions, headed by their regimental bands with Colours uncased and streaming in the breeze, marched inland.

'The advance of our armies this day over the vast plain was a sight never to be forgotten by anyone who witnessed it,' wrote Lieutenant Peard. 'The forest of bayonets of the advancing columns glistened in the bright sun, the heat of which was tempered by a soft sea breeze.'

At noon, having covered no more than three miles, Raglan called a halt for lunch on a ridge from where he and Saint Arnaud, together with their staff, could look down on the Alma Valley. Studying the enemy positions through their glasses, they quickly discovered just how strong a defensive position Menschikoff had chosen. The banks of the river were steep and on its opposite side were thick woods giving way to bare grassy slopes which rose to a plateau dominating the valley. 'Even at this distance we could see that it was a position of immense strength,' remembered Somerset Calthorpe, 'and what appeared at first sight as dark patches of underwood on the side of the hills, proved to be masses of infantry when examined with a telescope.'

The Russians in their turn, were observing the advance of the allied troops. Captain Robert Hodasevich recalled that:

At 12am the whole of the allied armies were in full view, and a more magnificent sight man never saw than when, at the distance of about two cannon shots from us, they began to deploy from marching columns. To the right, as we stood, went the red jackets, and I asked our Colonel who they were, and he informed me that they were the English. 'It would be good fun to fight with them', he added, 'as, though they may be good sailors, they must be bad soldiers; why, they would have no chance with us on dry land.'

The redcoats no doubt, would have been highly amused had they been aware of the remark for, as John Hume of the 55 Regiment was quick to point out: 'The Russians must have felt rather anxious when they saw from the heights above the Alma about sixty thousand men moving steadily towards their position. I don't think that there was the slightest doubt in any of our minds as to the result of the attack.'

The opening phase of the battle began in the early afternoon with a bombardment from the allied warships in the bay, while the French Legionnaires led by the Zouaves, crossed the River Bulganek at its mouth and began to climb a narrow twisting path up the cliff, unseen by the Russians, until they reached the summit. That General Bosquet's force was now separated from the British seems not to have been appreciated by the Russian Commander, for he neglected to commit his eight battalions in time and the French gained the plateau without encountering any appreciable opposition save that of a picket which was taken by surprise and quickly overcome.

A second French attack led by General d'Autemarre crossed the river by a ford with 3,000 men and twelve guns, eventually to join General Bosquet on the plateau after a climb of two hours, due to the guns having to be dragged to the top. Saint Arnaud, once he had confirmation that Bosquet had been joined by d'Autemarre, immediately ordered a general attack west of Bourliouk in front of Telegraph Hill, without waiting for the British or even notifying Lord Raglan.

It was now 1.00 p.m. and, after a pause to allow the French to make some progress, Raglan at last gave the order for a frontal attack on Kourgane Hill. In the lead was the Light Division supported by the Guards and the Highland Brigade. Next came the 2nd Division closely followed by the 3rd, with Cathcart's 4th Division bringing up the rear as a reserve.

The advance which had begun with enthusiasm by the Fusiliers soon degenerated into something approaching a shambles with the 7 Royal Fusiliers following too closely upon the heels of the 95 Foot. An attempt to change formation from close column into line, resulted in total confusion when the two regiments became hopelessly entangled. Raglan from his vantage point on the ridge, could see what was happening and dispatched an aide with instructions to halt the advance. The 1st and 3rd Divisions, still marching in column, were brought to a halt while still out of range of the Russian guns, but the Light and 2nd Divisions were less fortunate, being obliged to lie down under an artillery fire of grape and round shot for more than an hour. Many of the redcoats were experiencing their baptism of fire and to some it came as something of a shock. 'Most of us for the first time found ourselves under a hot fire of round shot and shell – a curious and by no means pleasant experience,' wrote Captain John Hume. 'There was an involuntary movement amongst the men to cower and crowd together when the first round shot passed over us, and there were few who did not duck their heads.'

'I know I felt horribly sick,' confessed young Timothy Gowing, 'and I must acknowledge that I felt very uncomfortable.'

His discomfort was soon forgotten, however, when at 3.00 p.m. he and his comrades resumed their advance towards the Great Redoubt. The Light Division and the Fusiliers in particular, were to suffer the consequence of being among the first to cross the river. 'The vineyards by the stream were full of Russian riflemen who kept up a heavy fire on our troops,' wrote Lieutenant Peard, 'and the grape and canister shot together with a heavy fire of musketry which fell among them, mowed them down by hundreds.'

The Russian sharpshooters on the opposite bank, were armed with the Minie rifle, which had a rifled barrel and a range of 1,000 yards. A weapon of far greater accuracy than the ubiquitous musket. In fording the river the Fusiliers fell victim to this superior weapon, vividly recalled by Corporal Gowing:

Our men were falling very fast. Into the river we dashed, nearly up to our armpits, with our ammunition and rifles on the tops of our heads to keep them dry. We scrambled out the best way we could

26

and commenced to scale the hill. We were only about six hundred yards from the mouths of the guns, the thunderbolts of war were, therefore, not far apart, and death loves a crowd.

It was strictly against orders for any soldier to offer assistance to the wounded who were to be left for the bandsmen acting as medical orderlies. William Russell, who accompanied the Fusiliers, wrote of one particular incident:

> The front of the Russian line above us had burst into a volume of flame and white smoke ... the shot came flying close to me, one indeed killing one of the two bandsmen who were carrying a litter close to my side ... it knocked away the side of his face, and he fell dead – a horrible sight ...

Once across the river and through the burning village of Bourliouk set on fire by Russian shells, Gowing's company found themselves climbing the slope towards the Great Redoubt and facing Russian cannon fire, which at first they treated with contempt. 'As soon as the enemy's round shot came hopping along, we simply did the polite – opened out and allowed them to pass on,' wrote the Fusilier Corporal with admirable panache, 'There is nothing lost by politeness even on a battlefield.'

Forcing their way through a tangle of vines and brushwood, the soldiers of the Light Division in line formation, swept forward pausing only to quench a burning thirst from bunches of grapes hanging invitingly in their path. As Gowing and his fellow Fusiliers neared the Great Redoubt, increasing numbers fell victim to the Russian cannon fire, but inspired by shouts of 'Forward the Welsh Fusiliers,' the redcoats pressed on up the slope as the lethal iron balls ricocheted over the ground to tear bloody furrows through their ranks. The Guards bringing up the rear, suffered no less than the brigades ahead of them, as Lieutenant Jocelyn Strange of the Scots Fusiliers reported:

> ... we were under fire almost immediately, their round shot flying through us and over us, everywhere. We kept on steadily advancing till we got to the river, when the fire of Grape and Rockets was something terrific. We were soon over the river, and instead of waiting under the Bank to recover our breath before rushing up the hill on their entrenchments as the Grenadiers and Coldstreams did,

27

my regiment rushed on. We were then about 80 yards from their entrenchments their men behind them, 20 and 30 deep, for they were standing on the hill and could fire over each other's heads on us. The fire for the next half hour was awful ... yet through it I was miraculously preserved ... 10 of my brother officers were down, and I lost one third of my Company. The Field was a dreadful sight after it was all over – too horrid to describe.

Fortunate was the soldier who met with a quick death, for those with shattered limbs or body wounds invariably faced a lengthy wait while medical orderlies searched the battlefield; followed by an uncertain future after surgeons had operated with unsterilized instruments and without anaesthetic on tables stained by the bodily fluids of numerous other casualties.

For the 2nd Division following close upon the heels of the Light Division, their view was obscured by the billowing clouds of dense black smoke from the burning village of Bourliouk which not only shrouded the enemy's position, but seriously impeded the redcoats endeavouring to deploy from column into line on the sloping ground. At one stage, the 98 Regiment became so entangled with the rear of the 7 Fusiliers, that the civilians watching on Telegraph Hill were encouraged to think that their artillery had brought the enemy to an untimely halt.

The troops under fire, desperately battling to contain the Russians, were stiffened in their resolve by the refusal of their officers to take cover and by the decision of the Duke of Cambridge, whose first battle this was, to bring up the 1st Division to support the hard pressed Light Division. At 3.30 p.m. the Duke put himself at the head of the Grenadiers and gave the order to cross the river and form up on the other side. The Grenadiers and Coldstreams were on the right and the Highlanders of the 42nd, 78th, and 93rd on the eastern slopes of the Kourgane.

Sir Colin Campbell had been given the task of attacking the heavily defended Russian right flank and as his troops waited impatiently under fire for his order to advance, this veteran of numerous Peninsula engagements, addressed the Highland Brigade thus:

Now, men, you are going into action. Remember this; whoever is wounded – I don't care what his rank is – whoever is wounded must lie where he falls till the bandsmen come to attend him .... Don't be

28

in a hurry about firing, your officers will tell you when it is time to open fire. Be steady, keep silence, fire low. Now men, the army will watch us; make me proud of the Highland Brigade.

Meanwhile, the confusion in the ranks of the Light Division had not gone unnoticed by Prince Menschikoff but any hope he may have entertained of avoiding defeat, disappeared with news that the French had succeeded in turning his left flank. There, west of Telegraph Hill, where the ground was so precipitous that it had been considered almost impossible for any body of troops to surmount, and quite out of the question for artillery, the Russians, without artillery cover of their own, had come up against the French who had quickly brought their field guns into action with disastrous results for the Russian troops. Caught between the musketry of the Zouaves and grapeshot from the field guns, the Minsky regiment, guarding the plateau, was forced to retire on Telegraph Hill leaving the Russian General's flank exposed and unprotected.

In a desperate attempt to prevent his flank from being turned, Menschikoff ordered up seven regiments of infantry and four batteries of artillery. But it was too late, for Canrobert's 1st Division was already on the plateau, and in leaving his command position four miles away on Kourgane Hill, the Russian Commander-in-Chief had compromised his ability to control the battle. Eventually, after waiting in vain for his reserve to arrive, Menschikoff decided that nothing could be accomplished by them, and ordered a return to Kourgane Hill leaving the French in possession of the plateau but lacking the necessary support to advance any further.

Back on Kourgane Hill, the redcoats of the Light Division now reinforced by the Guards, advanced towards the Great Redoubt. 'Up the hill we went,' wrote Corporal Gowing, 'The smoke was now so great that we could hardly see what we were doing, and our fellows were falling all round; it was a dirty rugged hill....' Within minutes a closely packed Russian column could be seen coming down to meet them. Captain Robert Hodasevich, from a neighbouring hill, watched the ragged line of redcoats as they prepared to meet the oncoming Russians: 'We had never before seen troops fight in lines of two deep. We did not think it possible for men to be found with sufficient morale to be able to attack in this apparently weak formation, our massive columns.'

It was doubtful whether that thought had ever crossed the mind of Sergeant Gowing and his fellow Fusiliers as they approached the grey coated Kazansky regiment. Once within small arms' range, they began to use their rifles to great effect. In the hands of the skilled riflemen of the Light Division, the greater fire power it gave them wreaked havoc among the closely packed Russian masses. Driving back the defending Kazansky regiment, Codrington's four battalions reached the Great Redoubt and a series of savage hand to hand encounters developed during which the dead and dying were trampled underfoot by men roused to a frenzy of bloodlust. Slowly the defenders were driven off and when the Russian field guns limbered up and withdrew, the four battalions of the 19th, 23rd, 33rd and 95th, and the 7 Fusiliers were left in possession of the Great Redoubt.

Prince Gorchakoff still possessed a strong reinforcement and when he brought up four battalions of the Vladimirsky regiment to attack the British left flank, they were at first mistaken for the French. As Codrington's men held their fire, a bugle sounded 'Retire'. There was never a satisfactory explanation for the call, but the redcoats, exhausted by the savage fighting and conditioned to obey orders without question, began to fall back on the river, leaving the stronghold to the oncoming Russian infantry who ruthlessly bayoneted the wounded left behind in the redoubt.

Sir William Codrington's brigade, acting in response to the bugle call, retreated in confusion colliding with the advancing Brigade of Guards, but fortunately neither of the Russian Generals, Menschikoff or Gorchakoff, who were both in the rear of their troops, were able to take advantage of the resulting chaos. Despite the impact of the Russians and the fierce exchange of musketry, the Guards pressed their advance to within 100 yards of the Russian line. 'The fire was so hot,' Hugh Annesley later informed his mother, 'that you could hardly conceive it possible for anything the size of a rabbit not to be killed.' He was not to escape unscathed, for struck in the cheek by a musket ball, he lost part of his tongue and almost all his teeth.

Lucan's horse artillery was now beginning to inflict serious losses not only upon the 3,000 strong Vladimirsky regiment but also on the Russian reserves. When an ammunition wagon exploded, the Russians, fearful of losing their guns, began to falter and it became apparent to Prince Mikhail Gorchakoff watching from Kourgane Hill, that a counterattack would achieve nothing, for the Sutherlands, Camerons and the Black Watch of Sir Colin Campbell's Highland Brigade had gained the slopes of Kourgane Hill to recapture the Great Redoubt untroubled by the Russian cavalry.

Colonel Sterling, in a letter to his family, praised the steadfastness of the men in the Highland Brigade who allowed nothing to deflect them from their objective:

> The men never looked back and took no notice of the wounded. They ascended in perfect silence and without firing a shot. On crowning the hill, we found a large body of Russians who vainly tried to stand before us. Our manoeuvre was perfectly decisive as we got on the flank of the Russians in the centre battery, into which we looked from the top of the hill, and I saw the Guards rush in as the Russians abandoned it. The Guards were not moved on quite as soon as our brigade, and suffered more, poor devils.

By late afternoon the Russians were in full retreat southward along the Sevastopol road, harassed by artillery fire from Kourgane Hill. A disillusioned Captain Hodasevich was with them:

> We passed numbers of unfortunate men who cried out to us for help we could not give them. Some asked for water to quench their intolerable thirst, whilst others begged hard to be put out of their agony by a speedy death. These sights and sounds had a very visible effect on the morale of the men, as they saw how little care was taken of them when they most required it.

The battle for the heights above the Alma had ended four hours after it had begun, but at a relatively high cost in terms of casualties. William Russell informed his readers:

> It was a sad sight to see the litters borne in from all quarters hour after hour. To watch the working parties as they wandered about the plain turning down the blankets which had been stretched over the wounded, to behold if they were yet alive or were food for the worms, and then adding many a habitant to the yawning pits which lay with insatiable mouths gaping on the hillside – or covering up the poor sufferers destined to pass another night of indescribable agony.

The Fusiliers had left almost half their number on the field dead or wounded. 'Some of those who had met death at the point of the bayonet, presented a picture painful to look upon,' wrote Timothy Gowing, 'others were actually smiling. Such was the field of the Alma.' Sergeant Gowing after rendering what assistance he could to the wounded, rejoined his regiment at the top of the hill and was made sergeant that very night.

Lord Raglan, in his report after the battle, listed the number of British casualties as 362 killed and 2,500 wounded, whilst the Russians eventually admitted to 1,800 dead and 3,900 wounded or missing. The French seemed to have escaped with remarkably few casualties, considering the numbers taking part – sixty killed and 1,200 wounded. However, these figures were very likely increased by the many who succumbed later to wounds or gangrene.

The surgeons in the hospitals did what they could with the limited means at their disposal but, as Somerset Calthorpe observed: 'The enormous number of wounded quite overpowered the unceasing efforts of the medical officers, who worked all night without rest, and many were quite knocked up, and had to give in for a certain time.' Colonel Anthony Sterling was left in no doubt as to what was necessary to remedy the situation at the hospital in Scutari:

> All we want is, to give the military surgeons leave to spend money, without the risk of being blamed for it afterwards. A more devoted set of men than the regimental surgeons I never saw, but they have been brought up all their lives under the tyranny of the Inspector-General whose object is to please the Government by keeping down the estimates, i.e., expending men instead of pennies.

Ten men from each company were assigned to burial duties on the day following the battle, and twenty-four huge mounds of earth, 500 yards from the river, were left to mark the last resting place of the many who had fallen. Commenting on the battle, Captain Bruce Hamley wrote:

> On the plain near the signal tower, where the struggle was hottest on the part of the French, our allies left a stone, inscribed 'Victoire de l'Alma' with the date. The English left no monument on their fatal hill, but it needs none. The inhabitants will return to the valley,

the burnt village will be rebuilt, the wasted vineyards re-planted, and tillage will efface the traces of the conflict; but tradition will for centuries continue to point, with no doubtful finger, to the spot where the British infantry, thinned by a storm of cannon shot, drove the battalions of the Tsar, with terrible slaughter, from one of the strongest positions in Europe.

That the Russians suffered such heavy casualties was explained in some detail by Captain Hodasevich's summing up of the Russian soldier's psyche:

> ... a Russian soldier forms part of a machine, which is composed of enormous masses of men that have never known thought and never will think. They are oppressed with blows and ill treatment; their understanding is kept down by their servitude and several laws to which they are subjected. It is an axiom in the Russian army 'that powers of reasoning are not expected in the ranks' and when this rule is broken by an inspiring fight he is frequently rewarded for it by a severe corporal punishment.

News of the allied success reached the Cabinet at Westminster on 1 October and was enthusiastically received by a relieved Foreign Secretary, who was inspired to write: 'Raglan has covered himself with glory, and his calmness and judgement in the field, as well as the modesty and the terseness of his dispatch would, I am sure, have made the old duke proud.' Even Queen Victoria who had expressed concern at the lengthy delays in receiving reports on the progress of the war, thought the news was 'glorious' although she sounded a cautious note by stating that she could not feel 'quite sure of its truth'. The Duke of Newcastle had no such reservation. In a letter written to Lord Raglan on the day he read the dispatch, which had been brought to London by Lord Burgheish on 9 October, he expressed the wish: 'God grant that you may live many years to enjoy the reputation you have won.'

In the court of the Tsar an air of despondency and general pessimism prevailed, deepened by eyewitness accounts from the battlefield which gave little credit to the army's performance. The Tsar refused to believe that his soldiers had conducted themselves in a less than honourable fashion, and in the opinion of Robert Hodasevich, a Pole who eventually seized an opportunity to desert to the allies, it was the high command who were responsible for the defeat. He wrote:

> If I might venture to give my opinion on the battle of the Alma, I should say that the Russians were beaten from the following causes – first: the troops were badly disposed upon the position; everyone acted as he thought fit; the battalions of reserve began to retreat without orders; our battalion also began to retire, following the example of the reserves. During the five hours that the battle went on we neither saw nor heard of our General of Division, or Brigadier, or Colonel. We did not during the whole time receive any orders from them either to advance or to retire; and when we retired, nobody knew whether we ought to go to the right or left.

Menschikoff's personal report and his decision to move the majority of his army out of Sevastopol did little to dispel the air of gloom, and the feeling grew in St Petersburg that it was only a matter of time before Sevastopol surrendered to the allied armies. There was a good reason for this air of despondency for, following Menschikoff's departure, the garrison had been weakened to the extent that just four reserve infantry battalions, four depot battalions, and seventeen battalions of naval personnel, with no experience of infantry duties, were all that remained to defend the city.

Despite the glowing tribute paid him by the Prime Minister and Lord Clarendon, Raglan did not escape criticism for his failure to pursue the retreating Russian army. His excuse that the heavy brigade he had requested, had not yet arrived from Varna cut little ice with Cardigan and Lucan, who believed that the Light Brigade should have been employed in pursuit of the Russians. Sergeant Albert Mitchell and his fellow troopers of the 13 Hussars, advancing up Kourgane Hill with a battery of Horse Artillery, heard the cheers of the infantry and realized that the battle was over. 'We pushed on in haste,' he wrote, 'expecting to be called into play at the top of the heights.'

'Many now thought the hour had come for us,' agreed Trooper Pennington, 'but cautious council would appear to have prevailed, for no pursuit was made, though I firmly believe we could have scattered the Russian horse and turned retreat into a rout.'

The sight of a defeated and disorganized army retreating rapidly towards Sevastopol certainly seemed to justify their expectations, but the only action taken was from Canrobert's artillery, which opened fire on the fleeing Russians from Telegraph Hill.

As night closed in, with the fighting at an end, the troops endeavoured to relax from the horrors of the day but found their rest disturbed by the cries and groans of the wounded, lying wherever they had fallen. Their pitiful cries certainly affected Albert Mitchell. 'We had already seen sufficient to harden our feelings, and make us callous to human suffering,' he confessed to his family, 'but I lay some time thinking very seriously and praying to God for protection from all dangers.'

The next day the troops, now refreshed, were stood at readiness to resume their march on Sevastopol, but when Raglan approached Saint Arnaud to suggest that the two armies seize the ground above the city, the French Marshal, already a very sick man, replied that his troops would first have to retrieve their packs from the river bank and were also fully occupied in attending to the wounded. Disappointed but unwilling to risk the camaraderie then existing, Lord Raglan did not press the point and the day was given over to succouring the wounded. In this, the French casualties fared better than those of their British ally. With the advantage of better medical attention, the French soldier stood a greater chance of recovery, even those suffering from potentially fatal illnesses such as cholera or dysentery.

'Our men were sent to the sea, three miles distant, on jolting arabas or tedious litters,' William Russell informed the readers of *The Times*. 'The French had well appointed covered hospital vans, to hold ten or twelve men, drawn by mules, and their wounded were sent in much greater comfort than our poor fellows.'

Not that the British soldier fared any better when he finally arrived at the port of Balaklava, as a horrified Mrs Duberly discovered:

I watched from over the taffrail of the Star of the South the embarkation of some Russian prisoners and the English soldiers – all wounded – for Scutari. The dignified indifference of the medical officer, who stood with his hands in his pockets, gossiping in the hospital doorway – the rough indecent way in which the poor howling wretches were hauled along the quay, and bundled, some with one, and others with both legs amputated, into the bottom of the boat, without a symptom of a stretcher or bed, was truly an edifying ex-emplification of the golden rule 'Do to others as you would be done by'.

For the wounded, even the four day sea voyage to the hospital at Scutari was a dreadful experience, with many dying before reaching Constantinople. One such was Lieutenant W.L. Braybrooke, who had been seriously wounded towards the end of the battle. Struck in the leg by a musket ball, he survived the amputation only to die from neglect on board the *Vulcan* en route to Scutari.

It was whilst supervising the transfer of the wounded to the hospital ships that Douglas Reid, the assistant surgeon of the 40 Foot, met Mrs Seacole:

> Here I made the acquaintance of a celebrated person, Mrs Seacole, a coloured woman, who, out of the goodness of her heart and at her own expense supplied hot tea to the poor sufferers whilst they were waiting to be lifted into the boats. I need not say how grateful they were for the warm and comforting beverage when they were benumbed with cold and exhausted by the long and trying journey from the front. She did not spare herself if she could do any good to the suffering soldiers. In rain and snow, in storm and tempest, day after day she was at her self-chosen post, with her stores and kettle, in any shelter she could find, brewing teas for all who wanted it, and they were many.

Mary Seacole, a stout forty-eight year-old Jamaican lady had read the reports of the journalist from *The Times* and, realizing that many of the soldiers she had known in Kingston, were now in the Crimea, she was determined to offer her services as a self trained nurse. Reaching London shortly after Florence Nightingale had sailed for Constantinople, she had failed to be accepted by the organization recruiting nurses for the Crimea, and also shamefully, by the management for the Crimean Fund. Undeterred, she made her own arrangements to travel to Balaklava and ultimately to Kadikoi where she set up a general store. Lady Alicia Blackwood explained:

> Mrs Seacole kept a general store which provided every variety of articles, both edible and otherwise. No doubt she paid a heavy price herself to provide for the demand, but if this were slightly

usuitiously (*sic*) added to on her behalf towards others, it was always remembered that she had, during the time of battle, and in time of fearful distress, personally spared no pains and no exertions to visit the field of woe, and minister with her own hands such things as could comfort, or alleviate the sufferings of those around her, freely giving to such as could not pay ...

It was not unusual for a casualty never to have seen a surgeon before being transferred to a hospital bound vessel, as Lieutenant Henry Clifford was at pains to explain in a letter home: 'Numbers of men wounded at Alma have been five days without having their wounds looked at by a medical man, and many men died from their wounds mortifying. All this is the fault of the Heads of the Medical Department, for quantities of medicine etc have been provided and sent out as far as Scutari and Varna.'

Even before the journey across the Bosporus could begin there remained the problem of conveying the seriously wounded the three miles to the transport vessels waiting in the bay. Mrs Duberly complained:

> We have no ambulance wagons, they are nearly all broken down, or the mules dead or the drivers are dead drunk. Our poor cavalry horses, as we know full well, are all unequal to the task of carrying down the sick, and the French have provided transports for us for some time. Why are we so helpless and broken down?

Shortcomings as serious as this could not be hidden from the newspaper correspondents and, before many days had passed, reports of the plight of the wounded were filling the columns of many London newspapers. In the meantime the march south to the River Katcha had begun and for much of the way the troops found the ground littered with discarded Russian equipment, including knapsacks and boxes of ammunition, but of the enemy there was not a sign.

In the early hours of 24 September the domes and spires of Sevastopol came into view from the surrounding hills. The allied commanders, however, had yet to agree on a plan and it was becoming increasingly clear to Lord Raglan that his French colleague was a very sick man. Later that morning, despite the anxiety raised by Saint Arnaud's physical condition, a council of war was held and a scheme, proposed by Raglan's Chief Engineer,

Sir John Burgoyne, was discussed and eventually approved by all parties. It called for an attack on Sevastopol from the south using Balaklava Bay, seven miles from the city, as a supply base. The alternative, an approach from the north, had been suggested but discarded, because naval surveillance had shown that the harbour was protected by forts both at the entrance and above on the cliffs. A further inland defence work known as the Star Fort, was surrounded by a ditch twelve feet deep and eighteen feet wide and furnished with forty-seven pieces of artillery. Any advance from north of the city would not only have to overcome this formidable barrier but would also risk heavy casualties from the guns of the ships in the harbour.

Now that Burgoyne's plan had been agreed by Lord Raglan and Saint Arnaud, despite opposition from Prince Napoleon, the allied army began its march on Sevastopol on 25 September taking care to avoid the area of swampy ground east of the city and reaching the village of Kadikoi the following morning. 'The country through which we marched was hilly and barren,' remembered William Russell. 'Amidst steep hillocks covered with thistles, and separated from each other at times by small patches of steppe, wound the road to Sebastopol – a mere beaten track marked with cart wheels, hoofs, and gun carriage wheels.' The march was beset by problems. There was no fodder or even water for the horses and the men fared little better, being on short rations or 'hard tack' as the army issue biscuits were more familiarly known.

From the plateau above Kadikoi the port of Balaklava could be seen, appearing to Henry Clifford as 'a most beautiful harbour, not more than two miles round – a basin in shape, where the water is almost like a mill pond, though deep enough for any line-of-battleship to come within a stone's throw of the shore'. Major Reynell Pack was equally impressed with the scenic beauty of the port, but in a letter home, he was at pains to point out the danger to shipping:

Balaklava Bay presents a grand appearance. High cliffs and detached rocks form its coast, and in a southerly wind, threaten destruction to any unfortunate ship that drags or breaks from her anchorage, affording to the passengers and sailors a poor chance for life for the sea then dashes in with such violence that, even if escape from the waves could be hoped for, the rocky shore allows no footing.

It was an observation that was to prove tragically correct on 14 November.

The water was undoubtedly deep, but the harbour was far too narrow being barely fifty yards wide, to serve as a base for both the allied forces. Since it had been surrendered to the British by a small force of militia which had been its sole defenders, it was agreed that the British would retain possession, leaving the French to use the less deep but wider harbours of Kamiesch and Kazatch. This meant that Raglan's army was positioned on the right when facing Sevastopol, whilst the French remained on the left with the sea to protect one flank, and the British the other. Thus the two armies held a rough semi-circle of land commanding the southern side of Sevastopol with the advantage of the high ground overlooking the city.

Dr Douglas Reid was singularly unimpressed by his bivouac area: 'Imagine a ploughed field after three days of heavy rain followed by a snow storm, and you may be able to form some idea of the ground on which our tents are pitched, then imagine a cutting wind on an open plain and a temperature of 22 degrees F, no shelter of any kind except a canvas tent, not a house or a wall or a tree anywhere within sight, and you may picture the situation.'

Captain Wombwell, an orderly officer to Lord Cardigan, drew attention to the particular difficulty the chosen site had for the cavalry: 'Where we are now encamped is near 7 miles from Balaklava where the forage is all landed, but the roads are in such a state, that it is impossible to get it up from there to our camp. The consequence is when it does come it is in very small quantities and the wretched animals do not get more than 2 handfuls a piece all day, hay we scarcely ever get, so you can easily imagine our horses are starved.'

On the day following Raglan's seizure of Balaklava Bay, Marshal Saint Arnaud resigned his command to General Francois Canrobert and took to his sick bed, dying three days later of a heart attack brought on by his cancer and the stress of command. The steamship *Bertheller* which conveyed the Marshal's body to Marseilles, also brought news of the allied army's advance, giving an impression that the fall of Sevastopol was just a matter of days. All Paris celebrated, but the politicians had disregarded the problems associated with an approaching Russian winter and the effect it would have on troops ill equipped and completely unprepared. For the soldiers in the trenches, the next month or two was to confront them with experience beyond their worst imaginings.

The British government, like the French, had every reason to encourage good news from the front, for public opinion, fed by alarming reports in the London newspapers, was beginning to question the desperate plight of the sick and wounded in the military hospitals where, if journalists such as William Howard Russell were to be believed, the soldiers were 'dying like flies'. His account was so disturbing that subsequent letters in *The Times* led to an appeal for a 'creature comfort' fund being launched. It met with an enthusiastic response from wealthy Victorian business men and the general public alike and resulted in sufficient funds to purchase a variety of comforts for the troops in the field.

Of greater benefit to the sufferers in the military hospital at Scutari was a question raised by a letter published in *The Times* on 14 October. It asked why the British did not have a similar scheme to the 'Sisters of Charity', a nursing organization employed by the French in their hospitals. It was read by a young woman from a wealthy family in Hampshire, who had long held an interest in nursing. She immediately contacted an influential friend, Mrs Sidney Herbert, with a proposal for an organization such as that of the French. After much argument, Florence Nightingale's suggestion was adopted by the Cabinet and she was given a budget of £1,000 and the grandiose title of 'Superintendent of the Female Nursing Establishment of the English General Hospitals in Turkey'.

The thirty-four year-old Miss Nightingale lost no time in recruiting a team of young women, most of whom had a religious background but little experience of nursing, but despite this shortcoming the scheme quickly proved a success, due chiefly to Florence Nightingale's superb organizational ability, and in little more than a fortnight, a party of thirty-eight nurses were on their way to Turkey. Sister Mary Aloysius, an Irish lady with, it would seem, definite ideas on dress, wrote:

> The ladies and paid nurses wore the same costume, and a very ugly one it was. It seemed to be contract work, and all the same size, so that the ladies who were tall had short dresses, and the ladies who

were small had long dresses. They consisted of grey tweed wrapped, worsted jackets, white caps, and short woollen cloaks, and to conclude, a frightful scarf of brown holland, embroidered in red with the words, 'Scutari Hospital'. That ladies could be found to walk into such a costume was certainly a triumph of grace over nature.

Miss Nightingale and her original group of twenty-four left England on 21 October travelling overland to Marseilles and, after a stormy passage in the P & O paddle steamer *Vectis,* during which Miss Nightingale was so violently sick that she was unable to dress or wash, disembarked at Constantinople on the 4 November en route to Scutari. Having arrived, they were appalled by the prevailing conditions. In a letter to her parents, Florence complained of filthy floors, overflowing privies and patients crowded together in rooms infested with vermin. Sister Mary was deeply affected by the suffering of the patients from her first day at Scutari.

> ... poor fellows, who with their wounds, had been tossing about on the Black Sea for two or three days, and sometimes more. Where were they to go. Not an available bed. They were laid on the floor one after another, till the beds were emptied of those dying of cholera and every other disease. Many died immediately after being brought in – their moans would pierce the heart – the look of agony in those poor dying faces will never leave my heart. They may well be called 'The Martyrs of the Crimea'.

The overcrowding at Scutari came as something of a shock to another nurse, Lady Alicia Blackwood, who described the facilities available:

> The great Barrack contained at this time about four thousand sick and wounded. Almost adjoining this was the Grand Hospital, it was smaller and contained about a thousand. Besides this there was a building used for stables now also converted into a temporary hospital, which received from one hundred to two hundred more. Two large hulks on the Bosporus were also filled; Such a state of things was sad indeed and required great activity and forethought to meet it, and here had been the failure.

It was not just the overcrowding that concerned Florence Nightingale. There was little in the way of medical facilities and she found that many of the doctors who were determined to find no fault with a system they were familiar with, obstructed her every move. With typical Victorian male prejudice, they quickly came to resent the presence of female nursing staff and even the medical orderlies did everything in their power to impede the women whose work might emphasize their own shortcomings. Happily, Florence Nightingale had the backing of concerned politicians who soon came to recognize the pressing need for an improvement in hospital administration, and not even dubious accusations that some Catholic nurses were proselytizing their faith, diminished their support. Unfortunately the government's gratitude did not extend beyond the nurses' service in the Crimea, for when they returned to England in April 1856, they were given no recognition by the War Office which did not even reimburse their travelling expenses. The only reward Florence Nightingale's nurses received was the sum of £230 from the Sultan, which they donated to the relief of the poor.

Now that an efficient supply base had been established at Balaklava Bay, preparations for the overthrow of Sevastopol began in earnest. Large calibre naval guns were sent ashore with 1,500 seamen to drag the heavy ordnance from the shore to the plateau, where they ultimately joined the siege train being assembled for a massive bombardment of the city. 'There are four drag ropes hooked on, one to each wheel,' explained Major Porter. 'Upon each of these twenty men are hauling with all their might over ground all soft and spongy from long continued rain, and the mud – true Crimean mud – as obstinate and tenacious as is everything Russian.'

The Russians of course, had not been idle and under the able direction of Lieutenant Colonel Franz Eduard Todleben, several barges laden with stone had been sunk in the narrow entrance of the harbour, and a cable strung across its mouth to prevent the entry of hostile craft, while ships' crews and the cannon from men-of-war scuttled in the harbour, had been added to the city's defences. These were being further strengthened by the addition of substantial earthworks and bastions, whilst on the more vulnerable south-eastern side, the Malakoff Tower stood as a formidable defence work, together with its heavy batteries and a trench system linking it with two other earthworks, the Lesser and Greater Redans. By the middle of October, as many as 340 cannon, some of large calibre, were in position and a floating bridge had been constructed across the harbour to facilitate supplies and reinforcements crossing from the north of the city. Somerset Calthorpe was certainly impressed: 'I think the Russian engineers have displayed great cleverness and ability in the manner in which they have up to the present time conducted the defence of Sevastopol. For some time past the deserters who have come over to us have perpetually mentioned the name of Todleben as the chief director of the works of the town.'

The allied troops were also engaged in the unpopular work of extending their trenches, but had Lord Raglan known that Menschikoff had just 18,000 troops in the city, a good proportion of which were disenchanted naval personnel in a near mutinous frame of mind, it is not unlikely that he would have overridden Canrobert's objection to an early attack on the city, whatever the chances of success. It might well have avoided the costly siege that was to span the next eleven months.

Chapter Three

A DAY OF DISASTER

As the days passed without any offensive action on the part of the allies, due in some measure to the difficulty of getting the siege guns into position and the need for a period of rest following the exhausting march of 26 September, Raglan warned the British ambassador in Turkey against expressing undue optimism. 'No one in government,' he told him, 'should expect the easy victories forecast by the newspapers.'

Following his success at the Alma, it had been Lord Raglan's intention to launch an immediate attack before the demoralized garrison troops had time to strengthen the city's defences, but Canrobert had advised him that without reinforcements and the support of heavy artillery, any such move would be little short of a military crime. Since, at that period of the campaign, there existed almost three miles of open ground between the allied positions and Sevastopol, it was probably sound advice.

By 3 October supplies were beginning to accumulate on the quay and landing stages of Balaklava in mountainous heaps and the waters of the harbour resembled a heaving mass of offal and raw sewage. Roger Fenton observed:

> The stench along the waterside is very bad, but they are taking pains to get rid of the filth. All the dead oxen and horses floating about the harbour have been towed out to sea. Do what they will, there is an immense quantity of putrefying matter which cannot be got rid of.

Lord Raglan to his credit, had done his best, but with insufficient labour, there was never any likelihood of the operation being

44

carried out efficiently and Captain John Hume of the 55th was probably justified in describing the road leading from the village to the harbour, as 'a real Slough of Despond'. 'It was now a sea of mud with broken down carts and wagons, dead animals lying about in all directions,' he wrote. 'As an Irish major said, "It was alive with dead animals".'

At a Staff conference on the 7th, it had been agreed that no orders would be given for an infantry assault on the city's outer defences such as the Malakoff and the Redan until they had been reduced by an intensive bombardment which was expected to begin on 17 October. The land bombardment was to be augmented by guns from the fleet, with the French firing on Forts Constantine and Alexander, while British ships turned their guns on the Malakoff Tower and the two Redans.

The next day the allies began work on their trenches, in which the French had by far the easier task, as Lieutenant Somerset Calthorpe explained: '...the ground we shall have to work upon is very rocky, the general depth of earth being not more than 18 inches. I understand the ground the French have got is very good soil, so they will have a great advantage over us when we commence making the trenches.' That his comment was pertinent was borne out by the fact that by 12 October the first French trench was just 1,200 yards from the Schwartz redoubt whilst the nearest British trench was more than a mile from the enemy batteries. Despite the lengthy stretch of open ground to be crossed before a storming party could hope to reach their objective, Lieutenant Dallas was quietly optimistic. In writing to his family that day, he stated:

> We are all the time preparing & have not fired a shot yet. How ominous it must seem to them, seeing us quietly sitting down round their city ... I expect that in a few days the whole town will be a heap of ruins, & that then we shall be sent to wherever we are intended to winter.

Much depended upon the progress made by the entrenching parties who in the bitter weather prevailing, suffered appalling hardships. Lieutenant Dunscombe of the 46 Regiment wrote of his experience in November:

... the whole time I was there I had nothing to eat or drink, as on account of the severity of the weather our rations could not be sent to us. The men suffered so severely from cold, hunger, and wet and every privation that out of 160 that we took with us last night to the entrenchments, we only brought away 98 of them this evening, all the others remained behind, either dead, dying or so bad with the cramps that they were unable to walk home.

Later in the year, Lieutenant Calthorpe found that conditions had altered very little:

I had to go all through the trenches yesterday, it was raining the greatest part of the time, and I never saw anything like the mud which we had to wade through. The men looked for the most part miserable and cold; everything they had on was wet through, and even when they returned to their tents they would have no dry clothes to put on.

On 17 October at 6.30 a.m., the long awaited bombardment began in earnest with the British and French artillery opening fire simultaneously. Noted Somerset Calthorpe: 'The roaring and whistling of the shot, as they flew through the air on their course of destruction, surpassed anything ever heard before. In a few moments everything was enveloped in smoke, so that we could only sit and guess and hope we were doing well.'

For two hours the domes and spires of Sevastopol were veiled in dense clouds of smoke with little retaliation from the Russians, but three hours after the start of the bombardment, a lucky or well directed Russian shell fell onto one of the principal French powder magazines, completely destroying a battery of five guns, and killing and injuring more than 150 men. Shortly afterwards a second explosion put another battery out of action and by 10.30 a.m. many of the French guns were silenced for the rest of the day. 'This disaster appeared quite to paralyse the French,' wrote Calthorpe, 'whilst it encouraged the Russians, who augmented their fire till they sent four shot to one from our allies.'

At noon, the ships in the Bay began to play their part in a four hour bombardment of Sevastopol. The French concentrated their fire against Fort Quarantine, a large casemated battery and other defences on the southern side of the harbour, whilst Sir Edward Lyons in *Agamemnon* directed his broadsides against Fort

Constantine to the north. Less experienced than the British, the French ships were more than a mile off shore, too great a range for their guns to be accurately targeted and little damage was done. The Royal Navy, in accordance with custom, was operating at a much closer range which whilst being more effective, made them vulnerable to fire from the Russian batteries and in less than two hours, *Albion* of 90 guns and *Arethusa* of 50 guns were disabled, the smaller *Retribution* lost her main mast, whilst the steamers *Firebrand* and *Triton* received damage to their paddle wheels and superstructure.

Lieutenant Dallas, in writing to his mother, was dismissive of the navy's contribution:

> The Fleet went in at them 3 days ago & I am told met with frightful loss and had no success. We could not see what they were doing from here on account of the dense smoke from our guns between us & them. They have not since fired a shot so that I am afraid they did not do much good.

Although the land based bombardment had been resumed following the disaster to the French magazine and continued for the next two days, it soon became apparent that, far from disabling the city's batteries or destroying its important outer defences such as the Malakoff Tower or the Redan, the damage inflicted was negligible and the bombardment was brought to a halt. Captain Reilly offered a plausible excuse with his explanation: 'The guns at this period were considerably worn and most needed replacing, but to bring up fresh guns was practically impossible as the roads had become impassable. So bad did conditions become that active operations of the siege were suspended.'

Lieutenant Dallas, in all probability, would have been far from satisfied with the Captain's explanation had he been aware of it for, as he told his father: 'We have not battered down the place at all in the way that our Engineers and Artillery led us to expect we should, & though I hear that the Authorities are quite satisfied with our progress, we who have hard work in the trenches, & don't see much visible result, are getting rather tired of it.' The disappointing results of the land and sea bombardment left the allied commanders in a frustrated and indecisive state of mind.

They were unable to prevent supplies or reinforcements from reaching Sevastopol, and the failure to reduce the city's outer defences made an attack on the city a hazardous undertaking. There also existed a possibility that the allied camp on the heights above Balaklava could be attacked by a Russian field army of unknown strength, for if the lines of communication and supply between Balaklava Bay and the plateau were cut, the British position in front of Sevastopol would become untenable. To ensure the success of just such an operation, the Russians had assembled 15,000 infantry, 4,000 cavalry, and seventy-eight field guns under the overall command of General Pavel Liprandi. He had ordered his infantry to assemble near the village of Tchorgoun, a picturesque hamlet surrounded by high hills to the north-east of Balaklava. The Russian General was confident that with the infantry, cavalry and artillery he possessed, he was strong enough to take the Fedioukine Hills and the Causeway Heights. Once this had been achieved, it would be relatively easy to attack and capture the port of Balaklava.

To counter this threat the allies had 1,200 Marines with naval guns brought ashore by the blue jackets who formed an inner defensive line, whilst nearly 1,000 Turkish troops, in hastily dug trenches on the Causeway Heights, guarded the outer line. Beyond this lay the North Valley and the Fedioukine Hills, and overlooking the South Valley Lucan's Cavalry Division which included the Light Brigade, awaited orders to deploy together with 650 men of the 93rd, and the guns of the Royal Artillery's 'W' battery.

The 25 October began with an early morning bombardment of the Turkish positions, from the Russian 12- and 18-pounder guns whose round shot soon led to the crumbling of Turkish resistance. From his vantage point above the Woronzoff road, Lord Raglan could see a strong force of Russian cavalry supported by infantry and artillery, advancing up the north valley towards the Turkish held redoubts and it alerted him to the threat it posed to Balaklava. The 1st and 4th Divisions were immediately directed into the south valley to reinforce Sir Colin Campbell's Highlanders, while General Canrobert acted equally swiftly by sending General Bosquet's Chasseurs d'Afrique in support.

As the Sutherland Highlanders were marching away, the buglers in the cavalry lines were already sounding 'Boot and Saddle' and the troopers of Lord Lucan's command were soon riding north to where the smoke of a distant engagement could be seen drifting above the Turkish redoubts. There, round shot and grape were wreaking havoc among the Turks, and believing themselves to be abandoned, groups of militia were soon fleeing for their lives, leaving the earthworks and the four guns it contained to the Russians; roundly condemned by Fanny Duberly watching from the cavalry lines, as 'brutal cowardice'. In fact, many of the more disciplined Turks formed up by the side of Sir Colin Campbell's Highlanders.

The 93rd for the moment hidden from the view of General Rykoff's Cossacks and Hussars, were all that stood between the Russians and the port of Balaklava. Sir Colin Campbell was quick to appreciate the gravity of the situation. 'Remember, there is no retreat, men,' he told them, 'you must die where you stand.' The Highlanders were drawn up on rising ground with the village of Kadikoi behind them and, as the Cossacks and Rykoff's Hussars came sweeping down towards them, the warning; 'Present!' rang out and a double line of Minie rifles extended as one, exploding to the word of command, 'Fire!' emptying saddles and leaving a struggling heap of men and horses on the ground.

William Howard Russell, watching from the Sapoune Hills above the village, described the Russian cavalry charge in graphic detail for the readers of *The Times*:

The ground flies beneath their horses feet: gathering speed at every stride, they dash on towards this red streak topped with a line of steel. The Russians come within 600 yards, down goes that line of steel in front, and out rings a thundering volley of Minie musketry. The distance is too great; the Russians are not checked, but still sweep onwards with the whole force of horse and men, through the smoke, here and there knocked over by the shot of our batteries above. With breathless suspense everyone waits the bursting of the wave upon the line of Gaelic rock; but ere they come within 150 yards, another deadly volley flashed from the levelled rifle, and carries death and terror into the Russians. They wheel about, open files right and left, and they fly back faster than they came.

What later became known as 'The Thin Red Line' had proved that when standing firm, disciplined infantry were quite capable of holding their own against cavalry even without forming a square.

Away to the left of Campbell's Highlanders, the Heavy Brigade of Lord Lucan's Cavalry Division, led by fifty-five year-old Sir James Scarlett, was drawn up at one end of the valley watched by Lord Raglan and his staff from the hillside above them. It had been brought up to protect the Turkish guns and was soon sighted by Russian cavalry coming over the Causeway Heights. The strong body of Russian horsemen, amounting to 3,000 troopers led in person by General Rykoff, advanced in two long lines from the higher ground, towards the unsuspecting Greys and Inniskilling Dragoons on the reverse side of the hill. Lord Raglan with the two French Generals Canrobert and Bosquet, could see from their vantage point on Sapoune Hill the danger facing the cavalry further up the valley, and an order was dispatched to Lord Lucan instructing him to withdraw to the western end of the Causeway Heights where he would be protected by a battery of French field guns. By the time the order reached Lucan the situation had changed. The mass of Russian cavalry had come under fire from the batteries on the Sapoune Heights, forcing General Rykoff to wheel left across the Causeway Heights putting him on a collision course with Scarlett's brigade who were outnumbered by odds of very nearly six to one.

The ground occupied by Brigadier General Scarlett was a mixture of rough scrub and tangled vines, hardly the most suitable for a cavalry action. Nevertheless, as soon as the Russians were sighted just 400 yards away, Scarlett ordered his bugler to sound the advance, followed shortly afterwards by the charge, and the two sets of horsemen met with a resounding clash of arms. For a few minutes all was a wild confusion of colour – scarlet, green, blue and dark grey, as the Heavy Brigade crashed into the centre of the enemy's line. Troop Sergeant Major Henry Franks of the 5 Dragoon Guards explained:

> It was rather hot work for a few minutes; there was no time to look about you. We soon became a struggling mass of half frenzied and desperate men, doing our best to kill each other. To quote Mr Russell's words, 'The Heavy Brigade went through the Russians like a sheet of paste board'.

Lieutenant Richard Temple Godman noted that:

The Greys and Inniskillings went first, then we came in support of the Greys. Their front must have been composed of three regiments, and a very strong column in their rear, in all I suppose about 1,500 or 2,000, whilst we were not more than 800. However, the charge sounded and at them went the first line ... as soon as they met all I saw was swords in the air in every direction, the pistols going off and everyone hacking away right and left ... the great bearskin caps high above the enemy. The 5th advanced and in they charged, yelling and shouting as hard as they could. For about five minutes neither would give way, and their column was so deep we could not cut through it. At length they turned and the whole ran as hard as they could pelt back up the hill, our men after them all broken up, and cutting them down right and left. We pursued about 300 yards, and then called off with much difficulty. The ground was strewn with swords, broken and whole, trumpets, carbines etc; while a quantity of men were scattered all along as far as we pursued.

Sergeant Major Gowing of the Royal Fusiliers reported:

At a distance it was impossible to see the many hand to hand encounters, the thick overcoats of the enemy, we knew well, would ward off many a blow. Our men, we found afterwards, went in with the point or with the fifth, sixth, or seventh cuts about the head ... if ever a body of cavalry were handled roughly, that column of Muscovites were. They bolted – that is, all that could – like a flock of sheep with a dog at their tails.

The Brigade had been bravely led by General Scarlett who had charged several horse lengths ahead of his men, as Gowing was pleased to confirm. 'How ever that gallant officer escaped was a miracle,' he wrote, 'for he led some thirty yards right into the jaws of death and came off without a scratch.'

'Why the Russians retreated in this way was a mystery to us,' wrote a bemused Henry Franks, 'as they outnumbered our Brigade, I should say by five to one.' An explanation perhaps, was not just the shock of collision with the heavier horses of Scarlett's brigade which caused the Russians to break off an engagement, which lasted no more than eight minutes, but the intervention of a troop of Horse Artillery. Galloping down from the higher ground, they had opened fire 'with admirable results' according to one gunner, causing the Russians to withdraw into the North

Valley before reforming behind a battery of eight cannon, with the day barely begun.

Whilst Scarlett's heavies had been engaged with General Rykoff's 6 Hussar Brigade, Cardigan's Light Brigade had been envious spectators just half a mile further up the valley on rising ground. Many of the officers of the 17 Lancers were impatient to get into the action and could not understand why Lord Cardigan did not give the order to engage the enemy. 'We could distinctly hear the din and shouts of our people, being only a few hundred yards off,' explained Loy-Smith. 'Our excitement became very great and I am of the opinion that nothing but the strict discipline under which we were held prevented us breaking loose to assist our comrades of the Heavies.' A window of opportunity had certainly existed, but Cardigan afterwards excused his failure to join the action by asserting that Lord Lucan had ordered him to remain in his present position and hold his ground.

The successful actions by the Heavy Brigade and Campbell's Highlanders had not averted the threat posed by the Russians to the port of Balaklava. Eleven of their Infantry Brigades and thirty-two guns still occupied the Causeway Heights, whilst further north on the other side of the valley, eight battalions, four cavalry squadrons, and fourteen cannon were firmly ensconced on the Fedioukine Heights. Encouraged by Sir James Scarlett's success, Lord Raglan wanted to drive the Russians from the Causeway Heights but lacked the necessary infantry to carry out the task. However, Lord Lucan's cavalry brigades were available and at 10.15 a.m. Raglan ordered him to deploy his cavalry as soon as possible, to recover the heights. 'They will be supported by infantry which has been ordered to advance on two fronts,' read his order to Lord Lucan down in the valley, who without further ado, instructed Cardigan to move the Light Brigade into the North Valley and face east, while he remained with the heavies behind a ridge of high ground to await the infantry before commencing a two pronged attack against the Russians on the Causeway Heights.

It was now almost 11.00 a.m. and looking down from the higher ground, Raglan was astonished to see the Light Brigade dismounted with the troopers lounging at their ease in the morning sun. The leading companies of the 1st Division were beginning to assemble in the South Valley when a member of his staff called that he could see the Russians removing the guns from the redoubts they had overrun. In the ethos of the times no greater humiliation could befall a commander than to lose his guns to the enemy, and Raglan did not intend to let that happen. General Airey, who had been his constant companion, was summoned to his side and Raglan quickly dictated an order which Airey was to emphasize came from the C.-in-C. himself.

> Lord Raglan wishes the cavalry to advance rapidly to the front and try to prevent the enemy from carrying away the guns. Troop of Horse Artillery may accompany. French cavalry is on your left. Immediate. R. Airey.

These imprecise instructions were given to his ADC Captain Lewis Nolan of the 15 Hussars, recognized as one of the best horsemen in the Division, with instructions to hand it to Lord Lucan without delay. Raglan's parting words to Nolan as he set spurs to his horse, were:

> Tell Lord Lucan the cavalry is to attack immediately.

Those few words and the erratic behaviour of the messenger, were to seal the fate of the Light Brigade. The thirty-five year-old captain was known to be headstrong, and earlier had voiced his criticism of Raglan's handling of the cavalry in conversation with the correspondent of *The Times*, who gathered the impression that he also held Lord Lucan in contempt. In fact Lucan had little time for Nolan whom he regarded as being disrespectful, and referring to the order given him, he looked up but could see no guns or the infantry support he had been promised. 'Attack, sir! Attack what? What guns, sir?'

'There my Lord', replied Nolan pointing vaguely towards the end of the valley where he supposed the redoubts to be; 'There are your guns!'

Unfortunately his gesture was at right angles to that intended by Lord Raglan, being in the direction of the Don Cossack battery at the far end of the North Valley, and the mystified Lucan, thinking that there had been a change of plan, said nothing but rode to where Lord Cardigan sat his horse. When Cardigan pointed out to him that the heights which flanked the valley were lined with infantry and artillery, Lucan assured him that it was a direct order from Lord Raglan. Cardigan, without seeing the order, turned in his saddle and quietly gave the word of command: 'The Brigade will advance.'

The Light Brigade faced a perilous journey of a mile and a half along the valley on the north side of which the Russians had eight infantry battalions, four squadrons of cavalry and fourteen cannon. On the Causeway Heights to the south, were sited thirty cannon and eleven battalions, whilst facing the Light Brigade at the end of the valley were twelve cannon and a mass of Russian cavalry.

In quick succession, following Cardigan's order, each officer took up the word of command: 'The Light Brigade will advance; Walk; March; Trot', and in a body, 673 men and horses moved off in two lines with the 17 Lancers on the left, and the 13 Light Dragoons on the right, followed by four squadrons of the 4 Dragoons and 11 Hussars, each line being 150 to 200 yards apart. William Pennington heard the order with something akin to amazement, 'For the madness of our errand was plain to the weakest judgement among us'. Moving off at a walk, Robert Farquharson, a trumpeter of the 4 Queen's Own Dragoons, wrote: 'This pace we kept at until we were fairly off the hill and into a heavily ploughed field below, which we continued until getting on to grass, when we got into a gallop, all the time being exposed to a galling fire in front from an eight-gun battery.'

As the Light Brigade increased its pace, Nolan, riding with the 17 Lancers, '...must have realized his mistake,' observed Pennington, 'for he was seen to gallop madly across the front of Lord Cardigan waving his sword and pointing frantically in the direction of the Causeway Heights on his right.' The reason for Nolan's late action will forever remain a mystery, for he was the first to fall, brought down by a fragment of shell which struck him full in his chest. The sword fell from Nolan's hand and his horse wheeled about, galloping back through the advancing brigade with its rider still erect in the saddle, eventually to fall dead close to the spot where Cardigan had given the order to charge.

The Heavy Brigade, forming up in the rear, also came under fire from the Russian batteries. Lucan was struck on his leg by a fragment of shell which killed his ADC and when he saw what confronted the Light Brigade, he cancelled the order to advance.

By waiting to give assistance to the Light Brigade on their return, Lucan's brigade was to be spared the heavy loss of men and horses suffered by Cardigan.

Trooper Pennington observed:

> As we advanced further down the valley, Lord Cardigan leading at a steady trot, round shot from the Fedioukine Hills and Causeway Heights came bowling in amongst us, making dire havoc, and bursting shells scattering broadcast their death-dealing horrors. Cannon shot tore the earth up, raising the dust in clouds, while men and horses in the leading ranks fell thick and fast.

As the Light Brigade thundered along the valley towards the grey coated infantry and the green painted guns, it became engulfed in the crossfire from each side of the valley and men and horses went down on every side. 'The first man of my troop who was struck,' recorded RSM Loy-Smith, 'was Private Young, a cannon ball taking off his right arm. I, being close on his right rear, fancied I felt the wind from it as it passed me.'

'Oaths and imprecations might be heard between the report of the guns and the bursting of the shells, as the men crowded and jostled each other in their endeavour to close to the centre,' wrote Sergeant Mitchell.

The heavy iron balls tore up the earth, raising clouds of dust. 'Riderless horses, maimed or unhurt, were galloping now between our intervals, rendered frantic by the deafening noise,' remembered Trooper Pennington, 'to the great distress of those of us who still rode on unhurt.'

Lieutenant Edward Seager, in describing his experience to a friend, wrote:

> We advanced at a trot and soon came within the crossfire from both hills, both of cannon & rifles, the fire was Tremendous, Shells bursting among us, Cannon balls tearing the earth up and Minie balls coming like hail. Still on we went, never altering our pace or breaking up in the least, except that our men and horses were gradually knocked over. Our men behaved well. Poor Fitzgibbons was shot through the body and fell, he was supposed to be dead. Clowes's horse was shot under him and the last that was seen of him, he was walking towards where he started from and we suppose he was taken prisoner or killed ...

Filling the gaps, the flanks closed in on the centre and riders who, in other circumstances, would never have committed such a discourtesy, could no longer be restrained from overtaking their officers. 'The galling fire to which we had been subjected raised our worst passions,' confessed Pennington, 'and we had all but one desire, and that was to silence the fellows who worked the fatal guns.'

Dozens of riderless horses, many wounded and wild with fright, but impelled by habit to wedge themselves into their old troop, competed with the rest in a race for the guns. 'As we neared the battery, a square of infantry that had been placed a little in advance of the guns, gave us a volley in flank,' wrote Loy-Smith. 'The very air hissed as the shower of bullets passed through us; I at this moment, felt that something had touched my left wrist. On looking down I saw that a bullet ... had blackened and cut the lace on my cuff.'

From his vantage point on the hill above Balaklava, Lieutenant Henry Clifford, '... saw shells bursting in the midst of the squadrons. Men and horses strewed the ground behind them. Yet on they went, and then the smoke of the murderous fire poured on them hid them from my sight.' Many of those watching from the safety of the hills, could not conceal their emotions and General Bosquet was heard to say, 'C'est magnifique, mais ce n'est pas la guerre'.

'The tears ran down my cheeks,' admitted Clifford, 'and the din of musketry pouring in their murderous fire on the brave gallant fellows rang in my ears.' In the hail of musketry, a ball struck Pennington's black mare on her hind leg and he was forced to dismount. 'A ball passed through my right leg, a shot from the left tilted my busby over my right ear,' wrote the Trooper of the 11 Hussars, 'while "Bess" received the *coupe de grace* which brought us both to earth.' Great was his relief when a sergeant major of the 8 Hussars, seeing his plight, handed him a riderless grey mare on which he eventually returned to the British lines.

'As we drew nearer, the guns in our front supplied us liberally with grape and canister which brought down men and horses in heaps,' recorded Albert Mitchell. 'We were now very close to the guns, for we were entering the smoke which hung in clouds to the front, I could see some of the gunners running from the guns to the rear.'

Despite the odds against it happening after a ride of eight minutes under such a murderous hail of gunfire, a majority reached the guns where many of the Russians had taken refuge behind the cannon's wheels or beneath the limbers, in a bid to escape the thrust of a lance or the sweep of a sabre. Behind them Russian cavalry moved forward to receive the oncoming Dragoons and Hussars of the Light Brigade. Lieutenant Seager told his parents:

> The men kept well together and bravely seconded us as we dashed at them (the Russian Lancers) they were three deep with lances levelled. I parried the first fellow's lance, the one behind him I cut over the head, which no doubt he will remember for some time, and as I was recovering my sword I found the third fellow making a tremendous point at my body – I had just time to receive his lance point on the hilt of my sword, it got through the bars, knocked the skin off the top of my knuckles and the point came out of the top joint of my little finger. I have only got a slight scratch that might look interesting in a drawing room.

Robert Farquharson, the trumpeter of the Light Dragoons, was not so fortunate:

> Just as we got into the melee my horse dropped. He had been hit by a bullet; but in addition to that, a Russian gunner with whom I was engaged, in attempting to cut me down missed his mark, the blow falling on the horse ... No sooner was I on the ground and saw that it was all over with my horse than I found the skirmish was past. I was left alone in the field.

In endeavouring to escape on a captured Cossack horse, a cannon shot put a stop to Farquharson's gallop to freedom, bringing his horse to the ground and in a few minutes he was surrounded by Russians and taken prisoner.

Controversy exists as to whether Lord Cardigan reached the guns. One argument has it that within yards of the Russian artillerymen his horse took fright at a sudden explosion and swerved away, galloping off with him to the rear. But, wrote Sergeant Major Henry Franks, 'It was stated at the time that Lord Cardigan's horse actually leapt over one of the Russian gun carriages, and I firmly believe it to be true'.

'The Light Brigade is now a skeleton, as all the regiments suffered more or less,' wrote Lieutenant Seager. Commenting on the part played by the 8 Hussars, he added: 'They gave us great credit for wheeling about and attacking the Lancers, it enabled the other regiments who were previously broken to get through them much more easily.'

Cornet George Clowes of the 8 Hussars was fortunate to survive the charge with a minor wound. Six weeks after being taken prisoner, having had his horse shot from under him, Clowes wrote to his father from Simpheropol describing his narrow escape:

> You will be glad to get a few lines from me to hear I am all right and very comfortable here...I will only say that I am very thankful that I did not share the fate of many of my brother officers for I had a pretty narrow escape, being hit hard on the back by a grape shot, but it only skimmed across, taking a few splinters of bone off my right shoulder blade...the people are excessively kind to us. We have lots of English books and we go where we like, only with a soldier to accompany us.

Earlier, Lieutenant Seager had notified the circumstances of Clowes's capture to his father: 'We could not pull up to look after those who fell, we were in the midst of a terrific fire and a body of Russian cavalry was about to attack our rear, which we avoided by wheeling about and charging them. Some one saw your son trying to make his way back with his sword in his hand on foot when it was supposed he was taken prisoner.' Cornet Clowes was eventually exchanged in August 1855, returning to Scutari the following month.

Another fortunate survivor was Robert Portal of the 4 Light Dragoons. Writing to his mother on 26 October, Captain Portal could hardly believe his luck:

> By a perfect miracle, I among a few more, was not touched by anything, except a piece of shell caught me in the back, but it was quite spent and did not hurt me in the least ... To give you an idea of the loss sustained by the Light Cavalry Brigade – in round numbers we mustered on parade 800 soldiers, last night we numbered 180. I numbered in my troop this morning on parade ten mounted men. Captain Nolan was shot dead the first shot, and we

think it was a judgement on him for having been the cause of our getting into such a mess ... It was altogether the maddest and most extra ordinary order ever given to Cavalry, and there is to be an inquiry instituted at once.

Those of his comrades who had reached the guns and engaged with the Russian artillerymen, having no support and with their horses blown, had been obliged to return through a murderous fire, pursued by Cossacks sent to cut their line of retreat. Seager, having got through the Russians, looked over his shoulder and noticed that,

> ... a large body of Lancers were coming on my left to cut us off. I put Malta to her speed and she soon got out of their reach, but the shot and rifle balls flew in great quantities, shells bursting just over my head with an awful crash. That any of the Light Cavalry Brigade returned through the cross fire kept up upon us, was through the great providence of God to whom I am grateful more than I can express.

That many who braved the initial charge up to the guns, did not survive the battle, was due to the vengeful Cossacks who showed no mercy to the fallen. Clifford, with the other watchers on the hill, was outraged by the behaviour of the Russians:

> I saw hundreds of our poor fellows lying on the ground, the Cossacks and Russian cavalry running them through as they lay, with their swords and lances. I believe the Russians treated our wounded shamefully in spite of our kindness to theirs at Alma. Our men will not forgive them and will pay them off in their own coin.

Lord Lucan lost no time in bringing up the heavy cavalry to the assistance of the survivors retiring before the enemy. They were not the only body to assist the Light Brigade, as Trooper Pennington makes clear: 'One cannot leave the "Valley of Death" without acknowledging the debt of gratitude due from the Light Brigade to the famed Chasseurs d'Afrique, who without hesitation sprang upon the enemy posted on the Fedioukine Hills. They silenced the batteries there, diverting all attacks upon the broken Light Brigade from that part of the field.'

At the midday roll call, of the 673 men that had formed the Light Brigade, only a mounted strength of 195 returned fit for action. Pennington, who numbered among them, recalled that:

> The first person I encountered as I rode in was a sergeant of the 13th Light Dragoons. He had been down the valley, and with his horse returned without a scratch. He rode up to me, and without a word exchanged he grasped my hand, moved by the perils we had escaped and shared. I judged his feelings by my own.

Trooper Pennington was later to contract camp fever of a most virulent kind in the winter of 1855, and was subsequently discharged as being unfit for further service.

Another cavalryman fortunate to escape serious injury, was Sergeant Albert Mitchell. Nearing the Russian guns his horse was struck by a shell and he was thrown to the ground, narrowly escaping being trampled underfoot as the 4 Light Dragoons galloped past. As he made his way back on foot, he met Lord Cardigan galloping away from the guns. 'Meeting me he pulled up,' recorded Mitchell, 'and in his usually stern, hoarse voice, said: "You had better make the best of your way back as fast as you can, or you will be taken prisoner".' Eventually Mitchell joined the survivors of his regiment, which numbered just thirteen who were still mounted and fit for duty.

'On that morning the brigade had mounted, I believe, six hundred and seven sabres and lances,' he wrote. 'Our regiment numbered a hundred and ten, or thereabouts, and by noon ours alone had lost eighty-six horses and upwards of fifty men killed, wounded, and missing.'

It is recorded that when the surviving members of the Light Brigade formed up for the roll call, Lord Cardigan rode forward to address them.

'Men!' he said, 'it is a mad brained trick, but no fault of mine.'

'Lord Raglan is very angry,' reported George Clowes to his father. 'He says he did not order us to go through such fire, but the man who carried the message from him to Lord Lucan is killed so I suppose the blame will all be laid to his account.'

Lord Raglan was indeed furious, and only later did he grudgingly concede that Cardigan was not so much to blame as Lucan, having merely carried out Lucan's orders. Lord Lucan was equally determined not to be made a scapegoat for the catastrophe, and was afterwards careful to send a copy of Raglan's original order to the British ambassador for safe keeping. Accompanying it was a letter from a staff officer who had witnessed the charge and was clearly of the opinion that it had been Cardigan and Nolan who were to blame. Both papers were eventually sent on to Clarendon, the Foreign Secretary, but did little to help Lucan's case. He was relieved of his command on 13 February 1855 but stayed on in another capacity and eventually reached the rank of Field Marshal.

Commenting upon the case, William Russell informed his readers that, 'The impression as far as I could ascertain, was that Lord Lucan was harshly and unjustly dealt with'. He had, of course, been a horrified witness to the charge of the Light Brigade and he made it quite clear that in his opinion, 'there had been some hideous blunder'.

Alfred, Lord Tennyson may well have read his comments for, a few weeks later, the Light Brigade's sacrifice was immortalized in his famous poem:

> Forward the Light Brigade!
> Was there a man dismayed?
> Not though the soldiers knew
> Some one had blundered:
> Their's not to make reply
> Their's not to reason why,
> Their's but to do or die:
> Into the valley of Death
> Rode the Six Hundred.

RSM Loy-Smith observed:

> Thus ended a day of disaster which might have been avoided if more forethought and discretion had been observed. I believe that had a few battalions of English or French infantry been posted in the redoubts to support the Turks, and more of our artillery been brought into action, and the cavalry properly commanded, the day would have ended very differently. General Liprandi might well ask our prisoners if we were drunk.

Later, when Liprandi addressed a group of prisoners, he told them: 'You are noble fellows and I am sincerely sorry for you.'

A total of fifty-six prisoners were taken by the Russians, of whom half died of wounds in captivity. The losses among the officer prisoners was even greater, as Lieutenant Jocelyn Strange was to discover. Writing to his father, he informed him:

> We sent in a flag of truce the other day to know how many of our cavalry officers had been taken prisoner, and their names. Captain Clowes of the 8th Hussars and Captain Chadwick of the 17th Lancers were just two of the twelve names submitted by the Russians who eventually returned to their regiments. The Russian officers were very civil and deplored the war very much; they were heartily sick of it and hoped the Emperor would make peace in the winter.

Perhaps the last comment on that fateful charge should be left to Lieutenant George Frederick Dallas who, in a letter dated 27 October, wrote:

> There is one universal feeling of disgust throughout the whole army at this murder, for it can be called nothing else. As a French Colonel said to me yesterday (who saw it all), They might as well have been ordered to charge the walls of Sebastopol. Who will answer for it, I don't know.

News of the 600's gallant charge reached Constantinople three days after the action at Balaklava and a report was sent to the Earl of Clarendon by Lord Stratford de Redcliffe, the British ambassador to the Porte. In it he assured Clarendon that it was merely a temporary setback. 'True or false,' he wrote, 'the impression still prevails that the allied armies will finally succeed in carrying the place (Sevastopol), though not perhaps, without a second, or even a third assault...'

Lord Raglan's view was not so sanguine. He was reluctant to expose Balaklava to further attacks and he did not have sufficient strength of infantry to capture the redoubts from Liprandi's forces on the Causeway Heights. That night, the first frosts of winter were felt by the Light Cavalrymen. It was to be a problem which would bedevil the British Commander-in-Chief for many weeks to come, but for now, his immediate task was to formulate a plan to lay siege to Sevastopol with his depleted forces while guarding against the possibility of a Russian counter-attack and the ever present threat posed by Liprandi's forces on his vulnerable right flank. A predicament which caused Trooper Pennington, when assessing the situation, to remark:

Our so called investment of Sebastopol was no investment, for here was Liprandi's command free to take the field at will, and a road always open by which the enemy could receive reinforcements. It will remain a mystery that with the command of the entire coast line, no serious attempt was made to prevent supplies and troops passing the narrow Isthmus of Perekop, which is only four miles wide and twenty in length.

Chapter Four

INKERMAN: A SOLDIER'S BATTLE

As October drew to a close, the weather worsened to the extent that Sergeant Gowing, having endured a spell in the trenches, was forced to admit in a letter to his parents:

> We had a rough 24 hours of it digging and making the trenches. It rained the whole time ... We were standing nearly up to our knees in mud and water, like a lot of drowned rats, nearly all night; the cold, bleak wind cutting through our thin clothing. As for the covering party, it was killing work laying down for hours in the cold mud. This is ten times worse than all the fighting. We are nearly worked to death night and day. We cannot move without sinking nearly to our ankles in mud ... I suppose we shall have leather medals for this one day – I mean those who have the good fortune to escape the shot and shell of the enemy, and the pestilence that surrounds us.

There was little comfort for the officers, as Lieutenant Curtis made clear in a letter to his brother: 'It must be borne in mind that we had no beds or mattresses to sleep on, only a blanket and a military cloak, and if a man had been on patrol or other duty, and had got a good drenching with rain, the cloak would not be a very desirable covering for his bed; but although these matters were not all that we could have desired, I never heard any grumbling or repining.'

Gowing's ordeal in the trenches as for many others, ended dramatically the day after Balaklava when a Russian reconnaissance in strength, was launched shortly after 1.00 p.m. from the Karabelnaya suburb of Sevastopol. A strong body of infantry led by Colonel Federoff, supported by two squadrons of Cossacks and four cannon, struck against the weakly defended right flank of the allied line, where the broken ground was occupied by the 2nd Division. Federoff's advance unseen over scrubland and along the Carenague ravine, was made with such rapidity that the pickets of the 49 Regiment on Home Ridge, were overcome before any support could reach them and it was only the intervention of a strong detachment from the Brigade of Guards that held up the enemy long enough for the 2nd Division to get under arms. The artillery, which accompanied it, opened to such good effect that the Russian field guns were obliged to limber up and retire from the field. The Russian infantry, left alone to face a punishing fire from field artillery in addition to the aggressive nature of the 2nd Division, retired in confusion after an engagement lasting little more than half an hour.

Lieutenant Somerset Calthorpe remembered:

We captured over 80 prisoners of whom two officers and 17 men were untouched. The troops had been told that the English were quite disheartened, so there was no difficulty in obtaining volunteers (for the attack). They must have been not a little surprised at the readiness with which they were met and repulsed by the British troops, whose numbers did not exceed 2,000 men.

Lord Raglan who had been notified of the engagement known as the 'Little Inkerman' arrived on the scene shortly after the Russians had retired and was no doubt relieved at the outcome, but it had alerted him to the fact that the 24,800 troops at his disposal were barely sufficient both to lay siege to Sevastopol and effectively defend his position against enemy attacks in the field. The 2nd Division in particular was perilously extended on a long front beyond the plain above Balaklava.

Shortage of manpower was not a problem which troubled General Liprandi, for he was receiving reinforcements almost on a daily basis. At the beginning of November, two divisions, the 10th and the 11th had arrived from Bessarabia to strengthen his army, a fact that did not escape the notice of Lieutenant Calthorpe: 'We hear from deserters, and indeed we can see, that large reinforcements are daily arriving to the Russian army. It is said that the Corps d'Armee under General Liprandi counts upward of 40,000 bayonets, and that he is expecting another division.' The growing strength of the enemy did not seem to worry the officers of the Headquarters Staff however, for as Somerset Calthorpe remarked: 'Though the Russians have a large disposable force, I doubt much whether they will have determination and courage enough to overcome British firmness and French gallantry.' His belief was shortly to be put to the test, for the Russians were preparing for what was to be the toughest battle yet, and which was afterwards aptly labelled as being 'The soldier's battle'.

Meanwhile the siege continued although not a few in Raglan's staff doubted whether the army had sufficient strength to storm the town before the onset of winter. The first frost after Balaklava was a reminder to Lord Raglan, who had been advised that 'in such weather no human creature can possibly resist cold during the night unless in a good house properly warmed, and in day-time unless properly dressed', but even before autumn was at an end, it was becoming obvious that the soldiers in the field were ill equipped, or prepared, for the bitter weather to come. Somerset Calthorpe confessed: 'The 29th was the first really cold day that we have had since we landed in the Crimea, and the contrast to the previous warmth was very great. Far more men go into hospital from the night work in the trenches than from any other cause; and even those not at work begin to feel the cold very much, being only under the cover of the tents, which are but poor protection against the inclement weather.'

The period spent in the trenches varied, but for the supervising officer his day was seldom less than twelve hours, during which time, as Lieutenant Dunscombe pointed out: 'The quantity of shot and shell that flew over our heads during this day was astonishing.'

'It is most unpleasant though very exciting work, to be shot at when in the trenches,' wrote Lieutenant Peard. 'We had to lie down constantly whenever shells fell near us, and it was impossible to judge where they would burst, or the direction of their deadly contents.'

In the opinion of William Simpson, an artist who was in the Crimea to record various aspects of the campaign, there could be no greater menace than the ordinary bullet. 'It was the rifle bullet I learned to dread,' he confessed. 'It comes stealthily, gives no warning, and no chance of dodging. The only hope of safety from it being careful to keep under cover.'

Occasionally such dangers were dismissed with a humorous remark similar to that heard by Sergeant Gowing: 'We had a very narrow escape from a huge shell that came hopping right into the midst of us; we just had time to throw ourselves down when it exploded and sent our breakfast flying in all directions. One of our officers enquired if any one was hurt, and a nice boy of ours answered that he was, "for, bedad, he had nothing to eat".' Temple Godman, in a letter which must have horrified his parents, complained:

> They say we are to winter here. I hope not, it is wretched work, and the cold gives one diarrhoea. We are so far from water we seldom get a wash, and every one is covered with lice which I pick out every morning regularly, but they come again. We are often turned out in the night and often sleep in our clothes for fear of an attack. I never take off anything for weeks together but trousers and coat, it is too cold to take off more.

Pressing though the question was of providing adequate shelter for the troops, of greater concern to Lord Raglan was the need to reinforce his weak right wing. At the beginning of November he had been notified by the Foreign Secretary that the 3, 62, and 90 Regiments would shortly be on the high seas together with a train of artillery, but it was made abundantly clear that their early arrival largely depended upon the availability of screw driven ships.

Prince Alexander Sergeevich Menschikoff although untroubled by questions of transport, was not without problems of his own. Under pressure, not least from the Tsar, to reduce the stress and anxiety of the artillery bombardment currently suffered by the citizens of Sevastopol, he was all too aware that failure would almost certainly lead to his dismissal as Commander-in-Chief. It was with this threat hanging over him, that he transferred his headquarters to the ruined village of Inkerman on 4 November in preparation for a major assault against the allies which, if successful, would force them to lift the siege and possibly drive them back to the sea.

Prince Menschikoff, a bluff unimaginative man, was not helped by the ill feeling which existed between himself and the Corps

Commander, General Dannenberg, who had arrived on 3 November with the 10th and 11th Divisions from Bessarabia. In fact the Russian leader had requested Gorchakoff to dispatch the reinforcements without their Commander, but he had been rebuffed; Gorchakoff having informed him that '...he could not have the benefits of the former without the disadvantages of the latter'. Dannenberg too, was a veteran of the Napoleonic Wars, but for all his experience it was said that his subordinates had little confidence in his ability after suffering defeat at the hands of the Turks a year earlier in Southern Romania due, to some degree, to his indecisiveness and inability to delegate command.

Captain Hodasevich reported:

> There were 12 regiments those of the 16th and 17th Divisions were less than 3,000 each, whilst those of the 19th and 11th were more than 3,000 men. In all some 40,000 bayonets and 120 guns also two battalions of riflemen. Under cover of the infantry occupying the heights, the artillery was to gain the heights by two roads, one to the left above the Quarry Ravine, and the other to the right by a road finished in July.

For the Grand Assault on three fronts, Menschikoff had 60,000 men and he intended to use the major part of his strength against Raglan's weakest point where the 2nd Division and the Guards were encamped, on a rocky scrub covered prominence overlooking the Tchernaya River known as Inkerman Ridge. Nineteen thousand men, under the command of General Soimonov, would leave Sevastopol, cross the Careenage Ravine and climb Inkerman Ridge, while 16,000 led by General Pavlov would advance from Inkerman village, cross the river and proceed along the numerous small ravines to Saddle Top Ridge. Two other diversionary attacks were to be made with the objective of preventing, or at least delaying, the French from coming to the aid of their ally. The first would be led by Prince Gorchakoff, with 22,000 men against the French on the Sapoune Hills overlooking Balaklava, aided by General Pavel Liprandi's 12th Infantry Division and a strong force of cavalry, while a smaller force led by General Timofeev was to leave the city and attack the allied trenches and earthworks in front of Sevastopol. As Captain Hodasevich disclosed: 'I learnt afterwards that, at the council of war that preceded the battle, General Liprandi had proposed to attack the heights of Balaklava, which, having succeeded, would have deprived the English of that harbour, of so much importance to them...the plan of General Liprandi was not received as he was only a general of division.'

Just under 60,000 men and an artillery strength of 234 guns was to be involved, including a combined force of 35,000 men in the two diversionary assaults. An altogether overwhelming force it would appear, when measured against Raglan's available strength of 8,600 men. Fortunately for the allies, the large scale troop movement planned by the Russians was likely to be restricted by the nature of the terrain – a series of ridges separated by ravines of varying depth, with rising ground covered with masses of brushwood and dense clumps of bushes.

Had Prince Menschikoff's emphasis on precise timing and coordination been observed, his ambitious plan might well have borne fruit but, happily for the allies, the Russian General Staff did not have the necessary experience to ensure it was carried out according to Menschikoff's instructions and, when General Dannenberg, who was unfamiliar with the territory, ordered Soimonov to advance west of the Careenage Ravine to the Victoria Ridge, it was disregarded without Dannenberg being informed; an oversight which was to throw the Russian infantry into confusion even before a shot had been fired.

When the advance began at 2.00 a.m. on Sunday, 5 November few of the Russians realized that they were about to go into battle against the victors of the Alma. 'No-one knew where we were being taken so early or why,' a Russian officer of the Tarutinsky Regiment admitted, 'although the night-time meal and extra cup of vodka and our route towards the enemy positions forced us to make a guess.'

As General Soimonov's columns began to make their way under cover of darkness along the Careenage Ravine, the clatter of dislodged stones was heard, but dismissed as nothing of special significance by the British pickets on Shell Hill. In fact, as Lieutenant George Carmichael explained:

On the assumption that in fog, an enemy would be more easily seen against the skyline from the base rather than the summit, the British pickets had been withdrawn from Shell Hill thus making it easy for the Russians to approach without detection. I remember hearing the clang of church bells in the town and the rumble of wheels in the valley but the latter noise raised no suspicion in my mind, as it was a nightly occurrence and had been reported previously and it was well known to all, that the enemy used this road during the night.

Lieutenant Calthorpe reported that:

Some of the men, on the outlying pickets in front of the 2nd and Light Divisions, more than once fancied they heard the sound of wheels passing under the heights between them and the harbour. Little did the watchers think that the wheels which they heard rumbling in the distance, were carrying the means of their destruction, and were forerunners of one of the bloodiest struggles in the history of modern warfare.

George Taylor thought that the pickets on Cossack Hill should have been on a higher state of alert, 'but much is said for them,' he admitted, 'on account of the badness of the weather, the dark background from which the Russians advanced, and the soft state of the soil, which muffled the wheels of the guns'.

The previous day had been wet and with the dawn, a steady drizzle leading to a mist growing denser every minute, effectively masked the advance of the Russian infantry. 'The gloomy character of the morning was unchanged,' wrote *The Times* correspondent, 'showers of rain fell through the fog and turned the ground into a clammy soil, like a freshly ploughed field.' The fog also led to confusion among the various Russian regiments. There was, as yet, no sign of General Pavlov whose troops had been prevented from crossing the Inkerman Bridge which was undergoing repair, but shortly before 6.00 a.m. there was an exchange of musketry when pickets of General Pennefather's 2nd Division were surprised on Shell Hill and suffered a number of casualties. Pennefather quickly brought up reinforcements and with the rapidly thickening fog bringing visibility down to a few dozen yards, the fighting on Shell Hill developed into a confused mêlée of personal encounters, with officers snatching up rifle and bayonet and laying about themselves with as much zeal as any private soldier. Captain Bruce Hamley observed:

On our part it was a confused and desperate struggle. Colonels of regiments led on small parties, and fought like subalterns, captains like privates. Once engaged every man was his own General. The enemy was in front and must be beaten back.

Lieutenant Peard reported that: 'The greatest confusion prevailed, and our Generals could not tell where to go, or which way to turn, on account of the fog, which screened the enemy from our view. Their position was only indicated by the rattle of musketry which poured into our lines with deadly effect.'

The fire power of the 95th had been reduced to some extent by the inclement weather. Lieutenant Carmichael wrote: 'The rifles of many of the men, who had been out the previous night would not at first go off from their damp condition but the rifles of the fallen men were to be had. My Colour Sergt. Saxton was one of those in this predicament, but I handed him one thrown down by a gigantic Guardsman, who was shot through the mouth by my side, and who reeled off to the rear choking with blood.'

The noise of battle was heard by the French and a concerned General Bosquet at once offered his assistance, only for it to be politely declined; a decision quickly reversed by Lord Raglan who dispatched a staff officer to him with an urgent request that he support the hard pressed British troops. General Bosquet indeed lost no time in ordering up his division but, since it was two miles distant with much of the ground covered with thick brushwood, the division's progress was necessarily slow, although the French were eventually to lend their support at a critical moment when the Guards were on the point of defeat at the Sandbag Battery. Two brigades of cavalry had been called out early in the morning, but were never used, much to the annoyance of Sergeant Major Henry Franks of the 5 Dragoons, who was obliged to admit:

We remained on the Field during the whole day, but for all the use we were we might as well have been in our tents. The fog never cleared away, and it was so dark in consequence, that the Cavalry were never engaged at all. In fact we never saw a Russian soldier during the battle.

Scarcely had shots been exchanged between the parties on Shell Hill, before the Russian artillery began its bombardment of the defences around Balaklava. The shells did little harm but the noise of gunfire alerted Sir Colin Campbell to the danger and shortly afterwards Lord Raglan, already aware of the engagement on the extreme right of his line, received a report that French pickets on the heights above Balaklava Valley, could see Liprandi's troops advancing rapidly towards the Black Sea port.

Raglan at once ordered the horses to be saddled and, with his staff, was soon mounted and prepared to ride where he would be most needed. For a moment he was undecided as to which area was the more important, feeling that one of the attacks must be intended as a feint. Realizing, however, that his right flank was the weakest and difficult to defend, he decided that the Russian advance against Balaklava could be safely left to Sir Colin Campbell's Highlanders, and that his presence with the 2nd Division was of crucial importance. By now, reinforcements, in the shape of the Light Division and the 1st Division commanded by the Duke of Cambridge, together with Cathcart's 4th Division, had arrived and the sight of the Zouaves sent by General Bosquet, lifted the morale of the hard pressed troops around the Sandbag Battery.

Lord Raglan and his staff arrived in the camp of the 2nd Division at 6.00 a.m. and he at once set about assessing the situation and the strength of the enemy's force. The officers on his staff had been taken aback by the chaos and the number of casualties which confronted them. 'Tents were every moment being knocked over by shot or blown to pieces by exploding shell,' remembered Lieutenant Calthorpe. 'The scene of confusion which the camp exhibited was frightful. Many bodies were lying about of men who had never even seen the enemy – possibly were hardly aware of their vicinity...'

The Russian bombardment from a commanding slope known as Cossack Hill, little more than 800 yards away, was causing other problems, for the drizzling rain held the smoke of battle close to the ground, effectively obscuring everything beyond a few yards and making it far from easy for Raglan to determine the deployment of the enemy troops and dispossess them of the ground they had already won. Captain Bruce Hamley observed:

Rarely has such an artillery fire been so concentrated and for so long on an equally confined place ... the resistless cannon shot in whose rush there seems something vindictive, as if each were best

72

ridden by some angry demon; crashing through the bodies of men and horses, and darting from the ground on a second course of mischief ... it was difficult to stave off the thought that, in the next instant, your arm or leg may be dangling from your body a crushed and bloody mess, or your spirit driven through a hideous wound across the margin of the undiscovered country.

The artillery on Cossack Hill was certainly causing much damage and inflicting many casualties, but of greater concern to Lord Raglan were reports that the Russian infantry was advancing in heavy columns on the road from Inkerman and along the Careenage and Quarry Ravines. In fact a brigade of the Light Division had become aware of a strong force of Russians climbing a ravine close to the Inkerman road. Charging out of the mist at the point of the bayonet whilst just thirty yards away, General Buller's men took the Russian soldiers by surprise. In a matter of minutes the 77 and 88 Foot drove the astonished Russians headlong down the slope before returning to the crest of the hill.

The Sandbag Battery, an emplacement made for two field guns, now assumed a position of crucial importance to the redcoats due to the position it occupied on a spur of the Inkerman Heights overlooking two ravines, one on each side, which merged into the valley of the Tchernaya. The 41 Welsh and the 49 Hertfordshire regiments commanded by Brigadier General Adams were ordered to take three cannon and consolidate the redoubt against enemy attack.

The two regiments had scarcely occupied the site before it was subjected to a heavy bombardment from Russian artillery on Cossack Hill. Adams lost little time in instructing his men to lie flat in order to minimize casualties, but Captain Hamley in the act of bringing up a field gun to protect the right flank, had his horse struck by a round shot which brought them both to the ground:

> This was the poor fellow's last field. A sergeant of artillery ran to extricate me; I was in the act of steadying myself on his shoulder, when a shot carried off his thigh, and he fell backward on me uttering cries as if of amazement at the suddenness of his misfortune.

Shortly after the incident involving Captain Hamley, the Russian cannonade ceased and their infantry began to swarm up the sides of the ravine towards the Sandbag Battery and begin the first of a series of hard fought actions in which the redoubt was repeatedly won and lost. The accurate fire from Minié rifles held off the Russians for the greater part of a quarter of an hour despite odds of ten to one, before it became apparent that the redcoats were in grave danger of being encircled, and the two regiments were ordered to retire upon the main body of the 2nd Division.

The Sandbag Battery was now in the possession of grey coated Russian infantry but reinforcements had reached the Light Division from Cambridge's 1st and Cathcart's 4th Division. The French too, had responded to a plea for support, and the sight of a battalion of Zouaves and another of Tirailleurs with four companies of Chasseurs d'Afrique coming to the aid of the hard pressed Light Division, raised cheers which could be heard above the noise of gunfire. Loy-Smith recalled:

> The Chasseurs d'Afrique now went past us at a gallop and passed over the brow of the hill. We halted about 200 yards from the top. The enemy must have known we were there, for they dropped their cannon balls just over the brow of the hill so that they passed through us about breast high. One struck a horse's head knocking it to pieces, then took off Sergeant Breese's arm, taking the three bars and leaving the crown.

Then, as *The Times* journalist dramatically alluded to the next phase of the battle: 'There commenced the bloodiest struggle ever witnessed since war cursed the earth.'

The Sandbag Battery quickly became the focus of ferocious hand to hand fighting with the Guards determined to regain possession, despite having come upon the scene tired after spending twenty-four hours in the trenches. Trampling the bodies of the dead and wounded as they surged forward, they neither gave or received quarter in a mêlée of hand to hand encounters. The Royal Fusiliers also played a prominent part, slashing and stabbing with their bayonets in a frenzy of blood lust which Timothy Gowing, caught up in the fighting as the Russian columns strove to retain the redoubt, explained in a letter to his father: 'The bayonet was used with terrible effect by all regiments. The enemy driven on by their brave officers, had to – and did literally – climb over the heaps of their slain countrymen and ours to renew the blood thirsty contest, but they had to go back time after time much quicker than they came.' Gowing himself received two bayonet wounds, one in each thigh. Fortunately, having hobbled away from the conflict, he was quickly attended by a surgeon and eventually sent to Malta. His subsequent treatment could not be described as either immediate or caring. 'We were packed on board any how – to live or die,' he remembered but, once his wounds were healed, Gowing was back on active service with his regiment in a little more than three months.

Just as the Guards and Fusiliers had successfully wrested the Sandbag Battery from the grip of the Russians, Lord Raglan and his staff arrived, anxious to see for themselves and determine the feasibility of holding the position against a numerically superior enemy. The site was of some importance as the ridge behind the Sandbag Battery formed a natural cover across the front of the 2nd Division's camp.

To the surprise of the staff, although the Russian artillery maintained a continuous cannonade, their infantry exhibited a marked reluctance to attack and Lord Raglan seized the opportunity of a temporary lull, to order up the 4th Division commanded by Sir George Cathcart, with orders to support the 2nd Division and the Brigade of Guards. According to Lieutenant Somerset Calthorpe: 'Now occurred one of the fatal errors of the day. Sir George Cathcart, seeing the inactive state of the Russian infantry, fancied that by descending the slope of the ravine, and turning round by the right of the Guards and the Sandbag Battery, he might attack the enemy's left flank and strike a severe blow, if not entirely throw them into disorder and confusion.' In disobeying Raglan's order to reinforce the Guards in the Sandbag Battery, Sir George Cathcart almost presented General Dannenberg with an opportunity to split the British line and win the day, but to be fair to Sir George, he believed that he would be striking a severe blow against Pavlov's columns on the Russian left flank, and without waiting for Raglan's approval, he ordered his brigade down the slope in the expectation of getting close to the Russian column without being detected.

In a letter to his parents, Lieutenant Dallas of 46 Regiment, wrote: 'I do not think "Guy Fawkes" day was ever celebrated by more gunpowder and fire.'

He went on to describe the charge down the Kitspur by the 400 men of the 4th Division as, '...a most splendid headlong charge on them, pushing them down the steep side of the mountain in utter confusion'. With them went Lieutenant Carmichael:

> We pushed the pursuit down the hill, and partly up the other side, and others followed the fugitives down the hollow or ravine itself. The men were scattered and were beginning to run very short of ammunition. I noticed first at this time, and the men near me also remarked that those following us, but a good deal further to the rear, were turning back, and soon after cries were raised evidently for us, 'Come back, you are cut off'.

'When a few of us got nearly to the top from whence we had started, to our astonishment a most astounding fire opened on us, from the very place we had come up from,' commented Dallas. 'We were so close to the enemy,' he added, 'that they threw stones, & clods of earth in our faces.' Despite the call to retire, Lieutenant Carmichael was unconvinced:

> I could see no cause for retreat thinking it was a false alarm, but the smoke and mist rolling away for a minute, a heavy Russian column became visible forming to our left on the high ground covered by a strong fringe of skirmishers extended at an interval of only two or three paces. It seemed to me more than doubtful if we could reach the Sandbag Battery before them.

General Cathcart turning in his saddle saw, to his dismay, that a battalion of Russian troops were lining the opposite side of the ravine he had just vacated and immediately sent an aide to recall the remainder of 46 and 68 Regiments who were still engaged with the enemy. The Russians, part of a column intent upon regaining possession of the Sandbag Battery, immediately discharged a volley with lethal effect on the fifty redcoats who had reached the summit, and among the many who fell, was Sir George Cathcart, shot through the heart.

The Sandbag Battery once again came under attack with the Coldstream Guards defending it with determination and vigour but, despite the enemy's losses being far in excess of those of the defenders, superior numbers eventually told in an unequal struggle and the Coldstreams, after losing a third of their strength and having exhausted their ammunition, were forced to retreat to the relative security of the ridge, leaving behind their wounded who were barbarously bayoneted by the Russians as they overran the redoubt.

It was now 10.30 a.m. and with fortune favouring the enemy, several battalions of French troops, together with two batteries of field artillery, made a timely intervention in support of the British right flank where the Brigade of Guards and the rapidly shrinking 4th Division were fiercely engaged with the Russians. Sergeant Gowing confessed:

> Our Fourth Division fought at a disadvantage, having been armed with the old Brown Bess musket, against the needle-rifle which the enemy were armed with; our weapons were almost as much use as a broom stick. We had no supports or reserves; but every man, as fast as he could reach the field, went straight at them with a shout that seemed to strike terror into them. And so the fight went on hour after hour.

With the Zouaves and the Chasseurs d'Afrique playing a prominent part, a general advance on the right was resumed and the Russians, seeing a number of French troops among the attackers, were misled into believing that the British had doubled their strength and the Sandbag Battery was abandoned with little show of resistance.

The allies, having once again occupied the Battery, were not allowed to savour their success for long. Within minutes a sustained cannonade from twenty-four large calibre and sixteen lighter field guns positioned on Cossack Hill, began to pound the whole length of the ridge, smashing through brushwood, ploughing up the ground and obliging the troops to lie flat, in order to avoid an excess of casualties from ricocheting shot.

Shortly before midday further reinforcements in the shape of three infantry battalions and two batteries of field artillery were sent by General Canrobert to be placed at the disposal of Lord Raglan. The twelve artillery pieces were especially welcome and were immediately employed in a harassing fire against the Russian columns assembling on the Inkerman road, whilst the infantry were sent forward to support units of the 2nd and Light Divisions, currently taking cover from the enemy's cannonade.

As the French breasted the crest of the hill in a line four deep, they too came under fire from the Russian artillery and began to take casualties. The horrific spectacle of men being mangled by round shot proved so nerve-racking for many of the inexperienced young soldiers, whose first taste of battle this was, that a mild panic set in. Despite repeated exhortations from their officers, a sizeable majority retired down the hill to a safer position watched by Lord Raglan and his staff. 'I cannot describe the sinking sensation one felt on observing our allies give way,' confessed Lieutenant Calthorpe. 'It was the only time that I ever observed Lord Raglan's countenance change.'

Eventually they were persuaded to form up in columns of companies instead of a line four deep and led back into action. Again, casualties led to a wavering in the ranks but, encouraged by the behaviour of the men in the 2nd Division, and a seeming reluctance on the part of the enemy's infantry to engage them, the French troops fought gallantly with their British ally for the remainder of the day. *The Times* correspondent told his readers:

> At twelve o'clock the battle of Inkerman seemed to have been won but the day which had cleared up about eleven, so as to enable us to see the enemy, again became obscured. Rain and fog set in, and as we could not pursue the Russians who were retiring under the shelter of their artillery, we formed in front of our lines and the enemy ... fell back upon the works and retreated in immense confusion, across the Inkerman Bridge.

By early afternoon it became obvious to the Russian General that his chance of winning the day was fast disappearing. The arrival of further large calibre cannon on the British right wing, which quickly reduced the fire power of the Russian artillery on Shell Hill and Cossack Hill to cover their retreating infantry, was followed by a successful attack by the men of 21 and 88 Foot, which forced the gunners to limber up and gallop off the field, leaving the Russian infantry unprotected. As Captain Hodasevich reported: 'During the retreat, or rather flight, we lost a great many men from our ignorance of the ground; everyone ran according to his own judgement, and many found themselves at the top of high precipitous rocks or quarries and such was the panic that had taken possession of the men that many of them, making the sign of the cross, threw themselves over and were dashed to pieces.'

When a weak winter sun began at last to disperse the mist, the sight of the enemy columns retiring brought renewed hope to the outnumbered and exhausted British battalions, which had suffered in equal measure from shot and shell, and close quarter fighting. Many of the redcoats had not eaten since the previous day and, despite the lift in morale, they were far too spent even to consider pursuing the retreating Russians. 'The whole camp was dismal,' reported John Hume, 'dead and wounded lying about in all directions, comrades missing and those who escaped were sad and weary, not withstanding the great victory that had been gained against such immense odds.'

The British troops were undoubtedly exhausted from the fierce fighting, but the same could not be said of the French. They had certainly suffered casualties, but there remained several brigades that had yet to see action and, if supported by their field artillery, were in a position to inflict much damage on the Russian infantry massing on the Inkerman road. When Lord Raglan pointed out to General Canrobert the advantages which might accrue from harassing the closely packed Russian columns however, the French General replied that he would only comply if the pursuit was joined by the Guards which, he said, '...had made such an impression upon his infantry'.

The Guards, however, were in no shape to launch an energetic pursuit, and the chance of striking a decisive blow against Dannenberg's retreating columns, which faced a hazardous crossing of the River Tchernaya by the only bridge, was lost. Although a battery of French artillery did open fire from the high ground on the Inkerman road, it inflicted only the minimum of casualties.

The fighting around the Sandbag Battery had been especially ferocious. Captain Bruce Hamley was appalled by what he saw when touring the battlefield:

Few sights can be imagined more strange and sad in their ghastliness than that of dead men lying in ranks shoulder to shoulder with upturned faces, and limbs composed, except where some stiffened arm and hand remain pointing upward. The faces and hands of the slain assume, immediately after death, the appearance of wax or clay, the lips parting show the teeth; the hair and the mustache (*sic*) become frowzy (*sic*), and the body of him who, half an hour before, was a smart soldier, wears a soiled and faded aspect.

Lieutenant Calthorpe, in describing the harrowing scene which confronted those who visited the site of the Sandbag Battery, was equally forthright: 'Within the circumference of a few yards round the work upwards of 700 dead were lying, the majority of them torn with the most ghastly wounds, for here raged the most desperate hand to hand conflicts. Upwards of 200 British soldiers were stretched upon the ground which they had so nobly held until death.' A cavalryman who took no part in the battle but visited the scene of fighting, was Captain Wombwell: 'I went over the battlefield and a more horrid sight you cannot imagine, The dead, dying, and wounded were lying so thick it was almost impossible to walk. I want to see no more fighting, it has pleased God to keep me safe through what I have seen, and I am now anxious to get home.'

Temple Godman, who visited the scene near the Sandbag Battery the following day, described it as being '...a terrible sight ...round which the bodies lie so thickly one can hardly walk'. Commenting on the Russian wounded he encountered, he added, '...they made signs for water; they were so thankful when we gave it to them. They say their Generals tell them never to spare the wounded. The consequence was they bayoneted all they came across. I wish they could see our men giving them water and their own rations of rum and biscuits.'

Lieutenant Jocelyn Strange was more forceful in expressing his indignation. 'The Russians behaved very atrociously to all the wounded on the field, bayoneting them in the most atrocious manner; more like a set of Caffres, than a civilized nation...'

In using mules to remove the wounded from the field, the French had by far the most efficient method for, unlike the British, they were able to retrieve casualties from even the most inaccessible of places without causing the victim too much discomfort. The British ambulance wagons were, as described by Somerset Calthorpe, '...great lumbering vehicles without springs which are far more difficult to move over broken ground than even a heavy piece of ordnance'. The plight of the wounded certainly left much to be desired and Robert Portal did not spare his family's feelings when he wrote:

> They are carried off the field, some not for twenty-four hours after the action and taken to a tent where they find hundreds of their brother soldiers all applying for the same relief from suffering that they ask themselves. A general care for the whole is all they can expect and all they get ... amputation takes place on any deal box that can be got and by the light of two tallow candles.

At least 700 of the Russian wounded, who had been abandoned, were not neglected by Lord Raglan, who ordered a fatigue party of Turkish troops to bring them into the camp hospitals before nightfall, but many were obliged to lie on the floor with their wounds undressed for many hours, despite the surgeons working to the best of their abilities. As for the dead, three days after the battle, they were still being recovered for burial. Bad as the situation was at Scutari, the wounded crowding the hospitals in Sevastopol fared even worse. Captain Robert Hodasevich, visiting the barracks on the north side of the harbour, wrote:

> On reaching the barracks the scene presented there was so replete with horrors that nothing will ever efface it from my memory, not only were the buildings full of miserable maimed objects, but the courtyards were crowded with the dead and dying, who lay there in their agony, with their ghastly wounds unwashed and undressed, in the dirt and dust. Not only were these unfortunate men unattended to, but the dead were not carried away. I felt sick at heart, and could understand why a Russian soldier prefers death on the field to a wound, however slight.

From the Russian prisoners brought in to the headquarters' camp for interrogation during the evening, it was ascertained that twelve regiments, each of four battalions, had taken part in the Inkerman battle, but it was thought that with the casualties sustained at the Alma, the total Russian strength could not have been much more than 50,000 employed in three great columns. The main objective of the Russian leaders had been to consolidate the high ground in front of the 2nd Division in order to construct batteries from which to enfilade the British positions which, had they done so, would almost certainly have resulted in the withdrawal of that division with the inevitable problems of maintaining the siege. That it did not succeed could be explained by the fact that the Russian attacks were largely uncoordinated and, crucially, the two diversionary attacks planned by Gorchakoff failed to take place.

The greater proportion of allied battle casualties had resulted from Russian artillery fire and from information supplied by prisoners, it was estimated that twenty-four pieces of heavy ordnance equivalent to the British 32-pounder howitzer, had been employed, in addition to ten batteries of field artillery. Since, in the Russian service, each battery comprised eight guns to the British six, it seemed that more than 100 cannon, large and small, had been used against the allies at various times during the day. The fighting around the Inkerman Ridge had been far more costly than that of the Alma. The British had lost 632 killed and 1,800 wounded, many of which subsequently died. French casualties amounted to 1,700 whilst the Russians had lost a third of their strength; in excess of 13,000.

In writing to his mother shortly after the battle, Lieutenant Morgan was possibly expressing the wishes of many of his comrades, when he wrote: 'I hope now it will soon be over for really I have had quite enough campaigning; it is so dreadful to see so many of one's best Friends killed all in one day.'

'It took three days to bury the dead and during that time the soldiers of the three countries were mixed up together, picking out and burying their own men,' recorded Henry Franks. 'Those men, although unable to speak each others language, fraternized together, exchanging and smoking each other's pipes, and when the grog was served out, in many cases drinking one another's health, in dumb show of course, but it seemed to be perfectly understood by everyone.'

In assessing the qualities of the fighting men, Timothy Gowing in his book, *A Soldier's Experiences*, reminds his readers that: 'This battle was not fought by men who were well fed, well clothed, or well housed, nor by an army that was well prepared; but, on the contrary, by men who were, so to speak, half starved, clothed in rags, and exposed to all the inclemencies of a rigorous climate, whilst they were attacked by hordes of men confident of victory, whose feelings had been wrought to madness by stimulants and priest craft.'

William Russell, in his usual eloquent fashion, wrote:

The battle of Inkerman admits of no description. It was a series of dreadful deeds of daring, of sanguinary hand-to-hand fights, of despairing rallies, of desperate assaults – in glens and valleys, in brushwood glades and remote dells, and from which the conquerors, Russian or British, issued only to engage fresh foes, till our old supremacy, so rudely assailed, was triumphantly asserted, and the battalions of the Tsar gave way before our steady courage and the chivalrous fire of France.

In Britain, the battle was regarded as having ended in something of a triumph and the usual congratulations followed. The Prime Minister requested Raglan to pass on the country's gratitude for the:

...cordial co-operation the French had shown, and the desire of the Queen to make known to the officers, non-commissioned officers and soldiers who have so gloriously won by their blood, freely shed, fresh honours for the army of a Country which sympathizes as deeply with their privations and exertions as it glories in their victories and exults in their fame.

Lord Raglan was elevated to the rank of Field Marshal, an honour which did not meet with universal approval. Lieutenant Dallas wrote:

We have heard that Lord Raglan is a Field Marshal. We are not so delighted with him, as you all seem to be at home. Nothing is done for us here. You will scarcely believe that the mail has been in since Saturday morning, this being Monday night, & except Ld R's own bag, not a single officer has yet received his letters ... it is shrewdly suspected that Ld. Raglan is at the bottom of it, as he does not like our accounts getting to England as soon as his.

Captain Robert Portal, in writing to his sister, was even more annoyed: 'Fancy making Lord Raglan a Field Marshal. What for? What has he done? He has left undone what he ought to have done, and done what he ought not to have done, all through.'

Another officer to criticize the promotion was Lieutenant Richard Temple Godman. 'I think Lord Raglan's promotion somewhat premature, they might have waited till this place falls,' he wrote, referring to Sevastopol, 'he is never seen and seems to take things precious easy.'

At a council of war on 7 November, Lord Raglan, in ebullient mood, proposed that a major assault be carried out against Sevastopol the very next day. This somewhat impetuous move was vehemently opposed by General Canrobert who held the view that battle casualties and sickness had so reduced the allied strength that any major move against the enemy would be inadvisable. With the British able to muster little more than 16,000 bayonets, with little chance of reinforcements, Raglan had no option but to recognize the French point of view that they confine themselves for the present to the defensive, and ensure that adequate measures be taken for wintering in the Crimea.

In a letter to his family, Lieutenant Henry Clifford summed up the situation with admirable foresight when he wrote: 'A large army quite at liberty and independent of the siege of Sebastopol has to be fought – winter is coming on – and we are far from our resources.'

The mood of the troops following the battle varied with their degree of personal satisfaction; elation at having beaten back a formidable enemy, and despair at the rapidly worsening conditions brought on by the incessant rain and gale force wind. Tents were continually being blown down and scattered, leaving the men soaked and shivering in their inadequate clothing. In the absence of suitable accommodation the troops were forced to improvise, and Lieutenant Calthorpe, when writing home, did not forget to praise their ingenuity:

> Some of the troops are beginning to make huts for themselves in their spare time ... they dig a trench some 20 feet long, 10 broad and three deep; then build a wall of loose stones inside the trench, and raise it two feet above the ground, and then the earth is thrown outside the wall, and banked up against it, so that the sides of the hut are quite air-tight. A roof is put on in the usual way; it is made with planks, when procurable but more frequently, from the want of the former, brushwood is used, supported on small rafters and afterwards covered with earth, plastered down. As no fireplace is put up, it being usually made in the centre of the hut, the smoke escaping, after the Irish fashion, by the doorway.

With the imminent approach of what was to prove a severe winter, despair became ever more widespread. Even so

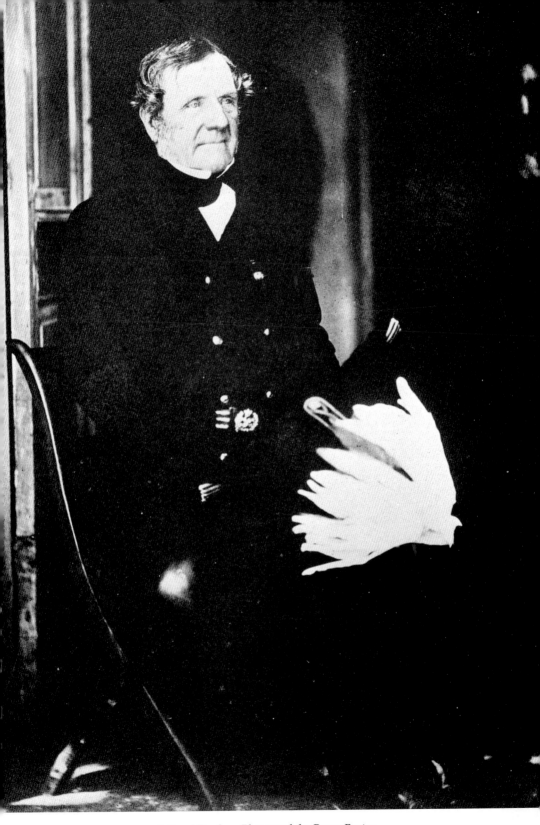

1. Lord Raglan. *Photograph by Roger Fenton*

2. The 93 Sutherland Highlanders at the Battle of Balaclava 1854. The Thin Red Line. *Watercolour by Richard Simkin.*

3. The Relief of the Light Brigade, 1854. *Oil on canvas by Richard Caton Woodville.*

4. Private John McDermond VC, 47 Regiment of Foot winning the VC by saving Colonel Haly, his Commanding Officer, at Inkerman 1854. Oil on paper by Louis William Desanges 1860.

5. Second Charge of the Guards at the Battle of Inkerman 1854.
Tinted lithograph by E. Mann after W. Simpson.

6. RHA Galloping into Action c.1855. *Charcoal and watercolour drawing by G. Bryant Campion.*

7. The Council of War held on the morning of the taking of the Mamelon. L. to R. Lord Raglan, Omar Pasha and General Pelissier. *Photograph by Roger Fenton 1855.*

8. The Capitulation of Kars, Crimean War 1855. *Oil on canvas by Thomas Jones Barker 1860*

distinguished a soldier as General Sir de Lacy Evans was of the opinion that there was nothing to be done but raise the siege and evacuate the Crimea. Lord Raglan, with his customary courtesy, pointed out that such a decision would be nothing short of lunacy. Even if there was enough shipping to evacuate the army, it would be unable to remove the siege train, and their French ally, to say nothing of the Turkish troops, would be left to their own devices. The presence of journalists such as William Howard Russell, who would have described the evacuation in painful detail to the British public, was another argument which made it certain that the army would winter as best it could while every resource was directed to maintaining the siege of Sevastopol.

Chapter Five

THE APPROACH OF WINTER

Lieutenant Godman wrote, in a letter to his brother:

> The winter is setting in and we have just had two days rain, the misery of which you can hardly realise. The horses up to their fetlocks in mud and slush, through which one must paddle to get to them, the saddles soaked, the tents so crowded that the men have no room in them for their arms, which must therefore lie in the rain ... The men are worse off, most having no change or only one of clothes – of course their clothes get wet in the daytime and their cloaks, and these they must sleep in as also their boots, for if they pulled them off they would never get them on again.

His letter was written on 11 November after which the appalling weather, with its bitter cold nights and periods of incessant rain and high winds, was to reach a peak which even hardened veterans found intolerable.

The next day the Crimea experienced a storm lasting for three days with winds approaching hurricane force during the night of 14 November. Vessels outside the harbour were torn from their moorings and blown ashore to be wrecked against the cliffs with great loss of life. Some, having waited several days to unload their cargo, had been prevented from seeking shelter by contrary winds. William Howard Russell was taken aback by what he saw in the harbour:

> At the narrow neck of the Harbour two or three large boats were lying, driven inland several yards from the water. The shores were lined with trusses of hay which had floated out of the wrecks

outside the harbour, and masts and spars of all sizes were stranded on the beach or floating about among the shipping.

In all, twenty-one transports were lost, together with their much needed winter clothing and provisions. Perhaps the most serious loss to the army being the 40,000 fur coats, leggings and boots aboard the steamship *Prince*, which broke up with just six surviving from its crew of 150. Writing home, Somerset Calthorpe considered it, '...a wonder that we have any ships left, and considering how entirely the army depend on the transports and fleet generally for their resources, it is a mercy that it was no worse'.

George Taylor, who a year or so earlier had sold his commission in the 95th and was now visiting the Crimea to meet up with old friends, did not hesitate to lay the blame for the disaster at the feet of the port authorities:

I must say, that this loss, or the most serious part of it, is attributable to our own mismanagement for all ships with stores on board should at once on their arrival have gone into the harbour of Balaklava; and those which had been discharged, should have come out to make room for them. The *Prince* especially, full of most requisite stores, essential to the comfort and health of the army, was left outside, with only one anchor, and the anchorage known to be insecure.

On the exposed plateau above Sevastopol the troops, many of whom were shoeless and with greatcoats worn to a shred, suffered severely from hypothermia brought on by the icy wind and driving rain. Colonel Sterling of the Highland Brigade wrote to his friends at home describing the battering they had undergone from the hurricane:

All the tents fell in about three minutes; in some the poles broke, in others the pegs drew. As to mine, the wind rushed in at the door, and split it right up; so that my servant and I spent an hour lying on the wet canvas, to keep it completely down, and to prevent the household goods from being blown away. Just at the first destruction of the tent the air was loaded with all sorts of articles – highland bonnets, shoes, chairs, bits of wood, and all the papers, news or official in the camp.

William Howard Russell in his dispatch to *The Times*, left his readers with a vivid impression of the storm:

> The sound of the rain, its heavy beating on the earth, had become gradually swallowed up by the noise of the rushing of the wind over the common, and by the flapping of the tents as they rocked more violently beneath its force ... Mud – and nothing but mud – flying before the wind, and drifting as though it were rain, covered the face of the earth as far as it was visible ... a harsh screaming sound, increasing in vehemence as it approached, struck us with horror. As it passed along we heard the snapping of tent poles and the sharp crack of timber and canvas ... towards twelve o'clock the wind became much colder. Sleet fell first, and then came a snow storm, which clothed the desolate landscape in white, till the tramp of men seamed it with trails of black mud ...

The 2nd Division, bivouacked on the plateau above Balaklava village, had suffered no less, as Russell was at pains to inform his readers:

> Looking over towards the hill occupied by the Second Division, we could see that the blast had there been of equal violence. The ridges, the plains and undulating tracts between the ravines so lately smiling in the Autumn sun, with row after row of neat white tents, was bare and desolate, the surfaces turned into sticky mud as black as ink, and the discoloured canvas rolled up in heaps all over it.

For the cavalrymen, it was the suffering of their horses which, for many, overrode their own discomfort. Captain Wombwell of the 17 Lancers, writing on 2 December, was not alone in expressing his concern: 'The weather here is dreadful, nothing but rain rain rain which nearly washed us out of our tents, and we have not a dry corner to put a thing in, the ground is over our ankles in mud, and the poor horses are standing up to their knees in wet mud and dying as fast as they can from cold, wet, and starvation.' Lieutenant Calthorpe was equally concerned in reporting the sufferings of the men and the horses exposed to the elements:

> A man of the 8 Hussars was found dead in the morning from cold, and several others died on the heights above Balaklava from the same cause. 24 horses of the Royal Artillery and 35 of the Cavalry Division, died during the day and night of the 14th. Numbers of

men had to go into hospital with paralysed limbs. Since there was no transport to take fodder up to the camp, the horses had to survive on a handful of barley a day, or whatever a caring rider was able to provide for his mount.

Loy-Smith was another officer moved to pity by the condition of his squadron's horses. 'They required but leading,' he suggested, 'being half-dead they followed us like dogs. It was piteous to see what cold and starvation had brought these poor animals to, that had been so beautiful and so full of life.'

'When a horse dropped dead in the lines, the others that could reach it would gnaw the hair off its skin,' wrote Sergeant Mitchell, 'and we had to be careful on going near them, or they would seize us by the beard and whiskers for the same purpose.'

Lieutenant Dallas, writing on 11 September to his family, did not forget to mention the plight of the horses:

> You will laugh at what I am going to tell you, but it is perfectly true. The horses have all been so starving that they have eaten each other's tails! & it is a fact that not one horse in ten of the Artillery has any hair at all left on that ornamental part of their persons, which adds considerably to their ghastly appearance.

In the aftermath of the storm, Raglan did his best to restore order and bring a little comfort to the troops by dispatching one of his staff officers to Constantinople to purchase warm clothing and other necessary articles for them. Fortunately, the British consul in Bucharest was able to report that, '...70 bales containing 2,184 fur coats and five boxes containing 545 dozens of woollen socks ...' were to be shipped to Balaklava with an additional 18,000 fur coats to be sent by the end of December. Welcome though these articles were, it was the provision of suitable winter quarters for the troops in the field that was most needed but, with the ever pressing problem of transport and distribution, it was to be many months before adequate provision was made, driving many officers and men to despair. Captain Robert Portal complained:

> We never shall be hutted; we never shall be fed; and why? Because Lord Raglan has placed his army on a hill with three miles of impassable roads leading to the top of it from the place where all these good things are supposed to be landed and stored. Nothing

would have been easier than to have made the road from Balaklava to the heights good when the weather was fine; now I believe it to be impossible, and the whole army is suffering the greatest misery with every comfort within a few miles of them.

It grieved Colonel Anthony Sterling that he could do nothing to alleviate the suffering of the men in the trenches or those on picket duty, and in a letter to his wife, he expressed his sympathy for their plight:

I found sad misery among the men; they have next to no fuel, almost all the roots, even of the brushwood, being exhausted. The consequence is, they cannot dry their stockings or shoes; they come in from the trenches with frost bitten toes, swelled feet, chilblains, etc; their shoes freeze and they cannot put them on. Many of the frost bitten men will lose their feet; many will recover; but the army, meantime, is cruelly weakened.

Lieutenant Clifford also expressed his sympathy:

The poor men are certainly suffering more than human nature can stand. They are dying off fast every day ... We have 55 men frostbitten in the Division. I saw one poor creature brought in, frostbitten in the feet, from the Trenches, and when his stockings were taken off, his toe nails and part of his flesh came off too. One man was found dead in his Tent this morning, frozen to death.

It was perhaps not surprising that cases of frostbite were by far the most numerous to be treated at this period in the General Hospital at Balaklava. Sister Mary Aloysius was appalled by the lack of foresight exhibited by the military authorities:

The men who came from the 'Front' as they called it, had only their linen suits – no other clothing. In most cases the flesh and clothes were frozen together; and as for the feet, the boots had to be cut off bit by bit, the flesh coming off with them – many pieces of the flesh I have seen remain in the boot. Poultices were applied with some oil brushed over them. In the morning, when these were removed – can I ever forget it – the sinews and bones were seen to be laid bare.

It was not only the men who suffered from the inadequacies of the military hospitals. The wives of soldiers who had been allowed to accompany their husbands, were also to be found in an abject state of misery. 'My heart bleeds for them,' Florence Nightingale told Lady Alicia Blackwood, 'and they are at our doors daily clamouring for everything; but it is impossible for me to attend them, my work is with the soldiers, not with their wives.' It says much for Lady Alicia's concern, that she immediately volunteered to undertake the work of looking after them. She quickly found the living conditions of these unfortunate women to be almost beyond belief:

> ... a poor soul in the agonies of death; she was lying on a heap of filthy black rags on the floor in a dark room containing about sixty women, from twenty-five to thirty men, and some infants. There were no beds or bedsteads whatever, a piece of Indian matting and a heap of rags was all anyone had, and these were strewn all over the floor ...

Lady Alicia Blackwood did what she could, and was not surprised to learn later, that the women had been ill for a week without medical help of any kind.

Drawing attention to the contrasting attitude between the British and French authorities towards the welfare of their serving soldiers, George Taylor wrote:

> While our men have nothing but their ordinary inferior greatcoats to wear in this dismal weather – The French have for their men white sheepskin coats, warm and neat looking, in addition to their usual clothing. They have made preparations for the winter, and we have not; They are making huts, and we are doing next to nothing.

The French, although their loss of equipment, due to the hurricane was no less severe, fared much better thanks to their organization and the fact that their supply base was much closer to the front line. They were constantly amazed by the inadequate rations served out to the British soldier but ready to respond generously to his request for food. Wrote one compassionate young French dragoon officer: 'In the absence of bread, which we are lacking in ourselves, we give them what we can but we never take their money. It is pitiful to see such superb men asking permission to gorge themselves on the dregs in our mess tins.' Lieutenant Henry Clifford admitted:

The French are far superior to us in everything but fighting. Their Engineers and Commissariat Departments are perfect, and their hospitals also. We have to depend on the kindness of the French to take our worst cases off the field of battle, and down to Balaklava on mules.

On the day following the havoc wreaked by the hurricane, the winds eased and an attempt was made to restore order. Tents were erected, and owners did what they could to retrieve their missing property. Colonel Sterling was fortunate to recover the contents of his trunk some 300 yards away in a vineyard. The one place where chaos reigned supreme, was the supply area and port of disembarkation. Fanny Duberly raged against the growing muddle which typified Balaklava:

> If anybody should ever wish to erect a 'Model Balaklava' in England, I will tell him the ingredients necessary. Take a village of ruined houses and hovels in the extreme state of imaginable dirt; allow the rain to pour into and outside them, until the whole place is a swamp of filth ankle-deep, catch about, on an average of 1,000 sick Turks with the plague, and cram them into the houses indiscriminately; kill about a 100 a day, and bury them so as to be scarcely covered with earth, leaving them to rot at leisure – taking care to keep up the supply. On to one part of the beach drive all the exhausted bat ponies, dying bullocks and worn out camels, and leave them to die of starvation. They will generally do so in about three days when they will soon begin to rot, and smell accordingly. Collect together from the water of the harbour all the offal of the animals slaughtered for the occupants of above a 100 ships, to say nothing of the inhabitants of the town – which, together with an occasional human body, whole or in parts, and the driftwood of the wrecks, pretty well covers the water – and stew them all up together in a narrow harbour, and you will have a tolerable imitation of the real essence of Balaklava.

An altogether colourful description from an officer's wife which could hardly have been more dramatic had it been written by a competent journalist such as William Howard Russell of *The Times*.

Major Reynell Pack who met *The Times* correspondent, described him as:

... stout, about five feet eleven inches in height, round face, black hair and whiskers, a pair of excessively bright intelligent eyes, dressed at the time like a sportsman, wearing a cap with a gold band. Agreeable in manner, witty in conversation, a jovial companion, an addition to a camp dinner, Mr Russell seldom fails to meet a hearty welcome among his legion of military acquaintances.

The writings of Russell and other journalists was to bring home to the British public the terrible sufferings of the troops who, unlike many of the officers, had no recourse to purchases from home and were left to face the rigours of a Russian winter on whatever sustenance an incompetent commissariat was able to furnish, which rarely rose above starvation level. Captain Earle's entry of 26 November in his journal, no doubt reflected the experience of many of his fellow officers at this time:

Returned from the trenches at 5 ?am. Went to bed and finding that the snow drift had occupied my place between the blankets was obliged to lie down in my clothes. Slept until 7 ? when I awoke and found that I had lost the feeling in my feet and my formerly damp hair had become a mass of icicles. Got up half frozen and by constant rubbing regained the use of my feet & called to my servant for firewood to make some coffee. There was neither one or the other. The commissariat had failed in their issue.

If one section of the allied force could be said to be worse off than the British, it was the Turks and even the redcoats suffering from shortages of every kind, were moved to do what they could to alleviate the suffering of the Ottoman contingent. Lieutenant Wolseley wrote:

The poor Turkish private was a still more melancholy figure in that 'slough of despond'. Starvation and want had reduced him to little more than a skeleton hidden away under the hood of his reddish-brown grego. No-one apparently took any interest in his health, comfort, or welfare. He looked the picture of resignation, accepting the position not only as his fate, the decree of Allah, but as if there was nothing in it to occasion surprise.

Lord Raglan was aware of the plight of the Turkish force and in a letter to the British ambassador in Constantinople he asked that the Porte be notified. This Stratford did and a few weeks later, HMS *Terrible* dropped anchor in Balaklava Bay having towed a Turkish hospital ship from Scutari to take on board the Ottoman sick and wounded.

The deteriorating weather, and the knowledge that Sevastopol showed no sign of surrendering, was having a dispiriting effect, not only on the ordinary British soldier, but also on a few high ranking officers. The Duke of Cambridge, on the verge of a nervous breakdown, had retired temporarily to Constantinople in November and Lord de Ros, the Quartermaster General, had also complained to Lord Raglan, that, 'my nerves are alas like a child's and they send me into tears'. He was quickly replaced by Brigadier General Richard Airey. Other high profile figures to leave the Crimea at this time, were Lord Paget of the 4 Dragoons and Lord Cardigan who, after a medical board had confirmed him unfit for further military service, was to sail for home on 8 December never to return. Seager, now a captain, wrote: 'We have got rid of Lord Cardigan. If pomposity or bluster are the requisites for command, he is the man, he went up to the guns gallantly enough on the 25th but finding it no joke, he bolted and left the Brigade to get back the best way they could.'

Lieutenant Jocelyn Strange expressed the attitude of many junior officers to the continuing failure to take Sevastopol, when he wrote: 'So here we have another winter staring us in the face, & our men only half clothed; in short, if we could not have taken this place by a *coup de main*, as was at first supposed, it ought never to have been attempted so late in the year. We have now fought two pitched battles, & several skirmishes, & lost an immense quantity of life & are not a bit nearer taking Sevastopol than before.'

Temple Godman was of much the same opinion and informed his father: 'I can't tell when the town is likely to be taken. Some say it will fall before Christmas, though why it should I can't see at the present rate of proceeding, for we never fire a gun hardly now. Others say that the place must be entirely invested first.'

Meanwhile parliament had reconvened on 12 December as Lord Aberdeen's coalition faced increasing criticism over its prosecution of the war. In the event Aberdeen weathered the storm after assuring members that adequate supplies and reinforcements were on their way to the Crimea and that steps had been taken to put right the deficiencies reported in the Press.

To satisfy the demand for extra troops, a Bill was passed enabling militiamen to transfer to the regular army, and for the acceptance of volunteers chiefly from Germany, who would be paid a bounty of £6 providing they met the minimum height regulation of five feet two inches and were at least thirty-five years of age. The measure was passed in both Houses but was far from popular with the general public as one parliamentarian noted. 'The Government proposal to engage foreigners, as soldiers to serve in the British army will be, I should think, a most unpopular movement,' suggested the MP. 'We see daily how little faith can be placed in the services of men who have no other interest than their pay to make them fight.'

Of far greater import to Government ministers, however, was the rising tide of resentment on the part of the population at the conditions being experienced by the troops in the Crimea; a view which the Press was quick to exploit. Edward Seager remarked: 'I see by the papers that the people in England are beginning to hear something like the truth respecting the position of our army here. The infantry are very badly off, the trenches are killing them very fast and they are so far off that they with difficulty get supplies.' *The Times*, which until then had supported the Prime Minister, made much of the army's grievances based upon letters written home by officers in the Crimea and on reports received from their war correspondents. Lord Raglan could not escape responsibility for the disasters which had befallen, '... the noblest army ever sent from these shores', and the influential editor of *The Times*, thirty-six year-old John Thadeus Delane, did not hesitate to criticize the newly created Field Marshal for the inadequate supply of food and clothing given out to the soldiers in the trenches. Even the Duke of Newcastle, who had been an enthusiastic supporter of Lord Raglan, wrote to him pointing out:

> ... reports reach me from time to time, of some of the Regiments under your command, and even of men in the trenches being on half, and in some instances quarter rations for two or three days together whilst there is no deficiency of food, and stores at Balaklava; I cannot entirely attribute this state of things if it exists to the badness of the roads, or to the interruptions caused by the bad weather.

George Frederick Dallas, in a letter to his family, voiced his concern for the soldiers in the trenches:

> The greatest trial here is seeing the sufferings of our men, without being in any way able to alleviate them. They are positively worked to death. If they were well fed instead of being half starved; & if the weather was fine and warm (instead of constant rain and wind) & if they had a change of clothes in their camp; if they had all these benefits I don't think any but the very strongest could stand it. As it is they die miserably, not singly but in tens!

Lord Raglan still enjoyed the support of not a few of his officers as Lieutenant Morgan's letter of 11 December to his mother, makes known: 'That infernal paper *the Times* has been abusing Lord Raglan more than ever; what an infamous shame it is, for not one word concerning the things they lay to Lord Raglan's charge is true, and instead of it being his fault the way things have been going on out here, is entirely the fault of that horrid mean minded Government under Lord Aberdeen.' Lieutenant Morgan of the Rifle Brigade was no doubt expressing the thoughts of many of his fellow officers when he wrote: 'I wish to goodness the siege was over, for I am heartily tired of sitting for twelve hours in a nasty cold, and often wet trench ... My regiment has dwindled down most fearfully. We came into the field 1,000 strong, and now have only 400 effective men.'

William Russell too, considered it his duty to bring the troops' plight to the notice of his readers:

> Hundreds of men had to go into the trenches at night with no covering but their greatcoats, and no protection for their feet but their regimental shoes. Many when they took off their shoes were unable to get their frozen feet into them again, and they might be seen bare-footed hopping along about the camp, with the thermometer at twenty degrees, and the snow half a foot deep on the ground.

The New Year saw a marked reversal in Lord Raglan's fortunes. From being the popular recipient of congratulatory messages following his success at Inkerman, he was now a target of disapproval from both public sources and disaffected officers. There can be little doubt that Raglan was dismayed by the amount of press coverage being given to complaints, many of them trivial, and to add to his troubles the French were beginning to question whether the British were able to prosecute the war on an equal footing. Certainly the French were adding considerably to their reserve in Constantinople, whilst the severe winter weather was seriously affecting the build up of supplies and troop numbers in Raglan's army.

In fairness to Raglan, the shortages the army was experiencing were as much to do with a government lack of foresight as they were to his administration and a poor commissariat. As previously mentioned, much of the criticism in the press resulted from letters written by disillusioned officers to their families, but at least two felt it their duty to condemn what they saw as disloyalty to the Commander-in-Chief. 'Some of the letters written by officers, are too bad, it is a great shame to publish them, however great the mismanagement might be,' Henry Clifford confided to his parents. 'I don't think it is the duty of officers to write complaints in the public papers, whatever they may think or see.'

Lieutenant Somerset Calthorpe was particularly annoyed by the reaction of The Times to the public mood: 'The Times seems to abuse everything and everybody out here, and to pooh-pooh the difficulties with which the commissariat have to contend, and to find fault with the endeavours made by the authorities, who I am sure, do all in their power, as far as circumstances will permit, to alleviate the overwork and sufferings of the soldiers.' Lieutenant Dallas again in writing to his parents took particular exception to an article he had read in The Times:

> The papers seem rather annoyed with us Regimental officers for not having died as quickly as the men. The answer is a very simple one. We fed and clothed ourselves, & Government did neither for the men. Unless we had all had some little means of our own, I think we should all have died in numbers enough to please The Times.

Warm clothing would have been the most acceptable Christmas present, for as Nicholas Dunscombe made clear: 'Very hard frost last night, and Christmas morning was ushered in by the most intense cold; never shall I forget my Christmas dinner in the Crimea; I made a sort of beef steak and plum pudding in the morning, intending to dine at five, but having no fire place (on account of the weather) did not succeed in getting it cooked until ten o'clock at night.'

Captain John Hume wrote:

> All the ships bells rang in the New Year. At first we thought the Russians were coming, the row was so great. We then remembered the occasion wished one another a 'Happy New Year', and so ended the eventful year 1854. The fall of Sebastopol seemed as far off as ever, while our fine army was reduced to less than 12,000 men to carry on the trenches and other duties before Sebastopol.

It was a fact that January brought a reminder of just how severe the winter could be in the Crimea with the temperature falling to 20 degrees Fahrenheit; the snow drifting to a foot deep, with a high wind whipping up the loose snow so as to almost blind the pickets. 'The troops suffer dreadfully from it,' commented Somerset Calthorpe; 'every endeavour is being made to get them better shelter than canvas tents. The wooden huts have arrived in great numbers at Balaklava, but, unfortunately, their great weight renders it a service of considerable difficulty bringing them up to the plateau.'

'The roads have been so bad between the camp and Balaklava,' Henry Clifford informed his father, 'we have had great difficulty in providing our siege guns with ammunition, our artillery horses dying three and four a night.' Certainly there could be no contemplation of any offensive action in the immediate future for the constant demands made on them by hundreds of near starving British soldiers had created an impression with the French that their ally was too enfeebled to consider a fresh assault on Sevastopol even had weather conditions permitted it and, as the worsening weather began to make serious inroads into Raglan's strength of 25,000 fighting troops, it seemed to many that there was no question but that the French would continue to maintain their dominance as the senior partner in the alliance.

As frost, snow, and bitter cold ushered in the new year, the mood in the Russian camp was one of satisfaction. Apart from Inkerman their army had not suffered a major defeat in the Crimea which might have jeopardized the security of Sevastopol; ice in the Baltic had ensured that the area would not be troubled again until the spring, and in the Caucasus the Turks were confined to Kars and Erzerum. As for the city's defences, Robert Hodasevich was convinced that earthworks which could so easily be changed or added to, rather than built of stone, offered by far the most effective protection against artillery bombardment: 'The batteries at Sevastopol were at first nothing but earth, loosely thrown up with the shovel, embrasures were plastered with moistened clay, but when this was discovered to be not enough, they were faced with stout wickerwork. Then facines were introduced, and finally gabions were employed.'

Nevertheless the Russians laboured under difficulties not dissimilar to those of the allies. Enough fodder to keep the horses alive was almost impossible to obtain and the Russians were obliged to feed them on ship's biscuits and oak leaves. Provisions for the garrison were also in short supply and ammunition was running low. Until the expected food stocks should arrive in the spring, the garrison was put under the severest rationing. Water too, was difficult to obtain, since the water table in the Crimea was far below the surface and it was not unknown for the Russians to dig wells in excess of 200 feet to keep the garrison supplied.

None of this seems to have bothered either the garrison or the civil population, as Leo Tolstoy pointed out late in 1854:

> The quayside contains a noisy jostle of soldiers in grey, sailors in black, and women in all sorts of colours. Peasant women are selling rolls, Russian *mushiks* with samovars are shouting 'Hotsbiten' (a honey and spice drink) and right here, lying about on the very first steps of the landing, are rusty cannon balls, shells, grapeshot and cast iron cannon of various calibres ... Not on a single face will you read the signs of flurry or dismay, nor even those of enthusiasm, readiness to die, resolve – of that there is none; you will see ordinary, everyday people, going about their ordinary, everyday business.

That his fellow officers did not seem to have held the British army in very high regard, was made clear to Hodasevich when he overheard a captain in his brigade explain to a another officer: 'The Englishmen go and return on the sea, but there is no fear that they will reach Sebastopol; they would be afraid to try; let them try on land, and we would give it to them in fine style. The French, we know, can fight, but the English, if they ever do make war, its only with savages, in a country a long way off.'

As winter intensified in the Crimea, operations came to a halt. Raglan's commissariat had all but collapsed, creating immense hardship for the troops in the field and it was perhaps as well that the Russians were also incapable of mounting offensive action. The shortcomings being exhibited by the military were having an effect upon Aberdeen's coalition government and when Parliament resumed after the Christmas break, it was on the point of collapse. Disraeli had added his voice to others complaining of the indifference and incompetence of Aberdeen's administration and, in a sarcastic aside, he pointed out that the government had sought to fight a major war while providing only for a minor one. Public opinion reflected his bitter criticism and Newcastle, the Secretary of State for War, survived calls for his replacement in favour of Lord Palmerston only by the support of fellow Peelites. It was fortunate that a rumour which began to circulate that Austria was willing to broker a peace treaty between the allies and Russia, diverted press criticism from the Prime Minister.

The rumour was welcomed by a majority of French politicians who were concerned that the war was becoming far too expensive. A few parliamentarians regarded such views with mixed feelings; chief among them being fears that Austrian participation would bring an end to the war before the Russians could be overwhelmingly defeated. On 12 January, Newcastle was concerned enough to advise Raglan to continue 'hostile operations against the enemy, without reference to the reports of negotiations which may reach you from various sources'.

Lord Aberdeen's administration was to survive just five days after the opening session of Parliament for when a back bencher, Mr John Roebuck, member for Sheffield, called for a Select Committee to examine the conduct of the War Office, his proposal was carried by 305 votes to 148. That, and the subsequent resignation of Lord John Russell from the cabinet, was enough to bring down George Hamilton Gordon 4th Earl of Aberdeen who, on 4 February, was replaced as Prime Minister by Lord Palmerston, much against the wishes of Queen Victoria. He did not find it easy to form an administration and of the previous coalition only Clarendon (Foreign Secretary), Gladstone

(Chancellor), Graham (First Lord of the Admiralty), and Herbert (Colonial Secretary), agreed to serve under him.

Inevitably, it was the War Office which saw the greatest changes. The separate offices of Secretary for War and Secretary at War were sensibly combined following the resignation of the Duke of Newcastle, and the position was given to a Scot who had some military experience and was acquainted with several of the senior officers serving in the Crimea. Lord Panmure was a bluff, rotund Scot who rejoiced in the sobriquet of 'The Bull' by reason of his girth. He had the misfortune of suffering from gout which perhaps did not help him in his assimilation of the complexities of office, but he was industrious. The public had every confidence that now Palmerston was in control, the Russian war would be brought to a speedy and successful conclusion once adequate supplies and reinforcements had reached the Crimea. Unfortunately, this encouraging start to the new administration did not last. Within days it was shaken by the resignation of William Gladstone, Sir Charles Graham, and Sidney Herbert, none of whom would accept Roebuck's proposal for a Committee of Enquiry when it was debated during the last week in February.

Palmerston, although he was distrusted by many in his own party, refused to resign and, in a demonstration of his ability, he improved the administration to such a degree that it achieved a greater efficiency than was at first thought possible. A mood of uncertainty had meanwhile spread to those in the Crimea closely affected by the politicians' view of how the war should be conducted. Worried by the fall of the Aberdeen coalition, Lord Raglan was dismayed to receive a letter from Panmure complaining about the lack of information the government was getting on operations currently being undertaken in the Crimea. Of greater concern was the closing paragraph which read: 'I see no reason, from anything which has come to my hand, to alter the opinion which is universally entertained here of the inefficiency of the general staff.'

Despite the implication that he and his staff were to blame, Lord Raglan, as befitting a man of honour, refused to condemn his aides by acknowledging the clamour from the House of Commons, and the press for the removal of senior staff officers and the commissariat. He was determined to rely upon the improving weather conditions and morale to minimize any further adverse criticism. In a dignified reply to Panmure's forthright accusation, he wrote:

> My Lord, I have passed a life of honour. I have served the Crown for above fifty years; I have for the greater portion of that time been connected with the business of the army ... and yet, having been placed in the most difficult position in which an officer was ever called upon to serve, and having successfully carried out most difficult operations, with the entire approbation of the Queen, which is now my only solace, I am charged with every species of neglect.

It says much for Panmure's mood that this appeal was ignored by the Secretary at War, who insisted upon change, and above all, the dismissal of Commissary General James Filder.

With the approach of spring and with it the campaigning season, Raglan had hopes that demands for the dismissals of General Richard Airey and Sir James Estcourt, both of whom had been criticized by Panmure, would be forgotten in the face of the urgent necessity for fresh supplies and extra troops. Raglan, however, could do nothing to prevent certain changes in personnel being imposed by the Secretary of State. Burgoyne, his senior engineer, was replaced by Major General H.D. Jones, Lord Rokeby was given command of the 1st Division in place of Cambridge, and Brigadier General J.L. Pennefather was appointed commander of the 2nd Division.

Of the changes made by Panmure, the departure of Sir John Burgoyne for England on 20 March, was the cause of much resentment. Lieutenant Calthorpe, for one, was at a loss to find a reason for the move. '... considering that he has the experience of up to fifty years of military life,' he commented, 'I think it would be difficult, at any rate in the English army, to find one better qualified to occupy the important place Sir John has filled since the commencement of the campaign.'

Among the changes it came as no surprise when Vice Admiral Dundas stepped down in favour of the more forceful Rear Admiral Sir Edmund Lyons but, in a controversial move, Lord Raglan was given a new Chief of Staff – Lieutenant General Sir James Simpson, a sixty-three year-old Scot with orders from Panmure to report directly to London on all matters appertaining to future campaigns. Simpson was not to prove so compliant to Panmure's wishes as that worthy might have hoped, however, describing Raglan, in his first report written on 16 April, as '… the most abused man I ever heard of', and his undivided support for Airey and Estcourt did much to stifle the criticism coming from Parliament.

Raglan's headquarters staff were not alone in suffering the adverse comments of journalists and politicians, for all was not well with the French High Command. François Canrobert was regarded by the Paris newspapers as being 'too amiable' to get the army moving, whilst Prince Napoleon faced condemnation for his failure to deploy the French 3rd Division to assist the British centre at Inkerman. The Russians too, were not without problems of their own making. Lack of resources and petty corruption among officials had always existed but, in the opinion of Captain Hodasevich, it was the blind confidence Prince Alexander Menschikoff placed in his generals, from hearing them boast of their past and future exploits, which most dismayed the junior officers. Now, in an attempt to reduce casualties, Menschikoff transferred his army to the north side of the city for the winter months where it would be free from artillery bombardment, ignoring accusations that he had abandoned the city to its fate. Menschikoff it seemed, had lost his taste for aggressive action and according to a member of his staff, spent most of his time 'just watching the weather'.

Prince Menschikoff however, was not prepared to relinquish command of his field army of 107,000 and, on learning that there were voices in St Petersburg urging Nicholas to replace him, he decided that a victory over a relatively unimportant Turkish garrison in Eupatoria would serve the dual purpose of raising morale and reinforcing his position in the eyes of the Tsar.

Plans were drawn up and on the evening of 16 February three columns totalling some 19,000 troops, under the command of General Khrulev, together with eighty cannon, having taken advantage of the undulating nature of the ground which served to conceal their movements, were drawn up in a curve fronting the Turkish entrenchments around the town without the Turks initially being aware of the fact.

Shortly after 6.00 a.m. the next day, the Russian artillery began a two hour bombardment which inflicted considerable damage on the poorly constructed defence works and succeeded in dismounting several of the Turkish cannon. But the attack which followed was not a success. The defenders, under the personal direction of Omar Pasha, behaved with courage and determination and were greatly assisted by a French warship and two British men-of-war lying off shore where their fire at long range, soon disrupted a large body of Cossacks covering the left flank of the infantry column about to attack The well directed fire of two field guns brought into action by a young officer from the East India Company, Lieutenant Colonel Cadell, was instrumental in checking the progress of the infantry columns and, with the help of the ships in the bay, was instrumental in causing both infantry and cavalry to retire.

The Russians on the extreme right did enjoy a measure of success by advancing a strong column of infantry equipped with scaling ladders under the covering fire of a troop of horse artillery. This column succeeded in penetrating the outer defences before being forced back by the garrison, who lined the parapets to pour in volleys of musketry at short range. A second assault fared no better in the face of a determined defence and, when a body of Turks sallied out to engage the Russians in close quarter fighting after shells and rockets from HMS *Valorous* had thrown the Russian reserves into a panic, Khrulev's troops were forced into a headlong retreat, pursued by the Turks who made no attempt to take prisoners.

General Khrulev, after three hours of fruitless endeavour which had cost his army nearly 800 casualties, and, in the face of his disastrous attempts to breach the defence works on the left and right of the town, decided to abandon an assault against the centre with his third column. At 10.00 a.m. he ordered a general retreat covered by a heavy cannonade from his artillery.

After the battle, many in the garrison were mystified to find the ground littered with numerous bundles of wooden sticks. 'From the statements of the few prisoners taken,' explained Lieutenant Somerset Calthorpe, 'it would appear that it was the intention of the enemy, if they succeeded in penetrating into any part of the town, to have set it on fire; and for this purpose, every infantry soldier had been provided with a small faggot of wood.'

This defeat convinced a disappointed Tsar Nicholas that it was time for Menschikoff to go and he was replaced by Prince

Mikhail Gorchakoff who had commanded the Russian army in Bessarabia. A further blow to the Tsar's confidence, already severely dented by his army's inability to defeat the Turks in Eupatoria, came with Austria's decision to enter into a treaty of alliance with Britain and France, although falling short of an active participation in the war.

The stress of sustaining a European war was affecting the Tsar's health and, in mid-February, after reviewing a detachment of troops in freezing weather against the advice of his doctors, he caught a severe cold and was obliged to take to his bed. His condition worsened and after a brave fight, on 2 March, Tsar Nicholas succumbed to pneumonia. 'We heard of Tsar Nicholas's death early in March,' reported Lieutenant Wolseley, '…but the Russian officers would not believe it, declaring it was impossible, for "God would not thus inflict Holy Russia in the midst of a great war".' He was succeeded by his son Alexander II who, in reply to peace overtures from the conference in Vienna, made it clear that they were making a serious mistake in believing that he would accept peace at any price, even given that the war was draining Russia's exchequer.

In Balaklava, the coming of spring and the reduction of the severe night frosts, enabled the work of clearing the port and harbour of the many rotting carcases, to proceed with something like efficiency. Order was restored to the mountain of stores and provisions heaped upon the landing stages. Supplies were arriving with increasing frequency including the sorely needed timber huts and, where lack of suitable transport had meant that they remained undisturbed for many weeks, there were now enough carts, mules, pack ponies and even camels to bring much needed military stores up to the plateau.

Of perhaps the greatest assistance in the movement of supplies, was the completion of a railway. An offer to construct one at cost price by the contractors Samuel Peto, was accepted by the Duke of Newcastle, and work had begun in late January to clear the area around the harbour. By the end of February, construction work had proceeded to such good effect that the first stretch of track had been completed up to the heights near Kadikoi, enabling horse drawn wagons assisted by a stationary engine at the summit of the steepest incline, to move supplies from the harbour to the camp. By 23 March the railway was fully operational and stocks of ammunition were building up on the plateau for the first time in seven weeks.

Mr Money, however, was not completely satisfied with the way in which it was being employed:

> Shot and shell it carried up, and to some extent commissariat stores, but it might easily have been made far more available for general purpose. Long strings of mules would often be seen wearily plodding by the side of the railway ... As slowly they toiled along, the giant slept inactive, whose strength could have relieved them of all their work, and left them fresh for that which he was unable to do.

One improvement much appreciated by the troops in the field, was an addition to the usual ration of salt beef and biscuit, of green vegetables and fruit, which soon had a noticeable effect in the men's improved health and stamina. Somerset Calthorpe was sufficiently impressed to record, in March: '...last week I understand, 500 men were discharged from the field hospital to return to their duty, and this week, they say upwards of 700 have come out. A month ago even a single man going back to the regiment would have been thought quite a wonder.'

With peace overtures at the Vienna Conference, which had begun on 15 March, approaching stalemate, it seemed that only a significant victory by the allies would force Russia to accept the four points on offer, namely:

1. Russia to renounce territorial claims in Serbia and the Principalities.
2. Freedom of navigation in the Danube.
3. Revision of the Straits Convention of 1841 governing the passage of the Dardenelles by ships of war.
4. Renunciation of a protectorate over the Orthodox Christians in the Ottoman Empire. The rights of Christians would instead be protected by a collective European guarantee.

Palmerston, arguing for Britain, was adamant that there could be no peace talks before Sevastopol had fallen, but the French were anxious to maintain negotiations which might bring Austria into the war as an active ally. Lord Raglan, knowing that with each passing day the Russians were adding to, and strengthening, the city's defences, was all for resuming the offensive, despite his divisions being woefully under strength. The over cautious François Canrobert who possessed eight full strength divisions to Raglan's depleted six, was well aware of this weakness and considered it unlikely that Raglan was in a position to defeat a counter-attack by Gorchakoff's forces, much less mount an assault on Sevastopol.

The Russians had spent the winter in strengthening their defences under the able direction of a young engineer, Lieutenant Colonel Franz Todleben. The most formidable of these, and generally regarded as being the key to Sevastopol since its capture threatened not only the harbour but the only means of retreat open to the Russians, was an edifice known as the Malakoff Tower, described by Marshal Pelissier as '... a sort of earthen citadel of 350 metres in length, and 150 metres in width' armed with eighteen guns of heavy calibre with strong redoubts to the east, including the Flagstaff Bastion and the Redan, both of which possessed 32-pounder cannon. Further earthworks had been constructed by the Russians on a mound in front of the Malakoff early in February, known by the French as the Mamelon Vert, and was attacked by them on 22 March. It proved to be a fruitless, if courageous, assault in which a battalion of Zouaves were surrounded and totally defeated. Since then, the position had been increased in size and strengthened to the extent that it now held a formidable arsenal of thirty large calibre cannon.

On 12 March Omar Pasha met Lord Raglan at his headquarters to discuss the provision of transports to take a part of his army from Varna to Eupatoria, and later that day a Council of War was held with the three commanders, plus the Admirals of the British and French fleets. The discussion involved a suggestion that 12,000 Egyptian troops, now at Constantinople, be brought to Eupatoria where their arrival would release 20,000 Turkish troops to join the French forces at Kamiesch.

The suggestion was not received with any enthusiasm by the British for, remembering the questionable behaviour of the Turkish gunners at Balaklava, Raglan and his staff did not have a very high regard for their fighting ability. This was a view shared by Lieutenant Calthorpe. 'I do not think the allied Generals expect much from these Turkish troops,' he wrote, 'except as making a diversion in our favour.' A further complication was the fact that the three armies were independently commanded. Added Calthorpe: 'Omar Pasha considers himself senior both to Lord Raglan and General Canrobert, as he has been a Marshal for more than a year. Unfortunately the French do not pay that respect to Omar Pasha that is due to his rank and command, and it requires all Lord Raglan's well known tact to keep the Commanders-in-Chief on that footing of cordiality so necessary to successful co-operation.'

An essential pre-requisite to any assault on Sevastopol was the destruction of the Malakoff Tower and its two redoubts to the east, the Flagstaff Bastion and the Redan, all of which were heavily armed with artillery, posing a serious threat to the assault force. Possession of these defence works by the allies would not only render the southern side of the town untenable, but it would relieve the troops of the uncomfortable duty of manning the trenches in front of Sevastopol, made particularly hazardous by the proximity of the Russian rifle pits. These excavations were manned by sharpshooters whose fire had proved deadly to anyone foolish enough to raise their head above the parapet. There was only one sure way of resolving the nuisance, as explained by Timothy Gowing: 'At a sign from the officers who are going to lead, the men creep over the top on all fours. Not a word is spoken but, at a given signal in they go – and in less time than it takes to write this, it is all over, the bayonet has done its work ... the pits are at once turned and made to face the enemy, or are converted into a trench.'

Gowing's account strikes a comparison with the activities of the heroes of a greater war some sixty years later, but the brave souls who volunteered on this occasion were usually drawn from several different battalions, in order to avoid an unduly heavy loss on one regiment.

Meanwhile the allied trenches in front of Sevastopol were subjected to a daily bombardment by various missiles, which sometimes proved to be an alarming experience even to a veteran as senior as Major Whitworth Porter of the Royal Engineers:

First there comes the round shot, rushing through the air with a sharp shrill shriek, very startling to the nerves of the young soldier; then a volley of grape, buzzing along with a sound not unlike that of a covey of birds very strong on the wing; next we have the gun shell, similar in its movements to the round shot but having in addition the unpleasant peculiarity, that when it reaches its destination it bursts into pieces, scattering small fragments of iron, in the most undesirable profusion in every direction. These are varied, every now and then, by a mortar shell, rising proudly and grandly in the air, easily to be discerned in the night by the fiery trail of its burning fuse, tracing a majestic curve high in mid air until having attained its extreme altitude, it commences to descend, falling faster and faster, till down it swoops onto the devoted spot against which it has been directed, making a sound in its passage through the air like the chirping of a pee-wit, or other small bird. Hand grenades, or small shells, of about the size of a man's closed fist, are discharged to the number of from twenty or thirty at a time out of a mortar. The effect of such a discharge in a dark night was really magnificent ... Imagine the sudden rise of five-and-twenty fiery meteors into the air, each leaving a long curved trail of light in its track, and, as they reach their destination, lighting up the atmosphere with short, fitful flares, as they burst in succession. But though thus pretty to look at, they were most awkward customers to deal with ... There was nothing for it, therefore, but to lie down on your face and wait patiently till the storm had burst, and the iron hail had ceased to fall.

To the men in the trenches it seemed that the numbers of Russian cannon increased with each passing day and it was widely accepted that, for any assault to be successful, their artillery would have to be softened up by the fiercest of artillery bombardments. Even so, the overthrow of the Russian defence works was going to be a costly affair and most of March was taken up with staff conferences debating the targets to be selected and the form the assault should take. Finally, it was agreed that the Flagstaff Bastion, and the Redan and Mamelon strongholds, would be subjected to a prolonged barrage of artillery fire following which, the British would attack the Redan, whilst the French being on the right of the siege line and numerically the stronger, would assault the Mamelon and Malakoff Tower bastions.

Acting as a spur to a swift solution, was the fact that peace negotiations at the Vienna Conference had reached a critical stage. Plans had been put in hand to limit the number of Russian warships in the Black Sea or, failing that, to neutralize it by stationing an allied naval presence equivalent in size to that of the

Russian fleet. Although tempting to the French, whose representative had suggested a reduction in the size of the Russian navy, it was unacceptable to the British, who could see no point in reducing the number of ships whilst the naval base at Sevastopol remained in Russian hands. Even with enthusiasm for the war showing a marked decline on both sides of the English Channel, it was apparent to the Horse Guards that acceptance of a compromise peace, without first achieving a military victory, would be a tacit admission of failure and with it, an acknowledgement that Britain's reputation for military greatness was no longer sustainable.

Chapter Six

KERTCH, THE MAMELON AND THE QUARRIES

Easter Monday, 9 April, a day of blustery wind and rain, began with the second bombardment of Sevastopol from an allied artillery strength of 500 guns of varying calibre, as recorded by Captain Hamley of the Royal Artillery: 'The morning broke darkly in wind and rain. The order to the artillery was to commence as soon as the targets were discernable (sic) and at 6.20 am the British opened fire with the French soon following. The Russians were caught unprepared and it was all of twenty minutes before they replied.'

Roger Fenton, seeking a good position for a future photograph of Sevastopol, had begun to climb Cathcart's Hill, when the bombardment opened. 'There was no stop to the awful commotion in the air,' he remembered. 'The 68-pounders especially almost burst the ears, and the shot from them sounded like an express train that had broken off the line and leapt up into the air ... as if all hell had broken loose and the legions of Lucifer were fighting in the air.'

'Although expected, yet when it began, we were somewhat taken by surprise,' admitted Major Reynell Pack. 'We subordinates were fairly puzzled; the want of clearance in the atmosphere, and the rain falling almost as heavily as in the tropics were enough of themselves to prevent the fire being effective; besides many of our advanced works and batteries were incomplete.'

The barrage intensified as the morning wore on but with visibility down to no more than fifty yards, Lieutenant Dallas

111

entertained no great hope that it would be effective. 'It has been a fearfully windy & rainy day, & we have not been able to see any distance,' he commented, 'so that the effect of the tremendous cannonade that has been kept up since 5am this morning, is a matter of surmise only.' Nicholas Dunscombe was equally pessimistic. 'The bombardment goes on as usual,' he observed, 'and may go on for eternity without the artillery doing any good, as the Russians repair by night the injury we do to the batteries by day ...'

That the bombardment did not bring the results expected of it, was no fault of the gunnery teams, as Bruce Hamley was at pains to point out: 'Drenched to the skin, and standing in thick mud, the artillery men and sailors worked their guns with admirable vigour ... the Russian gunners, fighting with the wind and rain in their faces, must have found the trial doubly severe.'

Despite the difficulties experienced by the artillerymen, Temple Godman was in agreement with the criticism of the artillery made by his brother officers: 'This is the fourth day of the second bombardment and we seem to be doing no good. The enemy keeps up his fire well, no-one is the least sanguine as to the result. Some talk of storming, but I hardly think this is likely ... if the bombardment fails, which there is every reason to think it will, I fear we shall never do anything as long as Sebastopol can communicate with the country.'

Just as the three officers had forecast, at the end of the nine days, the extent of damage to the city's defences was insufficient to justify an assault. It came as no surprise to Major Reynell Pack for, as he relates in his memoirs, many of the shells burst prematurely due to the fuses being up to fifty years old. Captain Reilly, whilst not disputing the fact, did his best to excuse the poor performance of his gunners by blaming the inclement weather. 'The weather told severely on the men and greatly increased their labours,' he wrote, 'the tackle used in working the heavy guns would not run, the ropes would not bite, and the hand spikes could obtain no purchase on the slippery boards of the mortar platforms, many of which were entirely covered with water.' Nevertheless, the Russians had suffered a considerable number of casualties from their working parties being more at risk due to the ever present need for repairs to the city's defences. Lieutenant Count Leo Tolstoy, who gathered much of the material for his classic work *War and Peace* from his experiences in Sevastopol and the Caucasus, leaves an interesting account of the impression the allied shelling made upon him. Attached to a battery, he heard a gunner shout a warning: 'Cannon!' and, he wrote:

> You heard the same shriek and thud, the same shower, or he yells 'Mortar!' and you hear the monotonous even somewhat pleasant whistle of the bomb, with which it is hard to connect the idea of horror. You hear the whistling approach you, increasing in speed, then you see the dark sphere, the impact on the earth, the stunning explosion of the bomb which can be felt. Accompanied by whistle and shriek, splinters fly about again, stones hurtle through the air, and mud be-spatters you. At those sounds you have a strange feeling of enjoyment and at the same time, of panic.

In sharp contrast with his somewhat light-hearted approach to the allied shelling, Tolstoy's visit to a hospital drew from him a more sombre account of the effect the bombardment had upon its victims and the staff who ministered to them:

> The pools of blood visible in the empty places, the hot breaths of several hundred men, and the steam rising from those who were working with the stretchers, produced a peculiar, dense, heavy, putrid atmosphere, in which the candles burnt dimly in the various parts of the room. Sisters of Mercy with calm faces and an expression not of vacant, womanish tearfully morbid compassion, but of active practical sympathy, flitter here and there among the bloody cloaks and shirts, stepping over the wounded, with medicine, water, bandages and lint.

Unlike the French, whose artillerymen had claimed to have all but destroyed the Flagstaff Battery and the Mamelon, the Royal Artillery, much to the annoyance of the infantry, had failed to inflict any significant damage to the Redan. It was abundantly clear to Raglan's engineers that, until the immensely strong earthworks of the Redan was reduced, it would be the height of folly to mount an infantry assault against it, although Raglan was of the opinion that an attack might just be successful with the cooperation of the French. This, however, Canrobert refused to sanction and on the 14th it was decided merely to maintain the bombardment for a few days longer, to the inevitable discomfort of the gunners. 'From the afternoon of Sunday to Tuesday morning the men were continually wet,' complained Captain Reilly. 'Their feet were so swollen from continued standing in and walking to and from the Batteries, that many were afraid to take their boots off lest they should not be able to get them on again.'

The Russian gunners were not slow to retaliate and, in referring to their employment, the *Times* correspondent noted, 'The Russians fired very well, but they were not generally equal as artillerymen to our men. About twelve o'clock in the day the Russians left off work to go to dinner, and our men followed their example; silence reigned almost uninterruptedly for two hours or more, and towards four o'clock the firing began again.'

To many of the men in the trenches, the siege was becoming more than a little irksome, as Jocelyn Strange pointed out in a letter to his father. 'I suppose there never was anything so tedious, uninteresting, and full of privations as this siege is. We are all of us quite sick of it, and blame the Government more and more every day for having sent us here so late in the year when all the summer was spent in idleness.'

George Frederick Dallas was similarly affected and in a letter to his family he did not conceal his anger at the incompetence of the High Command:

> The Russian batteries & works are as good & strong as ever. We are no nearer our end than we were months ago. There is one universal feeling of disgust and humiliation amongst us at this second ridiculous exhibition ... We are now, as we have been for months, ourselves the besieged in our corner of the Crimea. We have a most splendid army thrown away by our chiefs, either by their dissensions or their incompetence.

Whilst the shelling continued, albeit at a reduced rate to conserve ammunition, the allied General Staff met on 14 April to review the progress of the war and to discuss future operations. One noticeable absentee was General François Canrobert whose campaign plans had been largely dictated by Napoleon III from Paris. The Emperor had long held the view that Sevastopol could not be taken before it was completely invested and this, in turn, rested upon the Russian army being defeated in the field.

Panmure, the Secretary for War who had been present at the meeting in London between the Emperor Napoleon and the British Government, summarized what had been discussed for the benefit of Raglan, as follows:

> ... we entirely concur in the proposal to divide the allied forces into 3 Armies according to the document signed by Marshal Vaillant and myself referred to in His Majesty's dispatch to General Canrobert. One of these three armies will maintain the siege, a second under your own command is intended to advance on the heights of Inkerman and McKenzie's Farm so as to interpose between the town and the Russian army in the Field, and the third is intended to make such a diversion as shall engage the enemy's attention and by threatening or actually attacking his rear and you in your attack on his front.

Raglan, who received Panmure's dispatch in the second week of May, viewed it with mixed feelings. The cooperation that existed between the British and French armies appeared to be in danger of collapse. Although Raglan welcomed the contribution made by the Turks, Omar Pasha's preference was for an independent operation in Eupatoria, whilst Canrobert was eager to make use of the 13,000 Turkish troops who would shortly be arriving from Eupatoria, to bolster the strength of the French in front of Sevastopol. His suggestion that they could replace the British, who could use the opportunity to build up their reserves, was bitterly resented by Lord Raglan. Somerset Calthorpe in reporting the plan, commented:

> Lord Raglan, I understand, positively refuses to give up the English siege attacks to the Turks, as he had learned from past experience how little dependence can be placed upon our Mahometan allies; and he does not choose to risk even the possibility of English guns being again captured by the enemy, when under the protection of the Turks, and held up hereafter to the world at large as trophies from the English.

The Turkish Commander Omar Pasha, who considered himself to be an equal partner in the alliance, was quick to take offence, not so much from Lord Raglan's remark, as from an impression that the French had failed to show him the respect that he felt was his due by consulting Raglan rather than himself, concerning the disposition of Turkish troops. It said much for Raglan's diplomatic skills that he was, on this occasion, able to smooth over a potentially awkward situation.

The relationship between General Canrobert and Lord Raglan whilst still cordial, suffered from the disadvantage of Raglan's belief that he could no longer rely upon a man whose every decision was affected by the wishes of his Emperor to reduce losses and postpone offensive operations until the arrival of reinforcements. But, as the General subsequently pointed out to Lord Raglan, the daily losses incurred by the French in conducting the siege, were great enough without demanding the sacrifices that a massive assault on Sevastopol would entail. His argument, whilst appreciated by the British Commander, did not deflect his firmly held opinion that delay at the present time was tantamount to a wasted opportunity.

With the reinforcements expected early in May, the combined strength of the allies besieging Sevastopol was rapidly approaching 90,000 comprising 55,000 French, 20,000 British and 15,000 Sardinians, and it must have astonished the Russians that an assault against the town's southern defences did not follow a bombardment which continued without ceasing for more than a week. The reluctance to storm Sevastopol certainly puzzled the British and French troops waiting patiently in the trenches. To George Cavendish Taylor, a civilian observer in the Crimea, the continuing bombardment now seemed pointless. 'What annoys and distresses everyone is that all was for no defined object as the army were not prepared to storm the town,' he wrote. 'We say here that we did not take Sebastopol because the French would not fight by day, the English would not fight in the dark and the Turks won't fight at all.' 'The English have advanced their batteries to within 600 yards of the town, and they and their General all want to go in,' echoed a French admiral. 'The French have got within 60 yards of the town and their General won't go in!' That there was growing frustration, particularly among Raglan's troops, who suspected that they were playing second fiddle to the French, could not be denied. Not that any redcoat thought that he was less aggressive, but Canrobert's reluctance for offensive action had given rise to a suspicion that the French were less inclined to get to close quarters with the enemy than were the

British, whose overall strength, in comparison, was considerably weaker.

That an assault against the town's outer defence works was likely to reduce their numbers even further, was never very far from Henry Clifford's mind is made clear from a letter to his parents:

> If the assault is made by us on the Redan I think it will make a very big hole, not easily filled up, in our little army; but I am the last to wish to shirk any part of the work, and get the French, because they have more men, to do any of the dirty work for us. Depend upon it, tho' our loss may be very great, the work will be done when it is. The men are looking very well and are in good spirits ...

The French, although equally reluctant to risk the heavy casualties likely to result from an all out attack on Sevastopol, were nevertheless determined to clear the ground between their trenches and the Quarantine Fort – a large casemated battery – on the extreme left of their position, no matter how costly. This area contained a considerable number of Russian rifle pits linked by a trench, where sharpshooters had been inflicting daily losses on the French manning the trenches opposite which their staff considered to be unsustainable.

Accordingly on 13 April under cover of darkness, two columns, one 800 strong and the other of about 500, moved out of their advanced trenches to attack the Russians near the Quarantine Fort. The first column, after a prolonged struggle, was finally successful in capturing and holding all six rifle pits. The second column of 500 fared less well, being subjected to a murderous fire which inflicted heavy losses and forced the attackers to fall back on their own trenches. In the savage fighting which followed, the trenches changed hands several times before reinforcements were brought up and the attack renewed with such vigour that the Russians were forced to abandon their trench, leaving the French to advance their position 100 yards nearer the town. George Frederick Dallas had witnessed the French assault and described it in a letter to his family, as having taken place on:

> ... a very black night, there was the most furious fight I ever saw for about ? an hour on the same spot. We can see it from our camp and I never saw anything so beautiful as it was. The Russians lost

fearfully and the French followed them back into the battery from whence they sallied and destroyed it, which is considered a good thing.

Such clashes, even minor ones, were usually costly and on this occasion seventeen French officers and several hundred men fell victim to the savagery of the assault.

The following night Lord Raglan, accompanied by his headquarters staff, joined General Canrobert and his officers to witness the explosion of three mines, which had been placed between the advanced French sap and the Russian earthworks, with the objective of establishing a battery from which to fire on the inner defences of the town. In the event only two of the mines erupted, but such was their effect on the Russians that, thinking it preceded an assault against the town, they replied with every gun that could be brought to bear and the outer wall became lined with defenders who kept up an incessant small-arms fire together with showers of hand grenades directed at the allied trenches. 'It was a magnificent scene,' wrote Lieutenant Calthorpe, 'but our excitement was cut short by the rain, which fell in such quantity that we were all wet to the skin in a few minutes.'

The retaliation ceased after half an hour when the Russians realized that an attack against the town was not about to happen, but with the approach of daylight the work of establishing a link between the advance trench and the craters left by the mines, had to be abandoned by the French. The siege had now occupied the two armies for seven months and the prospect of taking Sevastopol seemed as far away as ever. Lieutenant Henry Clifford agreed with his parents that its fall was going to prove far from easy. 'The excitement about taking Sebastopol is, of course, not so great now in England, and no doubt many look upon it as hopeless,' he wrote in reply to a letter from his parents. 'I don't wonder at it after so long a siege. It will give France and England plenty to do yet to take it I think. We have got through one army already, and this will be pretty well used up by the time Sebastopol changes hands.'

There was no doubt that since Waterloo, the British army had been scandalously neglected. Confidence had grown in the ability of the Royal Navy to defend Britain's interests, and the expense of keeping a large regular army had not been considered necessary by succeeding governments. Apart from expeditions against poorly armed native tribes and the need to maintain a force in Ireland and India, the soldiers' chief employment had been in the suppression of civil riot. As a result, few serving in the Crimea had any experience of European warfare and most senior officers' knowledge of strategy had been influenced by the campaigns in Spain and Portugal.

Whatever the excuse for government economies, nothing could have excused the shameful neglect of the ordinary soldiers' welfare. Most barracks were overcrowded and badly ventilated – it has been stated that instead of the specified 400 cubic feet of space, with beds three feet apart, the soldier's bed was almost touching that of his neighbour. Meals were unappetizing and monotonous, usually salt pork and biscuit twice a day, or stringy beef and potatoes. Vegetables or fruit were seldom issued although, no doubt, the soldier if so inclined could buy or acquire them by other means. Drink was his one source of comfort and since raw spirit was cheap and plentiful in the regimental canteen, incidents of drunken brawling were of frequent occurrence.

Lord Palmerston was certainly conscious of the army's deficiencies, in particular the serious shortage of trained infantry, and he reproved Panmure for the fact that there was, as yet, no adequate supply of reservists for the Crimea. Although a Bill had been passed in 1854 to enable militia men to transfer to the army, response had been poor and the Bill's structure stopped short at compelling militia volunteers to replace the growing number of casualties in the regular army.

It was this acute shortage of trained troops which led the Government to pass the Foreign Enlistment Act – another controversial measure which sought to recruit mercenaries into the armed forces – and by the early summer of 1855 it had succeeded in establishing a German Legion and a Swiss body which, with the inclusion of a substantial number of Poles, was to grow to some 13,000 experienced troops which did something to reduce the embarrassment of the Horse Guards in being a junior partner in the alliance with the French.

A further scheme to resolve the pressing need to increase the strength of the Crimean expeditionary force was not so successful. It had been suggested that disaffected immigrants in North America would be interested in taking the Queen's bounty particularly if they were unemployed. Since this would undoubtedly infringe the Neutrality Act of 1818, it was necessary for recruits to be sent across the border to Canada in order to enlist, and a promising start was made on 10 April 1854 when the Lieutenant Governor reported that of the seventy recruits which had arrived in Halifax from Boston, only four had been rejected on medical grounds.

It was not to last. As the numbers of potential recruits increased, agents had to be appointed to direct those interested – chiefly former soldiers who had served in the Mexican war – to recruitment centres in Canada. Prominent among these agents were Henry Hertz, a Dane, working in Philadelphia with the British consul, and Max Strobel, a former Bavarian army officer, working in New York. Neither were particularly secretive and the authorities soon became aware of their pamphleteering activities. Other agents were arrested in Boston, Baltimore and Detroit and the border between the United States and Canada was made subject to stringent controls which included the surveillance of harbours. Such was the deteriorating relationship between the US and Great Britain which ensued that, on 22 June, Panmure ended the scheme which had attracted just 700 recruits, none of which ever reached Europe, at a cost to the Exchequer of £5,250.

Meanwhile in the Crimea, Lord Raglan found that discussing strategy with General Canrobert was becoming increasingly difficult. The French General, in his dealings with Raglan, was seldom in agreement with the tactics suggested or even with the target to be attacked. But then Canrobert had been put in an impossible situation; subjected to increasing pressure from the Emperor Napoleon III to conserve the strength of the French army he was, at the same time, being expected to maintain the siege and harass the Russian field forces in front of Sevastopol.

On 1 May after some prevarication on the part of General Canrobert, a plan for an amphibious attack on the port of Kertch was finally agreed. Kertch, a coastal town on the eastern edge of the Crimea near the Sea of Azov, and an important stage in the chain of supply to the Russians from Rostov and the Don, was too strong for the British army alone and Canrobert, although initially sceptical of the plan, agreed to supply an infantry division of 7,500 plus a squadron of French naval vessels, to add to the British contingent of 2,500 men and two batteries of artillery, the whole being under the overall command of General Sir George Brown.

The operation was to be conducted in the greatest secrecy with the allied fleet of fifty ships initially sailing north-west past Sevastopol as if heading towards Odessa, but eventually turning back towards Kertch. Amid much enthusiasm, the expedition sailed from Kamiesch Bay and Balaklava on the evening of the 3rd only for Lord Raglan to be informed six hours later by General Canrobert that he had received instructions from the Emperor, via the new telegraph line from Paris, to use the French ships to transport reinforcements from Constantinople, before resuming operations against Simferopol. No other offensive action was to be taken. In vain did Lord Raglan argue in favour of proceeding with the Kertch expedition, but Canrobert was adamant that the Emperor had left him with no alternative but to recall General d'Autemarre and the French squadron. Lord Raglan protested strongly, but without success, and a screw driven vessel was dispatched early the next day with orders terminating the expedition. Sir George Brown had Raglan's authority to continue with the operation should he feel there was a chance of success, but without French support it was always going to be a hazardous undertaking and, with the fleet just two hours from its destination, Sir George Brown reluctantly turned back towards the Crimea arriving without loss on 5 May. Never a popular general, his ignominious return, although no fault of his, drew forth some ribald comments at his expense. 'All kinds of jokes are afloat about Sir G. Brown's share in the affair,' commented Captain Earle. 'Some say that he forgot his razor and stock and was forced to return for them.' On a more serious note, Lieutenant Somerset Calthorpe depicted the feelings of everyone on Raglan's staff when he wrote: 'I can scarcely describe the indignation we all felt towards the French, which though not quite just, I am sure is very natural; and one will not be surprised that Lord Raglan feels how utterly impracticable it is to carry on a joint command with a man for whom it is impossible he can entertain that feeling of confidence so necessary to successful co-operation.'

Lieutenant Dallas, in a letter to his family, wrote of his fears for a repeat operation. 'The troops were landed again & if ever they again set out on the same errand they will find Kertch as strong as

Sevastopol; in a few hours it must have been ours as they were entirely unexpected by the enemy! Now they will of course have time to fortify it.'

General François Canrobert could not conceal the despair he felt for being associated with the cancelled operation, confessing to Colonel Hugh Rose that, '… no event in his life had caused him such regret and sorrow … because it had put him wrong with his friends, the English officers'. He was not without their sympathy, as Robert Portal made clear when writing to his sister. 'Canrobert gets all the blame for it, and has sunk very low indeed in the eyes of his army.' On 16 May Canrobert tendered his resignation, suggesting that Jean Jacques Pelissier should succeed him, whilst requesting that he might remain in the Crimea as a divisional general.

Pelissier who had risen from the ranks and had a reputation for being blunt, soon established his independence by making it known that he was not to be influenced by Napoleon III. In reorganizing the army into two corps and by ignoring the Emperor's instructions to conduct the war with three separate armies, he created a good impression in the British camp. 'Pelissier is certainly the Favourite in the French army and if he puts into practice here the decision they give him credit for, we have some hopes of doing something before long,' wrote an optimistic Henry Clifford.

Another delighted recipient of the news was Somerset Calthorpe:

> Early this morning (19 May) General Pelissier came to the English headquarters to announce to Lord Raglan in person the change which had taken place. He thought no time should be lost in taking immediate steps for the capture of Kertch, and also announced his intention of attacking the Ouvrages Blancs, to be directly followed, if not at the same time, by an attack on the Mamelon Vert; as he considers that, above all, the prosecution of the siege for the speedy reduction of Sevastopol; is of the first importance.

This encouraging announcement was welcomed by Lord Raglan who had every confidence that, on this occasion, the General's promises would be carried out and brought to a successful conclusion. Roger Fenton did not doubt that the operations promised by General Pelissier would take place, but at what cost?

General Pelissier is a very good personification of the French army for he is rough in his manner, though not without a certain bon homie. He cares nothing for the sacrifice of life and does not seem troubled with scruples of any kind. His face has an expression of brutal boldness, something like that of a wild boar.

At a Council of War on 20 May, attended by all of the allied generals, including Omar Pasha who had journeyed from Eupatoria, arrangements for the second expedition to Kertch were finalized. The French were to supply 7,500 men and three batteries, the Turks 5,000 men and a single battery, whilst the British contribution was to be 3,800 infantry, a single battery and a troop of cavalry. Sir George Brown was again appointed Commander-in-Chief with General d'Autemarre leading the French and Redschid Pasha the Turks.

After four days at sea, having sailed from Kazatch Bay on the evening of the 22nd, the allied fleet made its presence felt off Cape Takil with a brief bombardment, followed by an unopposed landing, during which the troops destroyed government buildings and an arsenal. Roger Fenton wrote:

A good many of the smaller Russian shopkeepers were still there, and many Greeks. They all looked very frightened and with good reason so far as the French and Turks were concerned. The windows were mostly smashed. The Turks and French putting in their heads to look for plunder and breaking the rest of the windows when they see that there is nothing for them.

Far greater destruction was to take place at Yenikale on the other side of the peninsula where the soldiers' interpretation of Brown's order to demolish any buildings which might prove useful to the Russians, resulted in widespread looting and vandalism, even to the extent of destroying Kertch's museum and its priceless collection of Hellenic art. 'There was a terrible scene,' admitted Fenton. 'French, Turks, and I am sorry to say a few Highlanders, were breaking into houses, smashing the windows, dragging out everything portable and breaking what they could not carry away.'

'I believe the churches are still untouched,' wrote George Taylor, 'but I hear from good authority that the priests would sell anything in them; and then, of course, assert that they had been plundered.'

William Howard Russell, who had sailed with the expedition, was appalled by the wanton destruction:

> The floor of the museum is covered for several inches in depth with the debris of broken glass, of vases, urns, statuary, the precious dust of their contents, and charred bits of wood and bone mingled with the fresh splinters of the shelves, desks, and cases in which they had been preserved. Not a single bit of anything that could be broken or burnt any smaller had been exempt from reduction by hammer or fire.

In gathering material to describe the looting of Kertch, William Russell found himself obstructed at every turn by the military authority. 'He had great difficulties to contend with,' observed George Taylor, 'as Sir George Brown refused to give him leave to land, saying that he would have no d——d newspaper correspondents there.' As it happened, Sir George's orders were ignored by Russell, for the General lacked the power to enforce them.

In a two week orgy of pillaging, which had seen several murders and the rape of Russian women, it had been the Turks who were the main offenders. But it could not be said that the British and French troops were blameless. Indeed, Sir George Brown was so concerned by the behaviour of his troops that he lost no time in sending fifty cavalrymen to patrol the streets and restore order. The measure brought little success and William Russell did not seek to excuse the behaviour of the English troops:

> We left ruin and complete desolation behind us. Sir George Brown, no doubt, was most anxious to prevent the pillage; but he had to deal with French and Turks as well as English and he did not succeed in checking rapine, license, and barbarous excess. Our attempts to prevent outrage and destruction were of the feeblest and most contemptible character.

Two days later, news of the town's capture was announced to the troops attending a Sunday service. Nicholas Dunscombe reported:

> At 11.00am we had a parade for divine service but a little after the commencement of it, Sir John Campbell made the clergyman stop the service and announced that the expedition to Kertch had been

successful, that it had been taken without loss on the Queen's birthday ... the news was received with three cheers for the Queen and three for the expedition; it was read to all the divisions on parade and the cheering was truly British; the Russians in Sebastopol must have heard it.

Lieutenant Dallas had yet to learn of the atrocities committed there when he wrote to his mother: 'I have not seen anybody yet that has come back from Kertch &c but I hear it was most delightful. They found in one house somewhere tubs of cream sunk in the earth, surrounded by ice! ... conceive coming on it iced!, when in a tight red coat and the thermometer 90 in the shade.'

Aside from the outrage which news of these atrocities caused, not only in St Petersburg but also in the United States, the value of Kertch and Yenikale to the allies, as Roger Fenton explained, '... is immense, as they can now cut off all supplies coming to the Russians from Asia and down the Sea of Azov, and can from here make attacks upon any port of the Asiatic coast of the Black Sea, or the ports of the Sea of Azov'.

News of the allies' successes in the Kertch peninsula did nothing to alter the Emperor Napoleon's views on the conduct of the war and, in a telegram from Paris, he made it clear to General Pelissier that he was never again to scatter his forces but to carry out the Emperor's plan to first defeat the Russian army in the Crimea and then invest Sevastopol before taking the town and destroying all its fortifications. This done, he pointed out, Pelissier would be able to evacuate the Crimea, and leave it to the Turks. Pelissier however, had his own plans to lay siege to Sevastopol and Napoleon's cable was ignored. It was not the first occasion he had put the Emperor's letters and dispatches into his pocket without reading them.

Following the allies' success at Kertch, Pelissier was encouraged to think that a successful assault on the Mamelon Vert would pave the way to the occupation of the Malakoff Tower and the Redan. Lord Raglan was of the same opinion and, at a combined staff meeting on 28 May, it was decided that following an intensive artillery bombardment, the French would carry the Mamelon Vert whilst the British attacked the Russian works in front of the Redan known as the Quarries.

This last position was, as its name implied, a sizeable excavation for the removal of gravel, lying half way between the British right flank and the Redan. 'It is hoped that if we are successful in our attack,' wrote Somerset Calthorpe, who was present at the meeting, 'we shall be able to push forward flying saps towards the Malakoff Redoubt from the Mamalon, and towards the Redan from the English right attack and by this means be near enough to make a final rush on their two great works of defence and carry them.'

It was in this confident mood that plans for an assault on the outer defence works around Sevastopol were agreed by the allied general staff and, as related by Lieutenant Wolseley: 'At 3pm, on June 6th, all the allied batteries opened fire, and the very earth seemed to shake and heave from the violent concussion of nearly 600 guns and mortars with which we pounded the Russian works. The heat told seriously upon our artillerymen and blue jackets, who worked hard at their guns all day. The roar of guns from both sides was terrific.'

'Its purpose,' stated Captain Edmund Reilly, 'was to reduce the fire from the Mamelon, White Works and the Quarries in front of the Redan. By 4.30pm the Mamelon and Malakoff were scarcely able to reply to the fire from the allied batteries.'

'The din was tremendous,' remembered Douglas Reid, the assistant surgeon of the 90 Foot. 'It is impossible to describe it. It was curious how the ear became accustomed to the booming of cannon. But the rattle of musketry put everyone on the *qui vive* – we knew then that a fight was going on.' The bombardment continued through the night, but at dawn the thunder of the artillery eased to an occasional rumble and the allied infantry waited for the signal which would send the French against the Mamelon and the British redcoats against the Quarries. Fanny Duberly voiced the hopes of many when she remarked to General Pierre Bosquet that hopefully '...this time the guns would not play an overture for another farce'. Turning to his companion, the Frenchman replied, 'Madame, in Paris there are always exhibitions, balls and parties taking place; but in ninety minutes time half of these brave fellows will be dead'.

The British headquarters' staff were also aware of the inevitability of heavy casualties but, like the French, were prepared to accept them in recognition that only a determined attack at this stage would bring the siege to an end.

By midday on 7 June many of the Russian batteries had been silenced, the outer works were in ruins, and it was thought that an assault on the Mamelon could be made with every expectation of a successful outcome at the expense of an acceptable casualty rate. Details of the attack had been decided at a Council of War some days previously. Four divisions of the French 2nd Corps were detailed for a twin assault against the Mamelon and the Ouvrages Blancs. General Camou was to attack the Mamelon on the left of the Careening Bay ravine, supported by General Brunet, whilst two other divisions led by Generals Mayran and Dulac attacked the Ouvrages Blancs on the right of the ravine, with two battalions of the Imperial Guard being held in reserve.

Late in the afternoon, Lord Raglan, accompanied by his staff, rode up to Cathcart's Hill to be greeted by men of the 4th Division in their shirt sleeves, who cheered him enthusiastically as he passed, but as usual in the face of demonstrations, he was overcome with embarrassment and did his best to ignore the cheering by conversing with his staff. 'Nothing could exceed the spirits of the troops,' commented Somerset Calthorpe, 'all the men, turning out of their huts and tents, crowded round the Staff, and made the whole plateau resound with their loud huzzas.' The French General Jacques Pelissier had also been warmly applauded by the British troops, which had affected him to the extent that he turned in his saddle and, with tears in his eyes, remarked: 'With troops in such high spirits as these we cannot but succeed.'

Lieutenant Dallas recorded:

At about 5pm we began to collect on the heights, the weather perfect, a delicious cool breeze blowing. Every gun we had was firing all it could to endeavour to silence the point to be attacked, & our eyes alternately strained through glasses, first on a flagstaff where the signal was to be raised, then on the Mamelon, the most important work to be taken. At about 6pm up went the Union Jack on the flagstaff & like magic the whole of the side of the Mamelon was covered with French (looking like ants) tearing up to the assault.

'Up swarmed the French over the green hill leading to the battery and at last we could see them jump over the parapet and bayonet the Russians out,' wrote Lieutenant Jocelyn Strange. 'They had taken it in exactly six minutes and a half.'

Lieutenant Henry Clifford had earlier seen several rockets describing a fiery arc against the evening sky, as a signal for four battalions of French infantry to leave their trenches and advance over the sixty yards of open ground towards the Mamelon Vert. An excited Clifford watched as they were followed by wave after wave of cheering French troops from the 50 Regiment sweeping across the ground and up the slope towards their objective, seemingly indifferent to the crackle of musketry. Caught by surprise and faced with several hundred bayonets, the Russian sharpshooters in the Rifle Pits took to their heels.

'It was as splendid as it was awful to see the brave Frenchmen running up under fire,' Clifford commented, 'and my heart beat as I never felt it before and the tears ran down my face when in less than ten minutes after they left the trenches I saw the "tricolour" flag flourishing over the parapet of the "Mamelon".' Another observer, George Frederick Dallas was similarly elated. 'The leading men get in & are followed by hundreds hopping on to the parapet & down the other side,' he wrote.

The French, having established a presence on the parapet of the redoubt, the work was lost to the Russians and, in less than fifteen minutes, the three regiments of General Camou's division were in possession of the Mamelon Vert for surprisingly few casualties. It had all seemed too easy for the impetuous Zouaves, and encouraged by their officers, they stormed through the Mamelon to mount an attack on the far more formidable defence works known as the Malakoff Tower. This bastion was well defended and Russian fire power decimated the tightly packed ranks of the Zouaves. In a fierce bout of hand to hand fighting, the Russians drove them back to the Mamelon, repossessing it and forcing the Zouaves to fall back upon their own trenches. A disappointed Henry Clifford reported, somewhat uncharitably:

They wavered, they turned, they fled. Back they came like a large wave, the grapeshot mowing them down in lines. At the Mamelon I thought; Thank God, they will be safe, they can make a stand, but a dark smoke came from it as they entered, the whole place was on fire, and over they came, the Russians close upon them over the slope ... at last we saw the French behind their own trench from which they had first started, not more advanced than if they had never left it.

The setback for the French was to be short lived for, in the space of half an hour, 50 Regiment, after a brief interval to recover, returned to the scene in another attempt to seize the Mamelon and clear the area around it. Lieutenant Calthorpe, in company with others of Raglan's staff, watched anxiously as the infantry, led by Colonel Brancion, breasted the slope in complete disregard of the numbers who fell. 'Nothing could be more magnificent than the advance of those troops,' wrote Calthorpe. 'A footing once obtained in the angle of the redoubt, the Mamelon was lost to the Russians, for the French troops now poured in everywhere along the surface of the works, and in the course of a quarter of an hour the whole assaulting column were in and about the Mamelon Redoubt.'

Whilst the 50th had battled with the Russian garrison to force an entry, a desperate struggle was underway for the possession of the Ouvrages Blancs or White Rocks, as it was known to the British. There, two brigades of General Mayran's division had advanced in column against the two earthworks in the face of a storm of musketry and grapeshot, which quickly threw the columns into confusion and threatened to bring their advance to a halt. Supported by General Dulac's brigade, the survivors rallied to drive the Russians from the first redoubt to a second, and stronger one, some way to the rear.

Although the enemy fought bravely, the French in a bloody hand to hand encounter forced them to fall back on a third and smaller works near Careening Bay and the harbour, overlooked by a battery in the town and several others on the north side of the harbour. The Russians were not left in possession of the work for long for the Zouaves, distinctive in their red fez and voluminous skirts, stormed on to drive the defenders down a steep slope towards the bay. Ironically, the Russians, manning the town batteries, seeing that the work had been abandoned by their own troops, brought every available cannon to bear, inflicting a number of casualties and obliging the French to evacuate the redoubt after spiking the few guns it contained. The one objective yet to fall to the allies, was the Quarries which had been fortified with a loop holed parapet around the perimeter, from which the Russian sharpshooters had maintained an accurate fire against the British trenches. It was essential that this position was captured for until it fell into British hands no advance could be made on the

Redan and Lord Raglan, conscious of the heavy casualties that had accompanied the French attacks on the Mamelon, gave the signal to advance with a heavy heart.

His plan called for 400 men from 7 Fusiliers, 31, 34, and 88 Regiments to leave the advance trench and turn the enemy's flanks. After capturing the position they were to press ahead as far as was practicable towards the Redan and give covering fire to a second party of 800 men whose task it would be to dig a trench linking the Quarries to the most advanced parallel. 'As the moment for the assault drew near,' remarked Lieutenant Wolseley, 'each man around me seemed instinctively to hold his breath in a state of pent up mental pressure.' Shortly after 7.00 p.m. the eagerly awaited signal was hoisted and 1,200 men left their trenches and advanced hurriedly towards the Quarries, supported by fire from the newly captured Mamelon Vert. So sudden was the appearance of the storming party that many of the defenders fled to the shelter of the Redan, leaving the remaining few to be bayoneted by troops who had not forgotten with what barbarity the Russians had treated the wounded at Inkerman. Just three prisoners were taken.

With the gravel pits now free of the enemy, working parties were brought up and, covered by the riflemen of the 31st and 34th, they quickly set to work throwing up a parapet facing the enemy and completing a link with the nearest trench to the Redan. Shortly after the work had been completed, a strong force of Russian infantry sallied out of the Little Redan between the Malakoff Tower and the Harbour to make the first of several attempts to regain the Quarries. 'The fighting then became desperate,' remembered Sergeant Gowing. 'The bayonet was freely used on both sides; but although the enemy were three or four to one they shrank back ... Thank God, I escaped once more, but it would be impossible for me to tell how.'

All the attempts made by the Russians were unsuccessful in the face of determined resistance and, although a number of casualties were sustained by the defenders, when darkness fell the Russians retired, harassed by musketry from the Quarries and supporting fire from the Mamelon. 'At times we were hard pushed,' confessed Sergeant Gowing, 'for we had no ammunition left, and had to do as we had done at Inkerman, viz: pitch stones at them ... we were now under good cover, the pick and shovel having been at it all night.'

'Repeated attacks were made during the night by the Russians and there was desperate fighting,' Douglas Reid confirmed. 'In holding the Quarries, our men were exposed to a very heavy fire from the Redan. We lost about 50 men a night until the breastwork was raised and strengthened.'

Despite delays caused by these night attacks, when dawn broke, the defences had been considerably strengthened and that day a flag of truce was raised, to allow the grim task of removing the dead by the troops of each country. Somerset Calthorpe had ridden down from the Careening Ravine:

> The ground of the scene of contest presented the same horrible appearance as the battlefield of Alma and Inkerman. Mutilated corpses and bodies covered with ghastly wounds met the eye all round ... The pale, upturned, happy faces of some, apparently in peaceful slumber, marked the instantaneous death which they had met, the dreadful contortions of those who had suffered agonizing deaths – were seen in both friend and foe. One battlefield is generally like another, the same features mark all ...

Another observer who visited the area under a flag of truce, was Lieutenant Dunscombe, who described the scene in a letter to his father:

> I took the opportunity of going down to see the Mamelon and Quarry. The stench from the dead bodies lying about was unbearable, as they had been lying there in the sun unburied for nearly two days. I entered into conversation with a Russian captain who spoke English most fluently. The Russians deserve the greatest credit for the way they fought the Mamelon, as the whole place was regularly honeycombed with shot and shell from our batteries ... they looked (the Russians) today very different to what they did when I saw them about a month ago, they look now sulky, miserable, and quite down in the mouth ...

Chapter Seven

LIONS COMMANDED BY ASSES

With the capture of the Mamelon and the Quarries, the successes of 8 June had given rise for hope that the dreary siege was drawing to a close. The allies were now in a good position to attack the key defence works of the Malakoff and the Redan which, if overthrown, would give them the entire command of the whole of the south side of Sevastopol.

Lieutenant Dallas had every confidence in the ability of the French and British troops to do so, and in a letter to his family he assured them: 'I have not the slightest doubt about the south side of the town being ours soon, and I imagine we are only waiting until the French make a battery on the Mamelon that they took. When it is made, it will command most of the place.' The proposed attack on the Malakoff would not be led by General Bosquet however, for he was to retain command for just seven more days before being replaced by the relatively inexperienced General Reynaud de Saint Jean d'Angely. His dismissal by General Pelissier had been as a consequence of insubordination and a failure to hand over a detailed plan of the Malakoff Tower found in the pocket of a dead Russian officer.

The change in command came as no surprise to the officers on Raglan's staff. Commenting on the dismissal, Lieutenant Somerset Calthorpe commented:

It is but just to General Pelissier to state, that on every occasion that he has proposed any offensive movement against the town, General Bosquet has always objected, and I understand, not infrequently in very strong terms, besides predicting all sorts of disasters and

132

defeat. Such being the case, General Pelissier felt that a man who had no confidence in the success of the operations was very unfit to be in command of them.

Bosquet's failure to pass on the captured documents in good time was to have a profound effect on the subsequent allied attacks on both the Malakoff Tower and the Redan. Both were formidable works well served by artillery and affording a good field of fire to the Russian infantry. Reinforced by masonry, it was going to take a heavy and sustained artillery bombardment to destroy the Malakoff, but on 10 June it was decided, after a study of Sevastopol's outer defences, that siege operations would continue and, at a Council of War six days later, a decision was reached that a major attack against these outer bastions of Sevastopol was perfectly feasible.

Lord Raglan, who was suffering from a mild attack of dysentery, raised no objection to the plan outlined by the French, which provided for three divisions to leave the trenches and attack the Little Redan and the Malakoff Tower. Following the capture of the Malakoff, the British would mount their attack on the Great Redan, it being considered too costly in terms of casualties to launch an assault before the Malakoff was taken, since its guns enfiladed the Redan.

'On Sunday June 17th the fourth bombardment of Sevastopol opened with a terrible crash, and from morning until night they kept it up as hard as they could load and fire,' wrote Timothy Gowing. 'The very earth seemed to shake beneath the crash of guns.'

'I was awoken at 3am this morning by the heavy firing from all the batteries ... the Colonel assembled all the officers in the reading room today, and told us the plan of attack,' reported Lieutenant Nicholas Dunscombe. 'We have received orders to parade at 1am tomorrow morning as quietly as possible, all the men are to carry extra ammunition in their haversacks and to have their water bottles filled.'

The artillery onslaught continued for the whole of that day with scarcely any retaliation from the Russian guns. When darkness fell, the bombardment ceased, with the exception of the heavy mortars which continued to pound the Malakoff and the Redan with bombs and shells, much to the satisfaction of the troops

133

waiting in their trenches for the signal which would determine their fate. That night, for reasons which were not entirely clear, Pelissier decided to advance the time of the French attack on the Malakoff to 3.00 a.m., an alteration to the original plan which Raglan considered to be a grave error, but he was left with little option but to modify his own orders to suit the revised timetable.

As the British troops left to join the French in the forward trenches early on the 18th – the anniversary of Waterloo – a bright moon and a sky brilliant with stars made it almost impossible for them to conceal their movements from the enemy who, thus warned, ensured that many more muskets were loaded and primed, and field guns dragged into positions which gave a good field of fire. 'The fact that the Russians expected to be attacked that morning came home to me in an instant,' remarked Wolseley, 'when upon the advance of our storming columns, I saw the superior slope of all their major works covered suddenly, as if by magic, with their soldiers.'

The Commander-in-Chief, with his staff, had ridden to a mortar battery which, whilst affording them a good view of both the Quarries and the Redan, was well within the range of the Russian guns. Raglan and his staff were shortly to become aware of this although Raglan chose to ignore the fact.

Lieutenant Somerset Calthorpe, who numbered among the thirty officers on Raglan's staff, was at a loss to explain a sudden burst of gunfire. 'We had not been in the mortar battery more than ten minutes, it being still quite dark, before we heard a heavy musketry fire going on upon the extreme right of the French Inkerman attack … it seemed as if a pitched battle was raging. We were all at a loss to imagine what it could be, as the signal had not been given …'

The situation for the attacking troops had been made even more confused by General Mayan in mistaking the fiery trail from the fuse of a French shell for a signal rocket, and giving a premature order for his column to advance. It left Pelissier with no alternative but to launch the other two divisions in support, and the planned coordinated attack was reduced to a shambles. A mass of French troops rushed towards the Malakoff in the face of a hail of musketry, canister and grape, which tore great gaps in the tightly packed formation. No body of troops could maintain order against such devastating fire power and the French attack soon disintegrated into a ragged and broken rush through the smoke toward the Malakoff and its formidable defences.

The slope up to the Russian stronghold soon became a killing ground littered with the dead, dying and helpless wounded, while those who could, desperately sought to evade the round shot ricocheting over the ground, the shrapnel bullets raining down upon their heads and, most deadly of all, the lethal sprays of canister. General Mayan himself paid the ultimate penalty for his rash decision, being twice wounded before being carried to the rear with a third wound which proved fatal. The rolling clouds of smoke and dust sweeping over the battlefield could not conceal the carnage from Lord Raglan and his staff, watching from the mortar battery behind the Quarries. They could see that the French attack was on the point of collapse, their broken columns thinned by an onslaught of lead and iron. Feeling that he was honour bound to relieve the pressure on the French, Raglan ordered an immediate advance on the Redan. Sir George Brown acted promptly by calling up two columns, one 500 strong led by General Sir John Campbell, commanding the 4th Division and another of similar strength commanded by Colonel Lacy Yea of the 7 Fusiliers. The storming column was accompanied by naval personnel carrying scaling ladders and sacks of wool to bridge the numerous ditches, the largest being fifteen feet wide and eleven feet deep, which scarred the quarter mile of broken ground between the trenches and the Redan.

'We all paraded and marched down full of hope and almost certain of success,' wrote Lieutenant Dallas bitterly. 'Instead of the result we so fondly anticipated, there ensued nothing but mismanagement and frightful carnage.' Given the lack of time in which to plan such a perilous assault, Sir George Brown could only hope that his troops would not encounter too many problems in vacating the trenches, but he was not optimistic. 'The troops moved out of the trench in anything but good order,' remembered Somerset Calthorpe. 'They had been arrayed along at about three deep, and immediately the signal was given, had to clamber over the parapet, and thus started in some confusion.'

The premature advance proved to be a grave error, for the element of surprise had been lost and the Russians were well prepared. At once a most tremendous fire of grape and musketry, which was so severe that many redcoats refused to leave the trench and follow their officers, met the stormers. Among the first to fall was General Sir John Campbell leading the attack against the west face of the Redan. Almost at the same moment Colonel Lacy Yea, several yards in front of his men, was struck in the neck by grapeshot whilst turning to encourage them. Fired by the example set by their leaders, riflemen and redcoats from the 33 Foot who had volunteered as a 'forlorn hope', made a determined rush towards the walls of the Redan followed by the sailors carrying ladders and sacks of wool, but the rush forward rapidly came to a halt, as men sought the protection offered by a ditch or a nearby shell hole.

Following the death of Lacy Yea, command of the 7 Fusiliers devolved upon Major Reynell Pack. Writing in the third person, he described what then happened: 'Scarcely had we assumed the direction of the regiment, when a ball from a minie rifle passed fiercely right through the fleshy part of our left leg cutting a round hole in the thick cloth of the trousers on entering and also another on leaving, and we were at once placed *hors de combat* and compelled to retire from the attack. As soldiers usually say, "every bullet has its billet".'

Captain Bruce Hamley, supporting the attack with his battery of field guns, was appalled by the chaos which ensued in the trenches:

In vain the officers stood up amid the iron shower and waved their swords; in vain the engineers returned to bring up the supports; the men could not be induced to quit the parapets in a body. Small parties of half a dozen, or half a score, ran out only to add to the slaughter. The party of artillerymen whose business it was to follow the assault column and spike the guns, sallied forth, led by their officers, and, of the twenty artillerymen only nine returned unwounded; whilst of the sailors who carried the scaling ladders, just one reached the abattis in front of the Redan where a few of the Royal Fusiliers, tried to pull it down.

Timothy Gowing, who numbered himself among the storming party, wrote in exasperation: 'We might just as well have tried to pull down the moon.'

'On each side of the embrasures of the left face of the Redan the enemy was standing up on the parapets in such crowds as apparently to hinder one another,' observed Major Reynell Pack.

'Doubtless within the work others were actively engaged loading and handing up arms, so that, in our advance, we were destroyed or placed *hors de combat* as expeditiously as possible.'

An unlooked for hazard in the shape of what might be considered an early form of the anti-personnel mine, faced the storming parties as they approached the Redan. These were boxes of gunpowder buried a few inches below the soil containing a fulminating tube of nitric acid within a thin metal tube. When trodden on, the glass tube within it fractured, and the acid making contact with the prepared ingredients, ignited the powder causing an explosion. 'Not only did it destroy anything near it,' commented John Hume, 'but it also threw out a quantity of bitumen so as to burn whatever it came to rest upon.'

In the torrent of grapeshot which met the redcoats running with their bodies bent, as if facing a storm, it was hardly surprising that those who survived to reach the abattis in front of the Redan, should seek the shelter afforded by a ditch or a fold in the ground. The officers had suffered so many casualties, at least eighty-five, that few orders had been given and the men, reduced to half their original number, dispirited and lacking leadership, joined their comrades in a panic stricken scramble back through the smoke to the safety of the trenches. In doing so they were not condemned by Lord Raglan who, seeing that the attack had been a dismal failure, ordered the artillery to give covering fire to the infantry in an attempt to restore something like order. 'The Russians when they saw us retreating, jumped up on the parapets, cheering loudly,' remembered John Hume. 'They threw everything they could lay hands on after us, and shot down a great number before we reached our trenches. A musket ball smashed my left arm.' Fortunately, Hume was spared the ordeal of amputation by an assistant surgeon from the 2nd Division.

'The whole affair is a very sad thing,' commented Lieutenant Dallas. 'It is the first time that our troops have been beaten. However, the feeling of the army is I think good, and they are burning to avenge their comrades' slaughter.'

'It was almost a miracle how any of the storming columns escaped,' mused Sergeant Gowing. 'My clothing was cut all to pieces – I had no fewer than nine shot holes through my trousers, coat and cap – but, I thank God, I was not touched. Out of my company, which went into action with 1 captain, 2 lieutenants, 4 sergeants, 4 corporals, 2 drummers and 90 men, all that came out with a whole skin were 13 men besides myself.'

For both the French and British General Staff the failure of the operation was disconcerting and indeed a few of the French commanders blamed their defeat on the British for failing to press forward with enough determination. Most British officers agreed that the attack had been ill conceived and bordered on the suicidal. George Frederick Dallas in a letter to his family, wrote: 'The whole affair was hideously mismanaged, and if it had all come off as intended, would, I think, have failed from the Russians being so perfectly prepared.' An excuse if not an explanation for the failure, was offered by Captain Hume. 'Our advance trench was too far from the Redan to give any body of men a chance of reaching the work in any kind of formation under the heavy fire of round shot, shell and grape. The only wonder was that any men who reached the abattis escaped unhurt.'

The most plausible explanation for the reluctance of the troops to press their advance, would seem to have been suggested by Mrs Duberly:

> Men who had been fighting behind batteries and gabions for nearly twelvemonth, could not be made to march steadily under fire from which they could get no cover. As Colonel Windham said, in speaking of the assault; 'The men, the moment they saw a gabion ran to it as they would to their wives, and would not leave its shelter'. Why not have taken all this into consideration and ordered the newly arrived regiments to lead the assault?

Lord Raglan had little choice but to order an assault for, as related by Douglas Reid: 'Had he given up the attack he would certainly have been accused of breach of faith. It would have been "Perfide de Albion" once more. Lord Raglan played the game, but it broke his heart.' Although morale suffered as a result of the failure to seize the Redan, at least one officer was reluctant to blame the Commander-in-Chief for the debacle. 'I have no doubt there will be a very great outcry against poor Lord Raglan in England when our would-be assault of the 18th is heard of and our sad loss,' wrote Lieutenant Henry Clifford to his father. 'Poor man! he has a hard part to play to satisfy our Government and the French too. It is hard to judge him and I am very careful how I speak of him to anyone.'

138

'In our confidence of success,' observed Roger Fenton, 'we had chosen this day in order that on the anniversary of Waterloo a victory common to both nations might efface from the minds of one the recollection of their former defeat, but we reckoned too proudly, and now the 18th of June will be a glorious day for the Russians.'

For each army the casualties suffered for a day of minimal gain, had been unacceptably high. One thousand six hundred killed and 2,900 wounded for the French and about 1,500 casualties for the British, including 100 officers. That the Russians had suffered even more so, was made clear to Lieutenant Calthorpe by a Russian officer. 'Losses!' the Russian told him in a voice choked with emotion: 'You do not know what the word means! You should see our batteries ... dead lie there in heaps and heaps! Troops cannot live under such a fire of hell as you poured upon us.'

Lieutenant Henry Clifford, as he stood near a huge pit into which the bloodstained corpses were tumbled, felt nothing but disgust: 'The sun was so hot that it was impossible to recognize the dead. Their bodies were swollen to an enormous size and their faces and hands quite black, and so dreadful was the stench that the men who were taking them off the field often vomited. This was all part of the Honour and Glory.'

Those who died of their wounds at Scutari were afforded little ceremony through no fault of the authorities. 'The remains of our poor soldiers were rolled in wrappers and laid side by side in a large grave,' reported Lady Alicia Blackwood, 'coffins for such numbers being out of the question. For many weeks the burials averaged over fifty per diem.'

A little more than an hour before the attack on the Redan, a brigade led by Major General Eyre had been sent by Lord Raglan to divert the attention of the enemy by attacking a position known as the Man of War harbour at the bottom of a ravine running between the old French and British trenches. It was to be made by 2,000 men taken from the 9, 18, 28, 38, and 44 Regiments and prior to descending the ravine, Eyre halted his troops to explain the operation and call for volunteers. There was no shortage of men willing to take part. An advance guard of 200 was quickly formed from each of the five regiments, and at 3.00 a.m. the newly formed column made its way down the ravine, meeting and making prisoners of two small groups of Russians without losing a man.

Ahead lay a cemetery known to be occupied by a strong force of the enemy. In the darkness it was impossible to estimate their numbers and, as Eyre's men advanced towards the position, they were greeted by the bright flashes of the enemy's muskets and the crackle of small-arms fire. The Russians however, after offering little more than a token resistance, sought the protection afforded by a group of houses at the foot of the ravine, and Eyre's men were able to take possession of the cemetery with just a few casualties.

Although his orders from Lord Raglan had been to turn his demonstration into a full scale attack only if the assault on the Redan was successful, after a short pause, General Eyre ordered an attack against the Russians on both sides of the ravine, and whilst men from the 18 Regiment drove the defenders from the houses on the left, a similar body from the 44th attacked and occupied those on the right of the ravine. Once it became known that the Russians had been driven from their shelter, a furious cannonade from the Barrack batteries was directed against Eyre's troops occupying the houses. 'At first they fired round shot at us,' stated Captain Hopton-Scott, 'and as every shot came through both walls one half of the house had crumbled down after a couple of hours. Had they continued it hardly one of us could have escaped; but fortunately they could not see the damage they were doing, or known the number collected there, for they gave that up, and took to shelling us.' Despite this, casualties mounted but the redcoats struggled to maintain a presence, even in the houses set ablaze by shells, but against artillery fire from the Barrack and Garden batteries it was always going to be a lost cause and Eyre sought permission from Lord Raglan to retire. In response to this request, the Field Marshal, who had notified General Pelissier of Eyre's operation, lost no time in dispatching an aide to Eyre instructing him to fall back from his present position if the French had not relieved him by nightfall.

For the remainder of that day Eyre's troops continued to suffer from the enemy's batteries and from Russian ships in the harbour, which led to numerous casualties among both officers and men. General Eyre did not escape injury, for later in the morning he suffered a grievous head wound which eventually made it necessary for him to delegate command to Colonel Adams of the

28 Regiment. With nightfall and no sign of the French, Adams ordered the column to retire with the wounded. Losses for what had been regarded as being no more than a diversionary operation, were altogether out of proportion to the numbers engaged. Thirty-one officers and 531 men killed or wounded from an original strength of 2,000. The failure of the attacks on the Redan and the Malakoff and the deaths of so many high ranking officers, had deeply affected Lord Raglan, who had watched the storming while he and his staff were under severe fire from the Russian artillery. As the days passed, the staff noticed a profound change in his appearance following criticism from the English press, and the news that a close friend, General Estcourt, was desperately ill with cholera. 'I fear that it has affected his health' commented Somerset Calthorpe. 'He looks far from well and has grown very much aged latterly.' It seemed that most of the Field officers had been gripped by a general air of depression for, in writing to his father, Lieutenant Jocelyn Strange admitted:

All our Generals have fallen ill since our disaster on Monday, and if things go on so, we shall have a set of very young Generals, so some good may arise out of it. The Russians at the Armistice for burial of the dead paid us the compliment of calling us 'Lions commanded by Asses'.

There was good reason to account for Lord Raglan's low state of health for, in addition to his sense of failure, on 23 June he was found to be suffering from acute dysentery. Three days later he took to his bed and, on the afternoon of the 28th, he died. The news was received by the army almost with disbelief. People '... looked at each other as if they had heard of the loss of some near relative,' remembered Timothy Gowing. 'We did not know until he was taken from us, how deeply we loved him.'

'The army is so quiet,' entered Mrs Duberly in her diary. 'Men speak in low voices words of regret.'

'He passed away quietly,' Lieutenant Henry Clifford informed his father, 'without leaving a single enemy.' A comment made by George Cavendish Taylor had some significance. 'It was strange that his last battle should have been a repulse, and on the anniversary of Waterloo,' he wrote.

The defeats at the Redan and the Malakoff had come as no surprise to Lieutenant Curtis:

> There was not the slightest attempt made to keep the matter secret, or any steps taken to prevent the enemy becoming aware of our intentions to attack them. If by any means the Russian Commander got the information, there was plenty of time for them to make preparations for their defence, and from what occurred afterwards I am of (the) opinion that the Russians knew the whole programme as well as we did ourselves.

For a time the Government was undecided as to who might replace Lord Raglan, but the appointment could not be postponed and Lieutenant General James Simpson was given temporary command. The sixty-three year-old had not sought the appointment and had, at times, shown a lack of confidence in his dealings with the problems faced by the army. In acknowledging the Government's choice, he begged Panmure to relieve him of it as soon as possible. 'I sincerely trust, my Lord, that a General of distinction will be sent out immediately ...' Lieutenant Dallas as ADC to Brigadier General Garrett, commanding the 4th Division, was one of many who had doubts about the appointment of General Simpson. 'I went with the Brigadier to call on General Simpson, our new chief,' he informed his father. 'He was very civil, but I fancy neither he himself nor anybody out here seems to think him much fitted for such an appointment. Who knows? Perhaps he may be the man.'

Ministers soon realized that a mistake had been made but it was to be November before a replacement was confirmed and prior to that Simpson's attention was to be drawn to an operation in the Baltic, and a Russian manoeuvre which threatened the French and Sardinian positions overlooking the Chernaya.

As early as September 1853 Sir George Hamilton Seymour, the British ambassador to St Petersburg, had raised concerns relating to the strength of the Russian Baltic fleet based in the heavily defended ports of Kronstadt and Sweaborg.

Sweaborg was the name given to a series of fortified islands in the Gulf of Finland, the most important of which being the isle of Vargon, just three miles from Finland's capital city, Helsingfors. Two years after the concerns raised by the ambassador, the

Admiralty decided the time was ripe for action and Captain Bartholomew Sulivan, a notable hydrographer and surveyor who had voyaged with Darwin, was asked to report on the strengths of the two Russian sea ports of Kronstadt and Sweaborg and advise on the amphibious force necessary to reduce them.

Sulivan was more than equal to the task, providing Rear Admiral Sir James Dundas, who had replaced Napier as Commander-in-Chief of the Baltic fleet, with an accurate estimate of the strength of the Russian defences and recommending that the expedition be confined to a naval force, the employment of troops being, in his opinion, completely unnecessary. Sulivan's report was endorsed by the Admiralty and warmly received by Napoleon III who had been notified of Britain's plan by Lord Clarendon, the Foreign Secretary, early in March. It had pleased the Emperor for he had long nurtured the belief that a naval success in the Gulf of Finland would be enough to persuade Sweden to join the allies in their campaign against Russia.

The fleet assigned to the task was entirely screw driven and included bomb ships armed with large calibre mortars, and rocket vessels, the whole being under the command of Sir Richard Dundas. The first British ships sailed from Spithead on 20 March bound for Kiel, with the remainder following two weeks later, intent upon enforcing a blockade to prevent essential supplies from getting through to Russia from the Baltic ports. In the event, it was to prove something of a diplomatic embarrassment, for the naval personnel became so frustrated by the reaction of the villagers when investigating breaches of the blockade along the Finnish coast, that it led to houses being torched and the occupants roughly handled.

On 1 June Admiral Penaud joined Dundas with the French fleet in the expectation of an operation against Kronstadt, but doubts had been raised on the advisability of attacking that port after Sulivan, in HMS *Merlin,* had made a further reconnaissance even to the extent of going ashore in Estonia to seek local information on the port's defences. What he discovered contrasted unfavourably with his previous report, for the Russians had not only added to the number of armed vessels, but had also strengthened its seaward defences by laying a great number of mines just a few feet below the surface. He also learned that a barrier of timber and stone had been built with an opening just sufficient to permit the passage of small craft, which would add to the difficulties faced by Admiral Dundas.

In the light of this knowledge, the Admiral decided that an attack against Kronstadt, with the resources at his disposal, would be both hazardous and doubtful of success, a point of view with which the Admiralty concurred and Kronstadt was ruled out of the operation. Sweaborg, however, did not pose such a problem and Dundas was confident that his ships were equal to the task. In this he was not being unduly optimistic for, although the port's defences had been strengthened, it was vulnerable to a close approach by rocket vessels and shallow draft floating batteries heavily armoured with 30-pounder guns, while the capital ships of Dundas' fleet were available some distance offshore to add their weight to the bombardment if necessary.

Early in the morning of 9 August, the mortar vessels or bomb ships as they were called, were ready to begin their destructive fire against Vargon, having just enough sail power to get them into position before being anchored fore and aft. By slackening or hauling on either cable, the position of the vessel could be adjusted and the twin mortars brought to the required bearing. These floating batteries were necessarily of much sturdier construction than most naval vessels, having timbers almost twice the thickness of other ships in order to withstand the massive recoil and downward shock from the mortars mounted in the centre of the foredeck.

After four hours, during which time the shells from the mortars had descended on the barracks to erupt in a lethal spray of iron fragments, causing numerous casualties and widespread destruction, there occurred a massive explosion in Fort Vargon. The magazine had erupted in a cloud of smoke and debris rising to several hundred feet, causing many inhabitants of Helsingfors to flee the city in fear of their lives. Shortly after midday a second powder magazine exploded in what a journalist from *The Times* colourfully described as '...a volcano in a state of eruption', which hurled round shot and shells high into the air and also started a chain of fires and several minor explosions.

The bombardment directed against various other works on the islands continued until early evening when the mortar vessels were forced to withdraw, their weapons rendered unserviceable from constant use. The night was comparatively quiet but in the

144

morning the task of destroying Sweaborg's defences was resumed and continued after nightfall when the darkness was rent by streaks of flame from the guns of the capital ships offshore, and the fiery trails of rockets tracing an erratic path towards their target.

Over the period of two days and nights, the Royal Navy alone had blasted over 1,000 tons of explosives into an area of three square miles at the expense of just one fatality and a dozen wounded. Some indication of the intensity of the bombardment may be gained from the fact that almost every sailor serving the guns was deafened for several hours after the action had been terminated. Sweaborg as a naval base had ceased to be of any further use to the Russians and twenty-three enemy vessels had been sunk by mortar shells or set on fire by rockets. When the ships of Admiral Dundas' fleet sailed back to home waters on 13 August, the success they had enjoyed emphasized the advantage to be gained by the employment of naval vessels against coastal defences to many interested observers. Not only was an action against Kronstadt reconsidered, but attention was focussed upon the Russian naval base at Kinburn. However, before this operation was undertaken, the French were to be involved in a fierce struggle with the Russians on the Fediukine Hills, a stretch of high ground overlooking the left bank of the River Tchernaya and flanking the northern end of the Balaklava Valley.

At the beginning of August, Tsar Alexander II, concerned at the ever growing casualty figures caused by the allied bombardment of Sevastopol, had advised Prince Gorchakoff that a successful major attack against the rear of the allied positions might result in the lifting of the siege. Gorchakoff had his doubts and pointed out to the Tsar that should the attack fail, it would in all likelihood result in the loss of Sevastopol. Alexander, although not going as far as to order Gorchakoff to carry out the attack, refused to change his stance on the matter and, at a Military Council held on the 9th, his suggestion was approved by a majority of the generals led by Liprandi. Not that many thought that Sevastopol could be saved, but it was hoped that a success in the field might gain Russia more favourable peace terms. The Fediukine Heights was occupied mainly by the French but further downstream of the Tchernaya, where the ground rose to a rocky hill opposite the village of Chorgun known as Mount

Hasfort, a 9,000 strong force of Sardinians and four batteries of artillery held an advantageous position overlooking a stone bridge which crossed the shallow river. In reserve behind the Sardinians was a large body of Turkish troops, while in the valley of Baidar stood a mixed force of French and British cavalry commanded by General d'Allouville.

The French presence on the Fediukine Hills consisted of three divisions of infantry, two of which had been sent there to recover from the severe losses they had suffered in assaulting the Mamelon and consequently were only at half strength, in total some 18,000 men and forty cannon. Four regiments of North African troops, together with five batteries of horse artillery, were held in reserve to the rear of the Fediukine Heights.

The Russian plan of attack devised by Prince Gorchakoff was first to drive the Sardinian outposts from the right bank of the Tchernaya guarding the Tractir Bridge, before establishing a part of his artillery to bombard Mount Hasfort on the opposite bank. At his disposal Prince Gorchakoff had a total of 35,000 men and 160 guns formed from two wings. The right wing comprising the 7th and 12th Divisions under the command of General Read and the left wing led by General Liprandi, consisting of the 6th and 17th Divisions.

Under cover of the artillery bombardment, General Liprandi was to advance along the valley and, passing through Chorgun, attack the Sardinian positions on Mount Hasfort. At the same time General Read would advance from the foot of the Mackenzie Farm Heights – a ridge of hills dominating the Balaklava Valley – towards the Fediukine Hills. Once this had been accomplished and the Sardinians driven out, it was hoped that the French camp would be forced to retire, and the Russians would have succeeded in their aim of dividing the allied forces in front of Sevastopol from their supports in the Balaklava Valley.

That night the 7th and 12th Divisions moved down from the Mackenzie Heights to their allotted positions. At dawn on 16 August, after attacking the Sardinians on the right bank of the river, a major part of General Liprandi's corps, concealed by a thick mist, advanced along the valley towards the village of Chorgun. Taking the Sardinian pickets by surprise and by driving them out, they succeeded in capturing Telegraph Hill. Liprandi's artillery then opened against the Sardinians on the Hasfort

Heights, while his reserve waited for an order from the Prince that would decide where it was to be deployed.

General Read's 7th and 12th Divisions had meanwhile assembled just out of range of the French artillery and the General took care to position a major part of his force in an advantageous position above the left bank of the Tchernaya. This had gone unnoticed by the French and the first indication they had of impending danger was the noise of cannon fire and the shock of having round shot bounding through their camp. Almost as astonished as the French, was Prince Gorchakoff. He had been about to order the advance of General Liprandi's troops when the rolling volleys of musketry coming from his right wing, as Read attacked with his two divisions ahead of schedule and without reinforcements, puzzled and annoyed him. The reason for General Read acting contrary to orders was never satisfactorily explained for, shortly afterwards, both he and his Chief of Staff were killed by shell fire. The French were quick to respond but the numerical superiority of the Russians attacking the stone bridge across the Tchernaya was overwhelming and the 12th Division was able to cross the river, which was never more than knee deep, in strength. The French guns then opened a telling fire against the mass of Russian infantry but were, themselves, shelled with equal vigour by the Russian artillery on the heights above the Tchernaya.

Read's troops, despite the loss of their General, continued to advance against the Fediukine Hills, all the while harassed by shell fire and musketry, before reaching an obstacle in the shape of an aqueduct taking water into the docks at Sevastopol. This unwelcome hazard, built just a few feet above the ground, broke up their columns, causing confusion and delay in the rear formations.

Despite suffering considerable loss, the Russians pressed on to face the French infantry at the western end of the heights but the French, lining the crest of the hill, poured such a volume of small-arms fire into their ranks that it virtually stopped the Russians in their tracks. There followed an exchange of musketry which lasted for almost half an hour before Read's troops retired to the shelter of the aqueduct, each side having suffered a considerable number of casualties.

On learning of this setback, Gorchakoff ordered the 7th Division to support the attack on the right and moving rapidly forward, Read's division crossed the Tchernaya further downstream followed by the 12th Division. The two Russian columns were engaged by General Camou's North African troops, who opened a heavy fire but succeeded only in slowing the Russians' progress, who with great determination advanced half way up the slope before encountering a headlong charge by the Zouaves. This broke up the leading files of Russians and brought the rest of the column to an untimely halt. Following a fierce bout of hand to hand fighting a further charge by the French infantry drove the survivors back to the aqueduct where the area soon became a killing ground as the Russians sought to re-cross the aqueduct and reform.

With neither side able to gain an advantage, by 10.00 a.m. the action had developed into an exchange of musketry and artillery until the Russians received a welcome reinforcement in the shape of battalions from the 6th Division which, acting on Gorchakoff's orders had abandoned the attack on Mount Hasfort and come to the aid of the 7th and 12th Divisions.

A fresh plan of action was now implemented with a brigade of the 17th Division moving between the village and the Tractir Bridge, into the Balaklava Valley. Aware of the Russians' intention, the French General La Marmora immediately dispatched a division to halt their progress, while additional troops were sent to reinforce those already on the high ground adjacent to Mount Hasfort. Here, a desperate battle was raging, during which the Sardinians distinguished themselves by eventually driving the Russians back across the river in the greatest confusion, inflicting many casualties at a relatively small cost to themselves.

The attack by the 7th and 12th Russian Divisions against the Fediukine Heights suffered a similar fate with grievous losses, not only from musketry but also from a tremendous fire of grape from seven French field batteries, and a battery of the Royal Artillery which had arrived upon the scene. The Russians, although in desperate straits, had not yet accepted defeat and, after crossing the aqueduct, reformed together with a large force of cavalry on their flank just out of range of the allied guns. An artillery duel then developed between Russian cannon and French field guns on the heights, without resolving the issue and after a passage of two hours, the Russian infantry were seen to be pulling back across the

Tchernaya towards the Mackenzie Farm Heights, where they had the advantage of higher ground. La Marmora was left to occupy the village and picket the heights from where he had been driven earlier that morning.

Sergeant Albert Mitchell, who had been sent with dispatches from headquarters, took the opportunity to divert his journey by riding towards the Tractir Bridge. 'The bridge,' he wrote, 'was almost blocked up with Russian infantry and Zouaves some of whom had fallen into the river. On either side of the bridge, too, the dead of each party were lying quite thickly, thus proving that many were killed by musketry fire before they were close enough to use the bayonet.' William Howard Russell, like Mitchell, had availed himself of the opportunity to visit the scene of the fiercest fighting. He informed readers of *The Times*:

> The aspect of the field, of the aqueduct, and of the river, was horrible beyond description. The bodies were closely packed in parties, and lay in files two and three deep, where the grape had torn through the columns. For two days the bodies rotted on the ground which lay beyond the French lines and the first Russian burying party did not come down until the 18th when the stench was so very great that the men could scarcely perform their loathsome task.

Thus the Battle of Tchernaya ended in defeat for the Russians after four hours of fighting, during which they had shown great determination and bravery. Their losses had been exceptionally heavy including three generals killed and seven wounded. 'I went on to the field in the evening, and had a good look round; on and at the Tractir Bridge the dead lay in heaps,' wrote Timothy Gowing. 'We had little to do with it; some of our Artillery were engaged and a portion of our Cavalry were formed up ready for a dash at them, but were not let loose.'

For the rest of August the allied generals were left anticipating further action in the area after learning that two divisions of the elite Grenadiers had recently arrived to reinforce the troops already on the plateau of the Mackenzie Heights. The expected engagement never materialized but it did have the result of obliging the allies to construct additional earthworks and batteries on the Fediukine and Hasfort Heights, while General Simpson thought it necessary to dispatch a brigade of Highlanders to support the right flank of the Sardinians and seal off the Balaklava Valley.

Before the end of October the government found itself drawn to the need to pacify the United States. The illegal recruitment by Britain of mercenaries in Boston had been raised by the US Secretary of State, and Parliament had been obliged to recognize that America was right to press the issue. As the weeks passed without the issue being resolved, America's resentment mounted to such an extent that its attitude was called into question by Parliament and its ambassador in London was summoned by the Foreign Office to answer a counter accusation that the United States was supplying arms and ammunition to the Russians. There was also a strong suspicion on the part of some parliamentarians that while Britain was fully engaged in the Crimea, American agents had been actively fermenting trouble in Ireland.

So impressed was Buchanan, the US ambassador, with Britain's argument – he was a prospective Democratic candidate in the forthcoming election – that he warned the Secretary of State that unless America modified its attitude, Britain was likely to go to war in partnership with France. Despite conciliatory moves, ill feeling between the two countries rumbled on through much of the autumn. It seemed likely that there would be a total breakdown of diplomatic relations when it was seen that Britain had a naval presence off the eastern seaboard, but with the Presidential election looming, America backed down and an awkward situation was averted.

Chapter Eight

THE FALL OF SEVASTOPOL

Although the allied attack on 18 June had been defeated, it was readily apparent to the Russians that another assault against Sevastopol's outer defences, such as the Malakoff and the Redan, was just a question of time. The intensity of the bombardment directed against the city had been such that in many areas damage was being inflicted faster than it could be repaired. Todleben had suffered a crippling wound and was no longer able to supervise the building of new works and many Russians, including Prince Gorchakoff, believed that the time had come to evacuate Sevastopol. The consensus of opinion at a staff meeting the Prince had convened, was indeed in favour of abandoning the south side of the city while holding the fort in the north, but this Gorchakoff rejected without offering any suggestion as to how the city was to be defended in the long term.

An air of pessimism also reigned in the British camp but for different reasons. The troops had become extremely frustrated with the time it was taking to overcome the resistance of the garrison and, in a letter dated 27 July, Captain Maxwell Earle complained of being heartily sick of the siege:

> There is nothing going forward at present, and we can look forward to nothing. Before the attack of the 18th of June when there was a hope of terminating the siege I took an interest in watching the operations of the enemy. Now whole days pass sometimes without my ever going 20 yards to look at the town.

A fortnight later, Lieutenant Dallas added his voice to the general feeling of resentment. 'We are rapidly approaching the end of

151

summer, & unless our Leaders feel perfectly certain of our being in the Town by the autumn, nothing can excuse their want of preparation & miserable supineness.'

In fact plans for the final assault against Sevastopol were to be drawn up in early September with instructions being given to the French sappers to dig a parallel trench closer to the city's outer defences. It had been long recognized that this was essential if casualties were to be kept to a minimum and, by 6 September, the most advanced French trench was no more than thirty yards from the Malakoff. The main objective had been decided by the French and it came as no surprise when it was revealed to be the Malakoff Tower; a semi-circular masonry construction which Pelissier regarded as being the key to the overthrow of Sevastopol, commanding as it did all the works on the eastern side of the city. The attack was to take place on 8 September, with General Bosquet restored to the command of 25,000 French troops while General Maurice Patrice MacMahon, a Frenchman of Irish descent who had replaced Canrobert, would lead with the 1st Division, supported by the Imperial Guard.

The British were to be given another opportunity to breach the heavily defended Great Redan with the 2nd and Light Divisions led by Major General Sir William Codrington. The Guards and the Highland Brigade were again being held in reserve. Unlike the French, the British troops still did not have the advantage of a short stretch of open ground between their trench and the Redan, the rocky nature of the ground having made it a hazardous and difficult task for the sappers to advance the trenches. These, as described by Captain Bruce Hamley, '...are nearly of the same description, two or three yards wide and two or three feet deep, with the earth thrown up to form a parapet towards the enemy. Sometimes the soil is clayey, but often bedded with stone, through which the workmen have painfully scooped a cover.' Such work could not be accomplished without loss of life which, at times, approached that of a minor engagement. 'We are sapping up to the Redan,' Nicholas Dunscombe informed his father, 'and we lose a man for every foot of ground we gain.' For just such a reason the 3,000 strong force of redcoats was faced with the unenviable task of crossing 200 yards of open ground, swept by all the fire power the defenders could bring to bear.

The French General, in discussing the attack with Lord Raglan, was confident of success and to ease the congestion in leaving the trench, he had wisely ordered his sappers to widen it and provide gabions for added protection. A thoughtful measure Codrington's troops would have welcomed, for their trenches were narrow, permitting the men to advance in single file only. Almost alone in expressing a high degree of optimism regarding the outcome of the attack was Captain Dallas who, in a letter dated 7 September to his father, wrote:

> I trust the troubles here are approaching their end. As I can by no means take any part or share in it, I don't mind telling you that the Grand Assault is tomorrow. The French at the Malakoff, & we at the Redan, & the French again everywhere else. I see no reason to anticipate anything but success, even granting that the Enemy know all about it.

The date of 8 September, and the order of attack when it was announced to the British troops, did little to raise their already low morale. Their sombre mood did not surprise Colonel Sterling. He was of the opinion that morale could only be raised by an example of good leadership. 'The heart is out of them,' he wrote. 'They ought to employ Eyre or Campbell for the assault if they wish to make a sure job of it, but then Codrington would not get the credit.'

Remembering that the previous attack against the Russian redoubts had been launched at dawn and had ended in failure, Pelissier decided to leave nothing to chance and he opted for the attack against the Malakoff to be made at midday, preceded by an artillery bombardment of sufficient strength to disturb the Russian gunners.

The morning of 5th began, as arranged, with a bombardment which continued for three days, causing Timothy Gowing to remark: 'On the morning September 5th, the last bombardment opened with a terrific shock; close on 1,500 guns and mortars were now blazing away at each other, the earth trembling a while – and so it continued all day.'

'The noise however deafening, was not what impressed you most,' commented G.H. Money. 'The earth seemed to shake and the air to vibrate – as each large gun belched forth its contents, it seemed as if nothing could equal the intensity of the devastation, except the earth opening up and swallowing the city.'

As arranged, the artillery onslaught was halted at noon on the 8th and the Zouaves and Colonial troops of the French 1st Division left their trenches and hurried across the forty yards of scrub towards the Malakoff Tower. The Zouaves in their red fezzes, embroidered jackets and red baggy trousers, were particularly valued for their fighting qualities as Captain Robert Portal readily acknowledged, but he was astonished to learn that they were not entirely composed of Algerians:

> They care for nothing and are great admirers of the English, who, they say, are the only troops like themselves, who never give way an inch. They have an immense number of Englishmen among them, which is very curious. There were four of them in camp the other day all speaking the broadest cockney dialect. One of them told me he had kept a pot house in Hammersmith, but got into trouble, left England, and enlisted in the Zouaves.

The Russians were taken completely by surprise by the French attack. Many were elderly veterans having dinner and, of the Russian artillery, only six cannons were manned and ready to open fire against the attackers. In a ferocious bout of hand to hand fighting the French battled their way across the embrasures and along the bastions, driving the defenders before them. In a space of little more than ten minutes, the Tricolour was seen to be streaming from its pole above the tower. Having taken the Malakoff, MacMahon was warned by Pelissier that the fortification was mined. Undeterred, the General is said to have muttered, 'J'y suis, J'y reste'. (Here I am, here I stay.)

'At about a quarter-past 12, up went the proud flag of France, with a shout that drowned for a time the roar of both cannon and musketry,' wrote Timothy Gowing. 'And now came our turn. We had waited for months for it, but it was a trying hour.'

According to Ensign Vieth:

> One hundred men of the Rifle Brigade led the assault followed by parties of the 3 Buffs, 41 and 62 Regiments amounting to 1,500 men in all, although not two thirds succeeded in reaching the embrasures. Here further misfortune overtook them. The ladders they carried – then only some half dozen – were found to be too

short. They had started out with twenty, having eight men told off to each ladder, and all but these few were left on the field smashed to pieces.

George Ranken admitted that:

The men, as they struggled up to the assault in support of the advance, seemed stunned and paralysed. Our Generals had left their reserves above an hours march in the rear, so that even if our soldiers had charged forwards, as they should have done, they would have probably found themselves compromised, surrounded by the enemy, and immolated before any assistance could have been brought to them.

No doubt Lord Raglan should have exercised his authority by ensuring that adequate reinforcement was in close support of the main attack. But judging from the remarks made by G.H. Money, it seems unlikely that it would have made an appreciable difference:

It was our misfortune that the reserve parties which lined the 5th or most advanced parallel, were composed mainly of boys, recently arrived, and new to the business. A feeling had gained ground among them, that the Redan was mined in every direction – and not all their officers could shake that conviction or induce the men to advance to their supposed certain destruction. Upon the result of this crisis turned the fortune of the day.

Unlike the French at the Malakoff, the redcoats were facing stiff opposition. Initially surprised, the Russians quickly recovered and their fire of musketry, discharged from behind loop-holed defence works, cut swathes through the onrushing infantry of the 23 Foot.
Sergeant Gowing wrote:

Our people were now at it in front ... we had a clear run of 200 yards under a murderous fire of grape, canister and musketry. How anyone lived to pass that 200 yards seemed a miracle. The musket balls whistled past us more like hail than anything else I can describe, and the grape shot cut our poor fellows to pieces. It seemed to me that we were rushing into the very jaws of death, but I, for one, reached the Redan without a scratch.

A few, like Gowing, surmounted the fifteen feet deep by eight feet wide ditch to reach the Redan, but they were quickly driven out and forced to retire after a savage mêlée in which rifle butt and bayonet were used to little effect, against the grey coated soldiers of the Selenginsky regiment.

Colonel Anthony Sterling leaves a blunt account of the troops failure to penetrate the defence works of the Redan:

> There was little of that dash and enthusiasm which might have been looked for from British soldiers in an assault; in fact it required all the efforts and examples of their officers to get their men on, and these were rendered most ineffective from the manner in which the various regiments soon got confused and jumbled together. I was near the counterscarp when I saw the whole living mass on the salient begin reeling and swaying to and fro; in a moment I found myself knocked down and lying on my face, with a number of men scrambling over me, their bayonets running through my clothes. In our trenches all was shame, rage, and fear; the men were crowded together and disorganized. It was hopeless to attempt to renew the attack with the same troops despite the devoted efforts of the officers to induce them to do so.

Somerset Calthorpe explained:

> Many officers most brilliantly distinguished themselves by the gallant manner in which they stood out in the open in order to induce their men to follow; but, among other difficulties, the men one and all believed that the Redan was mined. The English newspapers had done their best to din the fact into their ears ever since the first bombardment. This, doubtless, added to the disinclination to advance, but the real fact of the matter was, that there were not enough men.

It was certainly true that large numbers had refused to join the attack and given that a good many of the soldiers were young and inexperienced, 'callow youths' one officer called them, it is, as Mr Money pointed out, highly unlikely whether even a reinforcement of battle hardened veterans would have persuaded them to leave the safety of the trenches for a stretch of open ground swept by the murderous fire coming from the Redan. The few brave souls that did reach the ditch in front of the Redan were quickly driven out by the Russians, and among the more fortunate to return to the lines was Sergeant Timothy Gowing. He had received five wounds in different parts of his body and was unconscious when taken out of the ditch, having almost bled to death. His wounds were dressed and, he admits, '...a good cup of beef tea revived me; then I had to remain up to three months in hospital, but with careful attention, and a good strong constitution, I was, by that time, ready for them again.'

'There was a feeling of deep depression in camp all night,' William Russell informed the readers of *The Times*. 'We were painfully aware that our attack had failed.'

Henry Clifford echoed the correspondent's note of despair: 'What almost breaks my heart and nearly drove me mad,' he wrote, 'was to see our soldiers, our English soldiers that I was so proud of, run away ... was it right to sacrifice thousands of lives in attacking the Redan,' he asked, 'only because the French went at the Malakoff?'

Shortly after midnight it was noticed that there was an unusual absence of sound from the Redan and, wrote Frederick Vieth:

Some of the officers and a number of men too, volunteered to go and find out the reason, and finally creeping over the parapet they set out. They came back after a time and reported that they could hear nothing inside the fortress except the groans of the unfortunate wounded and dying, and they did not believe there was a living Russian in the place. They had not penetrated far into the interior for fear that the place might be mined.

Ranken, who went over the site after the battle, described what he found: 'The ditch near the salient was full of bodies, gabions, and debris, lying in horrible chaos together. Inside the Redan few bodies were to be seen, but a handful of our men having penetrated into the interior.'

Now that the French possessed the Malakoff Tower, Gorchakoff's position in Sevastopol was untenable and, during the evening while the allies were recovering from the trauma of the day's action, the Russian leader ordered what remained of his army to retire across a pontoon bridge and occupy the northern side of Sevastopol. Artillery fire was directed against the allied lines and, as the last of the Russian battalions left the ruins of the city, the night was split by explosions as various powder magazines were blown up, starting fires which burned for two days. 'At nine o'clock on September 8th, it was clear to the simplest mind,' wrote Money, 'that the Russians had determined to destroy and abandon the city. Explosion after explosion lit up the sky, and the buildings so exploded, continued to burn fiercely.'

Civilians, and as many of the wounded who could be evacuated, had been taken across the floating bridge before it was destroyed and, during the night, those ships that remained afloat were scuttled. The whole operation of evacuation went remarkably smoothly, save for a number of wagons and most of the artillery, being too heavy for the pontoon bridge, were either burnt or tumbled into the Bay.

The allies were at long last in possession of the southern half of the city and Captain Dallas could be excused for feeling elated by the victory:

> The more I hear of what is to be found in the Town, and of the strength of their works, & of its state, the more I congratulate myself on the termination of the siege. The place is full of all sorts of ammunition, thousands of guns that have never been used, all sorts of provisions and stores in profusion, and if they had not been completely surprised at the Malakoff, I don't know how we should have taken the place.

Referring to the Russians, he added:

> They have made, I imagine, the most glorious defence in the history of war, & their end was worthy of it, for knowing that the loss of the Malakoff must lead sooner or later to the capture of the whole place, they went away, having repulsed us at two, out of three, of the points of attack, & having fought at the other for nearly 5 hours, leaving us the smoking ruins of the Town.

In a sharply contrasting mood to that of Captain Dallas, Henry Clifford felt little exhilaration that the siege was finally over. Gazing around at the scene of desolation spread out before him and remembering his fallen comrades, he confessed: 'I stood in the Redan more humble, more dejected, and with a heavier heart than I have yet felt since I left home.' William Russell, on his way to

Sevastopol, first visited the scene of fighting which had taken place at the Redan in order to describe it to his readers:

> The scene in the ditch was appalling. The ladders were all knocked down or broken, so that it was difficult for the men to scale the other side – and the dead, the dying, the wounded, and the uninjured were all lying in piles together. The Russians came out of the embrasures, plied them with stones, grapeshot and the bayonet, but were soon forced to retire by the fire of our batteries and riflemen, and under cover of their fire a good many of our men escaped to the approaches.

Lieutenant Wolseley had been severely wounded in the head and face by a shell while in the trenches, and took no part in the final attack. Writing after the fall of Sevastopol, in a reflective mood he observed: 'So many of those around me in the engineer camp had fallen, that I felt my own time must come sooner or later. But what I had not contemplated was that I should live until the assault was delivered and yet be cut off from all share in it.' In later years as Sir Garnet Wolseley, he was to become one of the leading military figures of the Victorian age.

For those making their way into Sevastopol, almost every yard gave proof of the intensity of the allied bombardment, as Ensign Vieth explained:

> All about the path down to the town were scattered shot and broken shells, great stones, wood in splinters and debris of all description, making it difficult to guide the horses steps through it. In the houses below one saw great shot holes, walls pounded down, roofless buildings with broken chimneys, garden railings of iron wrenched and twisted into the most fantastic shapes, and streets pitted with deep holes. Our guns and mortars seemed to have searched out every spot, and dealt waste and destruction broadcast.

In spite of the destruction, Major George Ranken was quite impressed by what he saw of Sevastopol. 'Sebastopol is finely situated and laid out in broad spacious streets,' he noted. 'Some of the houses, though nothing in general remained of them but blackened disfigured walls, must have been very handsome and elegant.'

Lieutenant Temple Godman described the town as:

159

... a wonderful sight, cannon balls sticking in the house walls, and not one building but is riddled with rockets, bullets, shot and shells. Some that I went into were most horrible, mattresses soaked with blood and putrid, and dead men all colours of the rainbow, and among them the living. We were taking them away in cartloads, and the smell was such that the drivers were all as sick as dogs.

Lady Alicia Blackwood was spared the more gory sights in her exploration of the city, but she still found it to be: '... a mass of ruin, heaps of stone and pieces of exploded shells, and shot scattered in every direction; it was an awful picture of destruction; but the saddest sight was the rows and rows of graves, especially near the Malakoff ... All of this part of the Crimea was one vast cemetery ...'

Colonel Sir James Alexander viewed his ride through that part of Sevastopol with mixed feelings: 'I rode over the broken streets, and beside the burning houses with more comfort than if I had been on foot but, it was the entire wreck of a great city, every public building was more or less injured, a great many of the private homes completely so ...'

Since the French had played the major part in the capture of the city, it was decided that they should occupy that part of Sevastopol from Admiralty Creek west, and the British the Karabelnaia behind the Redan. Passports were at first required for visitors to the French sector but, by degrees, this was relaxed and eventually free passage was granted everywhere.

One of the first to explore the area occupied by the French was Captain Dunscombe, who set out on 13 September. 'I obtained a pass today and visited Sebastopol and the outworks,' he wrote. 'The barracks must have been once a magnificent building, but is greatly knocked about now from our shot and shell; in fact there is not an entire house in the town standing.' His one irritation was in being prevented from obtaining a souvenir. 'The French are permitted to go into the town and ransack it,' he complained, 'whereas we dare not take anything, this is not at all fair, but it is the fault of our Generals.'

Colonel Alexander admitted:

The most appalling sight in Sevastopol after its fall, was that of the great hospital inside the dockyard wall and the rear of the Great Redan. There were several chambers there filled with the dead and dying, to the number, it was said of 2,000, a hundred unburied officers lay in one room. Men living and dead were lying on pallets and on the flagstones and under the beds in every conceivable attitude – the smell was fearful in this chamber of torture.'

William Howard Russell found this description to be only too true and informed the readers of *The Times*: 'I confess it was impossible for me to stand the sight, which horrified our most experienced doctors. The deadly clammy stench, the smell of gangrened wounds, of corrupted blood, of rotting flesh, were intolerable and odious beyond endurance.'

What horrified George Taylor even more, was the plight of the living: 'All had been without food or drink since the Russians had left, and some, though unable to speak, raised their hands to their lips, signifying their wants. Many were too weak even to do this, and looked at us with a dull glassy stare, groaning and gurgling through blood which frothed and bubbled at their lips.'

An outbreak of plundering inevitably followed the occupation of the town which the British authorities, unlike the French, did their best to prevent. Taylor, who was himself prevented from carrying away an ornamental sword, wrote:

All our men were stopped by the pickets, and deprived of any plunder they had got, whilst the French were allowed to pass free, carrying off whatever they liked. Whatever our men had – no matter what rubbish, such as a kitten in a bird cage, an old fiddle, a tattered flag, an old musket, stools, chairs, frying pans, &c – they were compelled to put them down. It was absurd and gave rise to much murmuring and discontent.

Inevitably there were a few redcoats who, in spite of the severe restrictions, did succeed in possessing articles, however bizarre. 'I met one party who had been plundering a church,' remembered Captain Hamley. 'One was partly attired in the vestments of a priest. I told the adventurer with the alter (sic) cloth that the Bishop would excommunicate him; to which he replied by a gesture by no means flattering to episcopacy.'

In another incident reported by Sergeant Gowing: 'A stalwart Irish Grenadier, on being rebuked for pilfering, answered: "Sure an' your 'onor, them nice gentlemen they call Zouaves have been after emptying the place clean out. Troth, if the Divil would kindly go to sleep for only one minute them Zouaves would stole one of his horns, if it was only useful to keep his coffee in".'

The allies were reluctant to garrison the southern side of Sevastopol in strength because of Russian artillery fire from the north side of the harbour, and they were not prepared to take further offensive action following their seizure of the outer defence works. The next few weeks were spent in relative quiet, but it was not a policy approved by the politicians either in Paris or in London. An exasperated Napoleon III sent Jacques Pelissier, who had recently been promoted to Field Marshal rank, a list of options ranging from attacks on the Russians around the Mackenzie Heights, to offensive action in Bessarabia.

Ministers in London were equally belligerent advising Simpson that, rather than relying on rumours of an armistice, he should give the Russians no respite until they had been totally overthrown in the Crimea. This message was followed by a more forceful directive on 17 September when Panmure told him: 'We cannot tell why you are resting on your oars ... Don't waste your time in idleness.' In the light of that directive, it was perhaps not surprising that General Sir James Simpson should repeat his offer to resign.

Whilst the protracted siege of Sevastopol had engaged the full attention of the allied forces in the Crimea, a little known campaign had been underway in the mountainous area bordering Armenia and the Russian state of Georgia, since the middle of the summer. There, in Kars, Colonel William Fenwick Williams was occupied in a lengthy affair marshalling Ottoman forces against a numerically inferior, but nevertheless competent, Russian army. Williams was familiar with both the Caucasus area and the Ottoman army, having been attached to it early in his career. He was also aware of the corruption that existed among the Turkish officers and with the indiscipline prevalent among the lower ranks. Above all however, he laboured under a handicap of indifference to his requirements on the part of the Porte, while being ignored by the British and French high command in the Crimea.

During the winter of 1853 the Turks had suffered a series of defeats in Asia Minor at the hands of the Russians, which had forced a change in command. Abdi Pasha had been replaced by Ahmed Pasha, who had been given a considerable reinforcement of Armenian conscripts. Neither move was of any great value, for Ahmed Pasha was, if anything, more corrupt than his predecessor. Doctor Humphrey Sandwith who knew him well, wrote:

> His whole facilities were bent upon making money. He had in the first place to recover the sums he had already expended in bribes at Constantinople, and he had, besides, to make his fortune ... no chief can plunder without allowing a considerable licence to his subordinates, so that the poor soldier was fleeced by every officer than the major.

In the summer of 1854, the Ottoman forces were hit by a cholera epidemic in which the numbers of dead were concealed in order to preserve the allowances claimed by the senior officers, and consequently a year later the army found itself in desperate straits both in numbers and equipment. The success enjoyed by the Royal Navy on the eastern coast of the Black Sea did little to lessen the pressure from the Russians and, in late July, the Ottoman army suffered a heavy defeat at Bayezid which allowed the Russians to threaten the strategically important towns of Kars, and Erzerum more than 100 miles from Trebizond, an important supply port for the Turks.

Reinforcements were rushed to the area and Trebizond was made secure but, in the first week of August, the garrison at Kars was rashly tempted to offer battle at Kurekdere and, as a consequence of weak leadership, the Turkish infantry suffered appalling casualties. A reporter, writing in *The Times* issue of 7 August 1854, had no doubts as to where the blame lay:

> ... from the first cannon shot to the last straggling discharges of musketry, I can use no language too strong to express my mis-approbation of nearly four-fifths of the Turkish officers present. In accounting for the defeat of an army numbering nearly 40,000 men of all arms by a hostile force of less than one half that number, it is not sufficient to say that the management of the whole battle on the side of the Turks was a series of blunders from first to last ...

The journalist ended his article with a plea directed at the British government: 'I for one, earnestly entreat that Downing Street and the Tuileries will no longer leave Asia Minor to the mercy of intrigants and imbeciles.'

Westminster was certainly aware of a danger that the Russians could gain control of the overland route to Persia and, with it, the access they had long sought to the North-West Frontier. To guard against any such likelihood, Colonel Williams was sent to Kars as the British Commissioner, to assist the Ottoman forces in Asia Minor. Williams, when he arrived in Kars on 24 September 1854, discovered that the Russians, fortunately for the Turks, had withdrawn a large part of their army due to pressure elsewhere, which eased the plight of the 15,000 strong garrison, but did nothing to reassure Williams in the quality of the troops available to him.

'One of his first acts,' wrote Doctor Sandwith, who had journeyed to Kars from his practice in Constantinople, 'was to request a review of a certain regiment, which was accordingly drawn up; the muster roll was presented to him; nine hundred men were there in figures, – he had the men counted, there were but six hundred. Thus the pay, rations, etc, of the three hundred had gone to enrich the Turkish Colonel, while the Mushir took his share.'

On completing the inspection it came as no surprise to Dr Sandwith that Colonel Williams should be less than satisfied with what he had seen. The bulk of the infantry were poorly armed with flintlocks, and only the three battalions of Chasseurs possessed a useful rifle in the Minie. The Colonel was so taken aback by the 'ragged and threadbare' uniforms the troops were clad in that he requested 20,000 pairs of boots, and 10,000 shirts and trousers from Lord Stratford de Redcliffe as a matter of urgency. A later inspection disclosed the fact that the 2,200 strong body of cavalry were no better equipped having horses 'small and in bad condition' and with clothing little better than the infantry. The only part of the Ottoman army which did meet with Williams' approval, was the artillery. The horse drawn section possessed thirty-six field guns, the heavy artillery forty-two large calibre cannon and, in addition, there were eighty-four mountain guns, all in good order, while the senior gunner officer, Tahir Pasha, could boast of having been trained at Woolwich.

Despite Colonel Williams drawing attention to the men's low state of morale – they had not been paid for two years – most of the Turkish officers seemed interested, more in personal gain rather than their duties. Very little attention was paid by the Porte, and Colonel Williams and his staff were left alone to oversee the defence of Kars and Erzerum against the not unlikely resumption of hostilities by Prince Bebutov's army, which had defeated a large force of Ottoman troops at Basgedikler in December 1854; the survivors having fled to Kars. Doctor Humphrey Sandwith thought Kars, '...was a picturesque, mud built old city, situated at the foot of a cliff, with a fine mediaeval castle crowning a craggy hill in the centre, and a river running through the city, and through a deep cleft in the hills behind'. But his colourful first impression did not last, for he subsequently described Kars as, '... a true Asiatic town in all its Asiatic squalor. The streets are narrow and dirty and the people sordid in appearance, and the chief employment of the women appears to be the fabrication of *tezek*, or dried cow-dung for fuel, cakes of which are plastered over the walls of every house.' The perimeter of the town was protected by a ring of eight small forts connected by breastworks and trenches, and Tahir Pasha's artillery ensured that any attack by the Russians would meet with a warm reception. Much of the defence works had been initiated by an Irishman with the unlikely name of Guyon Pasha, who had been dismissed following his defeat at Kurekdere. Nevertheless the British Commissioner made sure that the soldiers at his disposal were put to work strengthening the existing earthworks and in ensuring a good field of fire. Doctor Sandwith, as he watched them labour, could not help but admire the work put in by Williams himself:

> During this time I often heard Turks remark that Williams Pasha worked as no other Pasha ever worked before. They admired him extravagantly, but could not understand him. Was he not a Pasha? Was he not therefore rich; and by his rank and wealth entitled to place, decorations, and everything else? Why then, should he work like a hammel – a common porter? This was incomprehensible to them.

On 7 June the Russians made their appearance and created quite an impression on Dr Humphrey Sandwith. 'About 10,00 o'clock the whole Russian army comes in sight, and a magnificent spectacle it is,' he recorded. 'About 40,000 men are in march towards our position, their cavalry numbering 10,000 are in advance and on each wing, vast grey bodies of infantry whose weapons gleam and flash in the morning sun.'

At that time it was discovered that the garrison was perilously low on ammunition, just one more example of the frustrations facing the British officers in their defence of Kars. Captain Thompson complained:

> We are placed here in a very tenable position, but with a lamentable lack of all the necessaries of war. We are very badly off for ammunition, food and clothing, and our army is in a sad state of discipline. The Russians are encamped on the other side of the valley on our front, about two miles and a half at most, and are only I think prevented from attacking us by the heavy ground in the valley, caused by the almost incessant rain we have had for the last ten days.

By the end of June, although the situation had not improved dramatically, Thompson's spirits had risen and, in a letter to his family, he advised them: 'I hope to come home and show you another medal in addition to my Burmah one, and that will repay me for the hard work of Kars. I have not had a dry thread on me for nearly a fortnight.'

Colonel Williams now held the temporary rank of brigadier general and, at Stratford's prompting, the Sultan was persuaded to grant him the title of Pasha. Unlike the Irishman, he was allowed to keep his surname instead of the customary Islamic adoption, but this honour did nothing to halt the numerous complaints he made concerning the abysmal state of the Ottoman forces and the lethargy of the Porte in putting matters right. It was not just the ragged appearance of the men or the fact that most were owed two years' arrears of pay, that he found unacceptable and, in his report to the ambassador in Therapia, he pointed out that '... drunkenness prevails to a great degree among those of higher rank,' before going on to name the officers he considered unfit for active service.

Stratford de Redcliffe was certainly aware of the corruption prevalent in the Ottoman administration, but he was irritated by the forthright manner in which Colonel Williams had written his report. Nonetheless, he presented it to the Porte, albeit rephrased in acceptable diplomatic fashion, at the end of November. The reply he received was encouraging, but nothing of consequence resulted and the Colonel and his team were left to carry on to the best of their ability. It proved to be an uphill struggle for, although it had been long recognized that the Russians had to be driven out of Asia Minor, every attempt made by the Turks to release troops from the Crimea had met with opposition from the French and, since Omar Pasha relied upon the allied navy to transport his men across the Black Sea to Trebizond, there was little more he could do other than ask the Porte to exert pressure on London and Paris.

Palmerston was willing to accede to the Turkish demands, but Napoleon III told Marshal Jean Vaillant:

> We have 60,000 men at the siege, the British 12,000. The Turks for whom we are fighting are never in the trenches, no more than the Sardinians ... if now they want to weaken the siege army by withdrawing Turkish troops, they will create a justified alienation in the French army. Furthermore, the great objective now is Sebastopol and not at Kars.

The response from the Porte had not satisfied Williams and, in answer to his repeated requests for assistance, Stratford requested that Colonel Atwell Lake of the Madras Engineers depart for Kars and assume responsibility for its defence. Much work was still to be done if the town were to withstand an onslaught from a strong Russian force led by Count Nikolai Muraviev advancing from Georgia. Colonel Lake on his arrival was quick to recognize the good work that Williams had done in raising the garrison's morale:

> He had to inspire courage and confidence in men who had in the previous year been signally defeated by the Russians in the battle of Kurukderi, and who had encountered such disasters and become so cruelly plundered of their pay by those in command of them that desertion had become an every day occurrence, and who were disorganized and demoralized to the last degree. Twenty-four months pay was due to them and their uniform was in rags.

Just seven days after Colonel Williams established his headquarters in the town, Russian reconnaissance parties were observed east of Kars and, on 16 June, an attack was made by a small force of infantry and cavalry which was easily repulsed by the garrison. Colonel Lake was nevertheless impressed by what he had seen of Muraviev's forces. 'The army of the Caucasus which has now set down before Kars was acknowledged to be one of the finest and best disciplined forces which the Russian empire could boast of and it well deserved its character,' he remarked. 'It was commanded by General Mouravieff (*sic*) in person, an officer of talent and energy who, during the long period of arduous service, has won for himself a name of which any soldier might be proud.'

It was an assessment which, in the months to come, was to be fully justified. The following month, July, was relatively uneventful, during which the Russians expanded their position outside the town and mounted just two minor attacks, one against the high ground to the east and the other on the southern defences, both of which the Turks defended with admirable determination. Muraviev, having discovered that the garrison was well able to resist attacks made upon them from whichever quarter, now changed his tactics, being content to invest the town and cut communication with Erzerum while awaiting the arrival of his heavy siege guns and mortars. Much to Williams' chagrin he could do nothing to obstruct these movements of the Russians, since his cavalry was completely unsuited for the task of harassment for, as Atwell Lake was at pains to point out: 'Their swords were too short, their lances too heavy, their uniforms torn and tattered, and their horses old, worn out, and therefore useless, and the men themselves such indifferent horsemen that they could scarcely keep their seats.'

It was not long before the garrison began to suffer from the consequences of the blockade and, at the beginning of September, Williams was obliged to put his men on half rations. Their reaction to this measure was predictable. Desertions became commonplace and, to make matters worse, after a while cholera made its appearance. '... small doles of provisions sparingly given to more than half starved beings, only enough, sometimes, to kindle fresh appetites without supporting life,' wrote Colonel Lake later. 'Women bringing their children to our doors and leaving them there to die – all these are a few features in that black and ghastly picture of horror and suffering that still clouds my memory like the hovering phantoms of some hideous dream.'

Captain Thompson endeavoured to make light of a grave situation: 'I am getting very tired of water as a beverage and begin to be of Mr H's opinion that a bottle of it well corked ought to last a lifetime,' he wrote. 'We have a capital cook who compounds messes for us, which I look at with aversion, and eat with considerable awe. I never venture to inquire of what animal or vegetable they are manufactured.'

The garrison's plight was becoming acute and, on 3 September, Brigadier General Williams managed to smuggle out a message to James Brant the British Consul in Erzerum asking him to notify Constantinople of their straightened circumstances, pointing out that should Kars fall, Erzerum must surely follow and '... a years campaign would be required to recover the two cities, which in the hands of the Russians might become impregnable'. With every expectation that his plea would soon be answered, Williams decided to increase the soldiers' meagre rations by thirty drachms of bread a day. 'A timely boon since the mortality has become alarming and still more so the frightful emaciation of our troops,' stated Doctor Sandwith. 'With hollow cheeks, tottering gait, and that peculiar feebleness of voice so characteristic of famine, they yet cling to their duties.'

Sixteen days after the fall of Sevastopol, the welcome news reached Kars, which gave the garrison reason to hope that the Russians would raise the siege. But to the dismay of the staff, Muraviev deployed his army for a major attack on the town which came six days later on the morning of 29 September. It was a bitterly fought contest with the main thrust of the Russian attack being directed against the heights above Kars where the Russians, advancing in column, were decimated by defenders equipped with the Minie rifle.

'This horrid carnage continued until the Russians, stopped by a mound of dead bodies and dislocated by the repeated discharges of grape, were brought to a standstill,' wrote Colonel Lake. 'The Turks there leaping over the breastwork and led on by the gallant Kmety, (the field commander Feyzi Pasha) a Hungarian, finished with bayonet the utter rout of their assailants.'

'... seven mortal hours of round shot, grape, and musketry, and the mountains of Armenia never before heard such music,' ventured General Williams, 'and God forbid that they ever should again! if the results are to be similarly estimated.'

At dusk the Russians retreated back to their lines. It had been a costly encounter for the garrison which had lost 1,000 men but the butcher's bill paid by Prince Muraviev had been close to six times that number. Thompson's artillery had played a major part in defeating the Russians but it had not been easy, as he readily admitted: 'Some seven or eight hundred Russians fell here, and I lost some twenty or thirty killed and wounded. They had nothing but small field pieces with them and I had large guns, or the event might have been different, but my thirty-two pounders carried more than double the distance that their guns did.'

'A day of hard fighting, of glorious triumph, and soul harrowing work,' Humphrey Sandwith called it. 'The loud hurrahs of the Russian host were mingled with the yells of the Turks, who fought like tigers, charging repeatedly with the bayonet.'

The repulse of the Russians, however, did not signal the end of the siege and when the first snows of winter spread a carpet over the ground, the Russian tents were replaced by huts, and the glow from the many bivouac fires betrayed the fact that, unlike the garrison, the Russians were not to suffer too much discomfort.

Up until then no attempt had been made to relieve Kars, despite the numerous pleas Williams had sent to the British ambassador in Constantinople, but in a last desperate appeal to James Brant on 19 November, Williams told him:

Tell Lords Clarendon and Redcliffe that the Russian army is hutted, and takes no notice of either Omar or Selim Pashas. They cannot have acted as they ought to have done. We divide our bread with the starving townspeople. No animal food for seven weeks. I kill horses in my stable secretly and send the meat to the hospital, which is now very crowded.

With food supplies dwindling at an alarming rate, the civil populace were suffering the initial stages of starvation. Dr Sandwith's diary entry for 14 November reads:

All the mosques, khans and large houses are full of invalids. The citizens nobly furnish us with beds, which however scarce suffice for our numbers. Women are seen gathering the dust from the flour depots to eat ... I observe people lying at the corners of streets, groaning and crying out that they are dying of hunger.

Captain Thompson sounded no less concerned when he wrote to his mother:

Unless we get English or French reinforcements in a month or two, there will not be a man of this army left alive. If the Russians don't kill us, we shall die of starvation, which is not by any means a pleasant alternative. Our communications are almost entirely cut off, and the country swarms with Cossacks and Armenians who are all hostile to us.

It had been obvious from early August that until Sevastopol fell, no approval would be given to the request to release Ottoman forces, and it was the end of September before a decision was taken in their favour but, by then, it was too late to be of much help to the garrison in Kars. An attempt to relieve the town was made by Selim Pasha during the last week of October with a landing at Trebizond, but his force got no further than Erzerum, and there it stayed.

In late November with barely two days' supplies remaining, General Williams had little choice but to offer his surrender to Count Muraviev. The Russian General was gracious in his acceptance. 'Let us arrange a capitulation that will satisfy the demands of war without outraging humanity,' he told the British General. Wrote Colonel Lake:

On 28th November 1855, the Turks laid down their arms. It was with the greatest difficulty that they could be persuaded to do so. The brave fellows wished to die at their posts, although worn out by famine, privations, and hardships. Indeed it required no little tact to prevent a serious disturbance.

Dr Sandwith observed that:

... early this morning the sounds of musketry are heard in all parts of the camp. The soldiers are emptying their muskets and piling arms. The people and the army have now learned that they are to capitulate; the word (*teslim*) is in every mouth ...

The garrison, in recognition of the brave resistance it had shown, was allowed to march out in an honourable fashion, led by General Williams and his staff who were afterwards invited to dine with General Muraviev and his officers. They were treated with every courtesy during their short imprisonment in Russia, and were repatriated the following spring – when Williams took

171

the opportunity to make it clear to Lord Clarendon that it was through no fault of the Ottoman soldiers, that he was obliged to surrender Kars. 'They fell dead at their posts, in their tents, and throughout the camp, as brave men should who cling to their duty through the slightest glimmer of hope of saving a place entrusted to their custody,' he informed the Foreign Secretary. Major Teesdale summed up the situation. 'The game has been played out, and we are prisoners,' he wrote. 'Still, even in our degradation, I cannot help feeling that the disgrace lies with those whose duty it was to help us; and not with us, who, I believe in my heart, have done all that men could do.'

Chapter Nine

THE ASSAULT ON KINBURN

The south side of Sevastopol, now in allied hands following a siege of almost a year, had left the allies with the vexing problem of the next phase of the campaign against the Russians. The French had played a major part in forcing them to evacuate the city, and they had justly claimed it as a victory, despite the fact that Gorchakoff's army was still largely intact. The Duke of Newcastle was joined by Napoleon in expressing disappointment at the failure on the part of the generals to prevent the Russians from taking up a powerful new position on the northern side of the harbour.

Following their debacle at the Redan, the British troops were exhausted and dispirited, wearied by the scenes of death and destruction and the awareness that in many instances they had shamefully neglected to support their officers whose losses had been severe. Unlike the mood prevailing in the British camp, the reaction among the French, particularly the politicians, was one of elation. The usual military honours to the commanders, quickly followed the successful occupation of the southern half of Sevastopol when General A.J. Pelissier was awarded a Marshal's baton and appointed a *Mushir* or Commander-in-Chief by the Sultan, much to the irritation of Sir James Simpson, who merely received the Légion d'honneur.

With the ignominious retreat from Moscow still a factor to be considered in his dealings with Russia, Napoleon III insisted that the war must continue until Russia was humbled and isolated from the rest of Europe, but it was a point of view which failed to meet with the approval of many of his countrymen. Whilst the fall

173

of Sevastopol was widely acclaimed, victory had only been achieved at a high cost in French lives, and it was a matter of concern whether the French exchequer would be able to sustain the cost of maintaining the army for a second winter.

Britain had no such financial difficulties, but Lord Palmerston's decision to support Napoleon's desire to continue the campaign was largely dictated by military pride. Conscious that the British army had not performed as well as the French during the closing stages of the siege, Palmerston, who held most generals in contempt, was of one mind with Napoleon that Russia should not be granted peace terms until she had been overwhelmingly defeated. In his decision to continue the war he had the support of Turkey, whose interests lay in Asia Minor and, oddly enough, in a similar desire on the part of the Tsar, who considered there was still much to be gained by maintaining the conflict. 'Sevastopol is not Moscow and the Crimea is not Russia,' Alexander II had told General Gorchakoff. 'Two years after we set fire to Moscow, our troops marched in the streets of Paris. We are still the same Russians and God is still with us.'

Peace terms at this stage of the campaign were not a prime consideration for ministers at Westminster and Panmure, after congratulating General Simpson on the success of the Sevastopol campaign, urged the Commander-in-Chief to ensure that his army was kept in readiness to resume the offensive. He followed this request on 26 September by a forceful reminder, in the form of a telegraph which must have caused considerable annoyance to Simpson's staff, by stating:

> The public are getting impatient to know what the Russians are about. The Government desire immediately to be informed whether either you or Pelissier have taken any steps whatever to ascertain this, and further they observe that nearly 3 weeks have elapsed in absolute idleness. This cannot go on and in justice to yourself and your army you must prevent it. Answer this on receipt.

This cable from the Secretary for War, did little to lift the bout of depression Simpson was undergoing and, to his relief, his repeated offer to resign was accepted by the Secretary for War on 28 September. Although the reason for his resignation was widely known, the War Office did its best to deflect any criticism by attributing it to ill health. 'Accordingly a little fiction was put forth to the effect that in consequence of weak health and infirmity, he wished the government to allow him to resign,' explained Douglas Reid to his family. 'Everyone understood the reason why, although in the trenches, at any rate, not much was said.'

After some thought, it was decided that his replacement should come from a general already serving in the field. Major General Sir William Codrington had earlier been thought of as the automatic successor. His leadership during the assault on the Redan had, however, demonstrated a decisive lack in the qualities expected of a general, according to the Duke of Newcastle, and it had taken the support of Lord Palmerston, who had no great regard for any general, before his appointment was confirmed on 15 October. No doubt Codrington's fluency in French had been a partial factor and, in a move to pacify other potential candidates, the army was divided into two corps, one command going to Sir Colin Campbell and the other to Brigadier William Eyre.

Opinion varied among the junior officers regarding Sir William Codrington's elevation to overall command. It was expected, but most were content to leave matters to the test of time. George Frederick Dallas, in a letter to his parents, wrote:

> You will ask me what we think about Codrington. It is perhaps an unfortunate moment to elevate him, as the miscarriage of our portion of the assault on the 18th is generally attributed to him in a great measure ... I fancy on the whole that his appointment is popular enough, & I think him a good man. This accounts for Sir Colin (Campbell) going away in such a hurry, he being senior to Codrington & having probably had a hint about the affair.

Hardships resulting from the mishaps of the previous winter had been recognized by the Government and the troops now possessed adequate winter clothing such as woollen jerseys, thick underwear, two pairs of woollen socks and long stockings. A fur cap, gloves and a greatcoat, along with a waterproof cape, completed the issue. Later in November, field stoves were shipped to Balaklava together with the long awaited wooden huts, although there still remained problems with their assembly, as pointed out by Captain Dallas in a letter to his family. 'We have

175

heaps of Huts come out, of various patterns, but unfortunately no one who knows how to put them together,' he wrote. 'I believe they have telegraphed home for the necessary conjurer, but until his arrival, they are lying about like melancholy Chinese puzzles.' The Rifle Brigade had similar problems, not so much with the assembly, as with transport. Lieutenant Frederic Morgan explained: 'We are gradually getting a wooden house or two up, but they being such a tremendous weight it is almost impossible to bring one up from Balaklava under 40 or 50 horses, or about 150 men; however, we have two completed in my regiment for hospitals for the sick.'

Exposure to sniper fire while observing the enemy, had long been a hazard in the trenches as Lieutenant Dunscombe would have been the first to acknowledge, having experienced a narrow shave himself. 'I saw a Russian head appear over a parapet,' he explained. 'I fired at him, and it appears that he saw me at the same time as the moment I had fired, a bullet struck the parapet close by me, and knocked all the earth over my face.'

A delivery of a thousand periscopes was naturally very welcome and these items together with adequate winter clothing, raised morale to the extent that before the first snows of winter made their appearance, entertainment such as race meetings and amateur theatricals became increasingly popular with all ranks. The only note of discord occurred with the introduction of independently owned canteens in Kadikoi which, if anything, encouraged incidents of drunkenness which did not escape the attention of the press. Captain Dallas complained to his parents:

The papers are full I see of our drunkenness out here. As they always do everything, they are hunting the subject to death, & talking dreadful nonsense about our losing by our own vices &c &c &c. There is not the least doubt that the men drink inordinately as English soldiers do & will when they get overpaid and under worked, but unfortunately for their argument about our expected frightful losses from that source, nothing can exceed the good health of the men. The French who, fortunately for them, are not dogged about by newspaper correspondents, drink in proportion to their means more than our soldiers ... They do not take the same notice of it as we do, and have not the disgusting publicity given to their punishment that we have.

The 63 Foot was probably no worse than many other regiments but Ensign Vieth, who had witnessed punishments for drink related offences, commented on such behaviour in his book *Recollections of the Crimea and Kinburn*:

> Whilst a fair percentage of steady men saved most of their pay by entrusting it to their officers, or the pay sergeant for safe keeping, there was always a certain number who cared for nothing but spending it on grog, and although excessive drinking entailed a very severe punishment, it failed as a deterrent. The penalty for the crime of habitual drunkenness was flogging. It was always a revolting sight. Once having undergone corporal punishment, the man often became utterly reckless, and seldom was out of trouble.

Now a permanent member of General Robert Garrett's staff, Captain Dallas certainly relished the advantages that his appointment as ADC had brought him. In a letter to his father dated 19 October, he wrote: 'I lead a very pleasant life now. In the first place the weather is quite perfect, half the battle with me always – then I have no tiresome Regimental Duty ... Altogether, I think I have found the employment suited to my energetic disposition, good pay, good food, & good company & no walking, & lots of forage for one's horses.'

October also brought good tidings to Nicholas Dunscombe of the 46 Regiment, who wrote on the 17th:

> I was agreeably surprised at receiving a letter by today's mail addressed to 'Captain Dunscombe', my promotion appeared in the Gazette of the 2nd inst. I must say that I have been very lucky as I have been only 2 years and 11 months in the service. I had the pleasure of a shake hands from Brigadier General Garrett, who congratulated me upon having 'got among the swells', as he styled it.

It was a rare event in the career of a young infantry officer at that time.

The afternoon of 13 November brought a signal catastrophe to the French *parc de siege* near Inkerman when 1,700 barrels of Russian and 800 barrels of French gunpowder exploded in three magazines, causing 240 French and 133 British deaths and injuries. The cause was believed to have been French artillerymen smoking while removing barrels of powder. George Frederick Dallas was riding towards the British powder magazine when, in his words:

> ... suddenly the whole earth seemed to open & one great flame rushed up into the sky. My horse, an English one & a very nervous one, wheeled round, but suddenly a succession of the most tremendous explosions in the air took place, many hundreds of yards up in the heavens & lasting like constant musketry for about 2 or 3 minutes ... Many thousand shells were sent up into the air & killed and wounded people to the distance of a mile. I owed my safety to my being too near, most of them going over me completely.

Ensign Vieth was sufficiently impressed to record the event in his memoirs:

> From the earth to the clouds above had risen what looked like a vast wall of smoke, flames and lurid vapour, whirling through which could be seen myriads of shapeless objects; a most appalling sight to break abruptly on one's vision without a second's warning. Then high in the air, and on all sides of this terrible upheaval came rapidly the reports of bursting shells, and I knew then the great magazine the French Artillery Park, near the division I had just come from, had blown up.

Just as dramatic was journalist William Howard Russell's description. 'The earth shook. The strongest houses rocked to and fro. Men fell as if the very ground upon which they stood was convulsed by an earthquake ...'

At this particular period of the war the welfare of the British troops showed a marked improvement, in sharp contrast to the French who began to suffer from the effects of an outbreak of cholera and typhus, caused by poor standards of hygiene. As the level of sickness mounted, their medical and commissariat services began to deteriorate, bringing Lieutenant Calthorpe to comment on their misfortune: '... nothing could be worse than the state of the French army during the first quarter of the year 1856. They appear to have been indifferently fed and badly clothed; typhus fever raging at the time among them drove immense numbers into hospital, where their state was truly deplorable.'

Earlier, the French troops had enjoyed a standard of medical care greatly superior to that of their British ally, but French hospital facilities were now acknowledged, even by their own troops, as being less than adequate. This rapid decline in the quality of care astonished the redcoats, as Major Ranken commented: 'I do not think this suffering is universal through the whole French army, but I am sure a great deal of real want and sickness exists, perhaps not more than might have been expected under the circumstances, but still painful to contrast with our own prosperity and abundance.'

Ironically, the British, who had been sustained by the French through most of the previous winter, were able to repay that debt by supplying warm clothing and provisions to their less fortunate comrades in the French army. Such was the outrage, once this became known in the Paris press, that it led to a campaign demanding that the veterans be returned to France. The French government soon gave in to the pressure and, early in November, the Imperial Guard was withdrawn and eight infantry regiments were transferred to Algeria.

This change in attitude by the French government did not bring all aggressive action to a halt, for before the onset of winter ruled out further campaigning, two operations were mounted against the Russians, one in Eupatoria during the last week of October when a body of French Light Cavalry and several battalions of infantry defeated a numerically superior Russian force causing it to withdraw and thus allowing the French to capture a battery of field guns. But, in the process, the opportunity of following up and inflicting an even greater humiliation upon the Russians was lost by General d'Alonville when he chose not to mount a pursuit. He did, however, have the excuse that he was merely acting in accordance with instructions from the French Chief of Staff, General de Martimprey, who had ordered a general reduction in offensive operations in the belief that negotiations in the winter would bring about an armistice.

The second, and by far the most important operation, took place on 17 October with the bombardment and capture of two forts at the mouth of the Dnieper – Ochakov and Kinburn. This was destined to be the last major engagement of the war, with the French, once again, playing a crucial role by supplying 6,000 troops commanded by General Achille Bazaine, as well as three battleships and a number of smaller gunboats.

On Sunday 7 October, a plan which had been drawn up at the end of September for the expedition, was put into operation when the Black Sea Fleet commanded by Admiral Bruat set sail from the ports of Kamiesch and Kazatch, together with a brigade of the 4th Division under Brigadier Spencer, with artillery and marines to the number of 3,000. The expedition to the Kinburn peninsula sought to conceal its real objective by sailing for Odessa, where it anchored the following afternoon before the astonished gaze of the citizens. 'What they dreaded might easily be imagined,' wrote Ensign Frederick Vieth, '... there stretched from end to end , for quite five miles an array of warships that could with the utmost ease, pound their fair city into fragments ... Church bells were heard ringing as the sun dipped behind the hill, and the city looked very peaceful; but just then a heavy fog came swiftly down and shut out everything, even our companion ships, from view.'

The fog lingered for two days and then, observed William Russell, 'On 11th October, the sun rose unclouded, Odessa looked more beautiful than ever.' The fleet then proceeded along the coast much to the alarm of the local inhabitants, eventually to drop anchor three miles west of Kinburn on the afternoon of 14 October after several days of rough weather. The next day HMS *Valorous,* flying Rear Admiral Sir Houston Stewart's flag, accompanied by several smaller vessels, forced a passage between Ochakov and the Kinburn peninsula into Dnieper Bay, where a mixed force of infantry and marines made an unopposed landing in Cherson Bay to cut off the fortress's communications and prevent any likely reinforcement from Ochakov.

Among the British troops there was some dispute as to whether a cutter, carrying men of the 17 Regiment was the first to battle through the surf, but Ensign Frederick Vieth writes:

> I was the subaltern that day carrying the Queen's Colour, Lacy, my chum, having the regimental one ... Scarcely had the boat touched when, grasping the shaft I jumped into the water and wading on shore drove the end of the staff into the sand, letting the Colour float on the breeze. It has been said that a boat of the 17th regiment landed first, but the fact remains that the Queen's Colour of the 63rd regiment was the first British flag on the soil of Russia proper.

It had been decided that three French ironclads should bring their considerable fire power to bear on Kinburn from 1,200 yards while the smaller vessels and the bomb ships were to engage the fort's sandbagged batteries from even closer range to cover the advance of the assault parties. Two days later on the 17th, as the expedition began to dig itself in and further supplies were landed, Kinburn was bombarded by the ironclads with little retaliation from the Russian shore batteries. But it had not been an easy matter getting the stores ashore because of a stiff breeze and the surf it threw up. The shallow draft boats, which were swept rapidly towards the beach, were fortunate to beach without mishap, but the swell proved too strong for an accurate naval bombardment from the smaller gunboats and it was quickly brought to a halt.

The trenches dug by both British and French troops were a half mile apart, one approaching the fort in Kinburn, and the other towards the small town of Cherson. The soil being sandy, progress was rapid and William Howard Russell watched the work on both with interest. 'The works are beginning to assume shape and to gather strength with every shovel of earth,' he told the readers of *The Times*, 'so that in a couple of days the Russians will find entrenchments between them and Kinburn whichever way they turn.'

Since it was the French whose trench had been directed towards Kinburn, it was they who undertook to sap up to within striking distance of the fort before making an assault on the town, whilst the British guarded against the possibility of a threat to their rear from Cherson.

Early that morning, the defending General Kokonovitch, alarmed by the approach of the French sapping towards his batteries, opened up a heavy fire on their parallels from 700 yards. The French were quick to reply, for the wind had dropped favouring the floating batteries and bomb vessels with a calm sea. This allowed them to sail in close to the southern side of the citadel from where they could shell the shore batteries exposed on the slopes, while allowing the battleships to direct a punishing fire against the fortress.

Shortly before midday a fire took hold of the Russian barracks, which quickly spread from one end of the building to the other, sending up a fiery column of blazing embers above the citadel while the heat and the acrid smoke prevented the gunners from serving the few large calibre cannon which remained serviceable.

Fed by a constant rain of mortar bombs and rockets from the floating batteries, a second fire took hold in the barracks, spreading to other buildings as the naval guns battered Kinburn into rubble.

As the day wore on and the destruction mounted and casualties increased, a white flag was raised from the fort, bringing the gunfire to a halt. Pinnaces sped towards the shore, returning after a short interval with the news that the garrison, given the right terms, was willing to lay down its arms to prevent further bloodshed.

Admiral Sir Houston Stewart, at the head of the British party was, no doubt, somewhat perturbed to find that the French general had already accepted General Kokonovitch's sword as a token of surrender, followed shortly afterwards by the garrison troops, many of whom under the influence of vodka, showed their feelings by dashing their muskets 'with as much ill grace as they could muster' at the feet of the victorious allies. 'On the whole,' observed Russell, 'they seemed "the worst lot" of Muscovite infantry I ever saw, and consisted of either old men or lads – the former fine soldier-like fellows enough, but the latter stupid, loutish, and diminutive.'

The terms of their surrender allowed the Russians to retain everything but their muskets and bayonets, although the officers were allowed to keep their swords, but before leaving for Constantinople most of the garrison sold their kit and everything else of value. 'The officers,' wrote The Times correspondent, 'bore their misfortune with dignity, as was evident from their grave demeanour and stern countenances. Few of them wore decorations and only one man was dressed in full uniform.'

Kokonovitch was requested to use his influence to see that no aggressive action would be taken against any of the allied troops who might enter Kinburn, to which he replied: 'I shall do so; but I must inform you that the flames of the burning barracks are, at this moment, very near the grand magazine.'

'I visited the fort the next day to see the result of our fire,' wrote Vieth. 'How they held out as long as they did seemed a marvel, when one looked around the interior. The fortifications were literally pounded into fragments, heavy guns broken, gun carriages in splinters or overturned and destruction was spread everywhere.' Captain Maxwell Earle's comments confirm what Vieth had reported.

'The place is actually shattered and I cannot imagine how they managed to remain inside for so long,' he wrote. 'They had lost about 60 men killed and wounded and I think all but 2 guns dismounted or *hors de combat*. About 60 guns have fallen into our hands and 1150 prisoners, 25 officers.'

There was one late alarm for the expedition when, on the morning of the 18th, the fort at Ochakov on the opposite side of the estuary, was blown up by the Russian garrison before it retreated to Nicholaieff, which gave rise to a rumour that General Liprandi was marching with 20,000 men towards Kinburn. Several British battalions were sent on a patrol to establish the truth of the rumour, and Frederick Vieth was sufficiently concerned to leave his impression of the four-day reconnaissance in which he had taken part:

Our expedition consisted of about 4,500 men and nearly 340 horses. The marching was very heavy, as the sand under our feet gave way at every step. Each man carried besides his knapsack, great-coat and rifle, sixty rounds of ball cartridge and his rations for three days in his haversack. Personally I found it hard enough, for in addition to my rations I had my great-coat, and the Queen's Colour in heavy oilskin covering – no light weight in itself. We marched only about ten miles that day and then bivouacked for the night ... on the evening of the fourth day of our expedition we returned, so very tired and dirty; and cold though the water was at this season of the year, many made a trip to the beach and had a dip in the sea.

Allied casualties for the whole operation had been remarkably light. Just two dead and thirty-two wounded. Vieth found the whole exercise to have been interesting if uneventful. For him, the one incident which he found to be amusing, occurred when one of his men managed to drink himself unconscious when apparently there was no alcohol to be had for miles. The man had, in fact, persuaded a Russian peasant to part with a bottle of 'raki', but what made the situation memorable for Ensign Vieth, was the fact that it had taken six men to carry the man who was 'six feet five inches in height, but only eighteen inches across the shoulders' back to the camp. When Vieth enquired of the officer of the picquet, why it had taken so many, he was told that he had felt it was necessary to send six , '... as the man was so d——d long he was afraid he would break in two'.

Generals Spencer and Bazaine, after selecting the troops who were to repair and garrison the fort, and leaving a few screw driven vessels to guard the estuary, re-embarked with the remaining French and British troops on 30 October, returning to Sevastopol early in November by which time the harbour and the southern half of the city had been in allied hands for almost three months.

The small part the British had played in the capture of Kinburn was apparently a source of irritation to Captain Earle. Writing to his mother on 5 November, he had this to say: 'It is really disheartening to find how much we are daily being reduced to a contingent to the French army. Pelissier has it all his own way and poor old Simpson's want of activity makes us all more or less slaves to the want of the former ... Are we for ever to be the tail end to every French undertaking?'

Kinburn and the earlier attack on Sweaborg had demonstrated, if further proof was necessary, that the allied fleet had the capability to cripple Russia's sea power, both in the Baltic and the Black Sea. But, as the first snows of winter made their appearance, far from contemplating further operations, Pelissier, now that Sevastopol had fallen, voiced his opinion that it was time to reduce the allied army by half to something approaching 70,000, despite the fact that the Russian army remained undefeated. His view found sympathetic support in Paris where Napoleon III argued that to continue the war would entail considerable expense which a depleted treasury could ill afford and was unlikely to bring the Russians to the negotiating table any sooner.

The new mood of pacifism in Paris did little to reassure the politicians at Westminster who felt such a move would merely encourage the Russians to view it as a sign of weakness which could be exploited in order to gain better terms. Indeed Lord Clarendon was sufficiently concerned to exert diplomatic pressure on Napoleon to keep his present force in the Crimea until at least the spring. Lord Lansdowne was sent to Paris with the promise of a joint allied War Council to be held in January to determine the future operations in the Baltic, if the Emperor would agree to maintain a presence in the Crimea.

Lansdowne's suggestion was well received by Napoleon, who agreed with him that it would be unwise to remove a large number of troops in the winter, but he insisted that he was determined not to undertake a third fruitless campaign in the Crimea. The British parliament, who were in a weak position to go it alone, were left with no alternative but to accept the Emperor's promise that he would at least refuse to yield to his generals' requests for further troop withdrawals.

Troop reinforcements of the right quality were becoming something of a problem for the British generals in the Crimea, as Sergeant Albert Mitchell was at pains to point out to the readers of his book, *Recollections of One of the Light Brigade*: 'Many of the recruits sent out to fill up the regiments, both cavalry and infantry, were not the stamp of men to enter on a campaign. Many being mere boys, with rounded faces and rosy cheeks, but in many instances died before they had been weeks in camp, many others being sent home before they had been there a week.' Colonel Sterling in his book *The Highland Brigade*, was doubtless correct in stating: 'The mistake that has been made has been a very common one in our country, viz, not keeping up certain military establishments in peace, because people took it into their heads that war would never come.'

Fortunately the number of troops available to Major General Sir William Codrington had, by now, increased dramatically with the addition of a second Ottoman corps of 20,000, under the command of Lieutenant General Sir Robert Vivian, who had spent a considerable part of his army life in command of sepoys in the East India Company, on active service in Burma. He was a capable and strict disciplinarian who lost no time in turning his new command into a reliable and useful addition to the British force. At long last, with the Foreign Legion battalions and the Sardinians, Codrington now had an army equal in strength to that of Marshal Pelissier's command.

The war, however, was becoming increasingly unpopular with the civil populace on both sides of the Channel and it was perhaps fortunate that with Sevastopol in allied hands, no further campaign was being planned in the Baltic or the Crimea, for Britain could now expect little cooperation from the Ottomans. The Sultan of Turkey was at variance with the British ambassador, Viscount Stratford de Redcliffe, who had returned to Constantinople from the Crimea to find that, in his absence, the Sultan had appointed his brother-in-law Mehmet Ali as Minister of Marine. Not only was Ali corrupt but he had previously been accused of the murder of his Christian mistress and, as a result, had been removed from public life at the insistence of the ambassador. His re-appointment now, was regarded by Stratford de Redcliffe as an insolent rebuff to the measures he had taken to reform the Sultan's court. So incensed was he that, on 3 September, he had written to Clarendon outlining his fears. '... if half of what is rumoured, to be true, the morals of the Palace are undergoing a melancholy decline. I hear of personal expenses threatening the Sovereign with serious pecuniary embarrassment, of vices no less pernicious than detestable, and of resentments kindled in a bosom, naturally just and generous, by the inconvenient fidelity of those who mark the progress of contamination and foresee its results.'

Stratford de Redcliffe's objection to the return of Mehmet Ali met with a noticeable lack of sympathy from the Sultan. While the ambassador had been away visiting the British forces in the Crimea, Turkish attitudes towards the reforming of the Court had hardened and the Sultan made it plain that any interference from London would be extremely disagreeable to him. Much to de Redcliffe's astonishment and anger, the new regime had the full support of the French ambassador to Turkey, Edouard de Thouvenel, who had replaced his predecessor, Benedetti.

Thouvenel further ingratiated himself with the Porte, not only by supporting Mehmet Ali, but by making it known that the British ambassador was reputed to have a less than tactful approach to diplomatic problems. All this had a depressing effect on Stratford de Redcliffe, who was feeling the strain of working long hours, and he admitted to Clarendon that he was unhappy at the thought of the war dragging on, and by his failure to persuade the Porte to mount a relief operation for the garrison at Kars. Eventually, realizing that his usefulness to the troops in the Crimea was drawing to a close, he directed his energies to improving the plight of Christian subjects in the Ottoman Empire and, in this, he was supported by the British and French governments for, during the winter of 1855, the allies were able to bring pressure to bear on Sultan Abd-el-Mejid to respect the rights of the many non Muslims in his country.

In January 1856 the allies met to establish plans for the further conduct of the war. François Canrobert, who still entertained hopes of persuading Sweden to join the allies, felt that a further success in the Baltic, such as the seizure of Kronstadt, would be sufficient to entice them, but the talks achieved little beyond the need to maintain a presence in the Crimea until such time as the Tsar acceded to the allies' terms of surrender. Canrobert's suggestion, although it had found favour with the British Admiralty, had stood little chance of approval for, as Stratford de Redcliffe explained in a letter to Lord Clarendon. '...Canrobert read a very wild scheme for attacking St. Petersburg by land with an army of 60,000 French and an equal number of troops not named, but which I believe were intended to be Swedes. However the scheme was so wild that he concluded by saying that it was impracticable, and that might have saved us the time occupied in reading it ...'

The conference broke up on 21 January with just one viable proposal – a French led attack on the Russian lines of communication from Eupatoria, with the British and Sardinians providing river borne support from Chernaia.

For the soldiers spending a second winter in the Crimea, there was little to occupy their time, save for the satisfying task of destroying the docks in Sevastopol. Most of the troops were aware that peace feelers were in the air, but they were not so naive as to believe that there would be no more fighting. The Russian strong points on the northern side of the city still posed a threat but, by the middle of February, Codrington was informing Panmure that further operations in the Crimea were unlikely.

In fact, by then, many of the veterans had left the Crimea, including Generals Bosquet and Neil, who had returned to Paris, while the British cavalry were at their winter quarters in Constantinople. So, too, was the formidable Mrs Duberly, who had bid a reluctant farewell to a Balaklava she now found to be 'fresh, healthy and even pretty ... rows of trees are planted down the centre street the railway runs, giving dignity and importance to the place,' she wrote. Mrs Henry Duberly also found time to pay a compliment to the correspondent of *The Times*. 'I think the thanks of the army, or a handsome national testimonial ought to be presented to Mr Russell, the eloquent and truthful correspondent of *The Times* as being the mainspring of this happy change.'

Colonel Sterling, disappointed at his failure to gain promotion, had earlier left for Malta. His absence was short lived however for, missing the excitement of the Crimea, he was back with the Highland Division in February. 'I do know war and I hate it,' he confessed, 'but I hate tyranny more, and would fight against it any day!'

He was not to get the opportunity in the Crimea for, with the approach of spring, the end of the conflict was in sight.

Chapter Ten

AN UNEASY PEACE

Apart from the entry into Sevastopol, the last few months of 1855 had been notable only for an inconsequential victory at the Black Sea port of Kinburn. There was a pressing need, particularly in British military circles, to maintain the war in the hope of gaining a spectacular late victory over the Russians. But the Government was realistic enough to accept the fact that Britain did not have the manpower to ensure the successful completion of further operations without the cooperation of the French, and it seemed inevitable that the war would shortly end with a negotiated peace. France had already acknowledged that fact, in spite of giving the impression of wanting to prosecute the war more firmly. The reality was that with the fall of Sevastopol, Count Walewski, the illegitimate son of Napoleon Bonaparte and now the French Minister of Affairs, had already begun secret talks with the Russians through Austrian diplomatic channels. The Russian exchequer was practically exhausted and providing that the allies did not seek humiliating terms, the Tsar had made it known that he was willing to accept Austria acting as an honest broker.

The original terms for a negotiated settlement were based upon an amendment to the 'Four Points' but, when it became known in London that the French Foreign Secretary was negotiating with the Russians through an intermediary, it aroused Clarendon's suspicions that Britain was being forced into 'playing second fiddle' to France in that country's desire to impose terms less harsh than the British Prime Minister thought necessary to curb Russian power.

Britain's influence, however, was waning. France, no matter how damaging it might be to the spirit of good relations, was intent on bringing the war to an end and since France was the dominant military power, it had left Clarendon with little alternative but to join her in the peace process.

From October 1855 to January 1856 the diplomatic negotiations continued apace with each negotiator being guided by self interest and with Britain maintaining a high degree of suspicion regarding Austria's motives. Palmerston, as befitting his reputation for gun-boat diplomacy, wanted to open the campaigning season in the spring, with an attack on Russia through Finland in the north and Georgia in the south. This, of course, was entirely out of the question, for Britain did not have the military means for such an undertaking, and so discussions continued between Napoleon III and Cowley in Paris, which the British ambassador found, at times, quite frustrating.

On 19 November following an unsatisfactory meeting with the Emperor, he could contain his exasperation no longer and wrote to Clarendon as follows:

> I will only add that both the Emperor, who has spoken to me on the subject, and Count Walewski (French foreign minister) are most anxious that the proposal of Count Buol (Austrian foreign minister) that Austria act as an intermediary should be favourably entertained by her Majesty's government. I have not given either of them hopes that this will be the case, though I have assured them of the constant desire of your colleagues to meet the wishes of the Imperial government, as far as your own sense of duty will admit it. I have dwelt more particularly on the great anxiety of her Majesty's government to avoid a repetition of the Vienna Conference by advancement of negotiations which can terminate in no practical result.

Events now took a turn for the worse as far as Britain was concerned when Walewski instructed the French ambassador to return to Vienna and reopen negotiations with Buol and give the impression that Britain agreed to his intervention. Buol however, was far from satisfied that the terms outlined by France were to Austria's advantage. Austrian influence and security in the area could be threatened by a proposed union of Moldavia and Wallachia and he was anxious for Russia to concede more of Bessarabia which would bring the Danube under Austrian control.

The French ambassador, anxious not to prejudice the negotiations at this stage, reluctantly conceded the point, providing that the two major powers retained the right to introduce special conditions to be known as the Fifth Point.

On 18 September, documents outlining the proposals were dispatched to the British Parliament for approval, where they met with a mixed response. Clarendon was of the opinion that the proposals would never be acceptable to the Tsar and therefore would ensure that the war would continue, whilst Queen Victoria thought that if Britain were to reject them outright, or if France refused to support a continuation of the conflict, it would leave Britain isolated and in an undesirable position.

Palmerston was adamant that Austria, a country which had taken no part in the war, should not be instrumental in drawing up the surrender terms. To him Britain's aim was clear – Russian military power had to be crushed, even if it meant fighting alone or simply with the support of Turkey. Palmerston's view, however, was very much in the minority and, when the proposals were discussed in Cabinet they were accepted subject to the Fifth Point, which would allow Britain to raise special conditions should it be in the European interest, being accepted by Austria. This last condition meant that negotiations dragged on well into the new year with Britain insisting that the Aaland Islands in the Baltic be demilitarized in order to protect Sweden from the possibility of Russian aggression occurring in the future.

This France found unacceptable and Napoleon even wrote a polite letter to Queen Victoria asking why Britain thought to question the Austrian initiative. The answer was probably not what the Emperor wished for, acting on the advice of her Prime Minister, the Queen replied that there could be no question of Austria making any territorial demands of Russia and that her government would not feel bound to the Austrian ultimatum.

Eventually a compromise was agreed. Britain dropped her request that the Sea of Azov be neutralized as a condition of the peace treaty but, whilst Waleswki agreed to include the demand for the Aaland Islands to be demilitarized, he signally failed to include it in the papers sent to the Austrian authorities, giving a false impression that there was full agreement on all five points.

Despite the bad feeling which resulted from this devious action on the part of the French foreign secretary, the final draft was dispatched to Vienna on 16 December before being sent on to St Petersburg, where the Austrian ambassador, Count Esterhazy, was instructed to give the Russians eight days in which to accept or refuse the five points outlined in the ultimatum. It was pointed out to Russia that, should she reject them, Austria would break off diplomatic relations and consult Britain and France on the next step, although she had no desire to go to war.

Britain, France and Austria were not alone in manoeuvring to protect their best interests. Tsar Alexander also believed that he could negotiate from a position of strength, encouraged by news at the end of November of General Muraviev's victory at Kars, which had given him a valuable bargaining ploy to set against demands by the allies. His army had yet to be decisively defeated in the field and through diplomatic channels he had learnt that France was anxious for peace. Despite the fact that the war was crippling Russia's exchequer, a recent visit to his army in the Crimea, where he had inspected additional regiments raised in Moscow, had encouraged him to feel that any further attempt on the part of the allies to bring pressure to bear could be successfully resisted.

The arrival of Count Esterhazy in St Petersburg on 28 December with the ultimatum, punctured the Tsar's optimistic air. At a hastily convened council, chaired by the Tsar on 1 January, his ministers discussed this latest development. The point was made by Count Kiselev that a continuation of the war would soon bleed Russia dry and, perhaps, lead to even more humiliating terms. If that should happen, he asked, what guarantee would Russia have that its frontiers would not be weakened by the loss of Poland, Finland and the Caucasus. Because of the blockade, no chemicals could be imported to supplement an almost exhausted stockpile of saltpetre and sulphur needed for the manufacture of gunpowder, and it was becoming increasingly difficult to bring in weapons and provisions from other parts of Russia.

Only one of those present wanted to fight on, but although the general feeling was that to continue the war would be an act of folly, no one was willing to accept the fact of peace at any price. On 5 January the Tsar made it known that he was in favour of most of the terms, but rejected the Fifth Point outright. It left Austria with little alternative but to sever diplomatic relations with Russia thirteen days later.

On the day that Austria took action, the Tsar received a further blow in the form of a telegraph from King Friedrich William of Prussia. It informed him that Prussia supported Austria's proposals and that if they were rejected, Prussia also would be obliged to break off relations between their two countries. Faced not only with the prospect of going to war with Austria, a country which he had once regarded as a friend, but now with the possibility of having Prussia ranged against him, the Tsar began to have second thoughts and, on 15 January, he again met with his advisers in the Winter Palace who assured him that Russia no longer had the means to continue the war and to do so would certainly risk further humiliation. The very next day Russian acceptance of the original terms on offer, were made known to Austria.

News of Russia's change of mind reached Paris on 19 January and was announced by Napoleon III to an allied Council of War the next day, despite Britain's objection to an early negotiated peace. 'England must consult her own interest and her own dignity,' the Foreign Secretary told Sir George Seymour, the British ambassador who, at one time, had represented his country's interest in St Petersburg. But, in a dispatch to Clarendon, Cowley informed the Foreign Secretary that the unanimous opinion in Paris, was 'far more Russian than English' in regard to the suggested proposal.

Lord Palmerston, however, remained clear that there could be no armistice unless Russia agreed to Britain's conditions relating to the Fifth Point in the peace proposal. Unless this was recognized, Cowley pointed out to Napoleon III, all the events of the past two years would have been for nothing and Russia would have escaped relatively unscathed.

Austria was well aware of Britain's position regarding the peace negotiations but Foreign Minister Buol was adamant that Britain could not depart from the ultimatum signed on 14 November without compromising Austria's position with Russia, and now that Russia had committed herself, Buol sought to assure Seymour that Britain's special conditions could be discussed at the Conference and he promised Austria's support for Britain's demands over the Aaland Islands. It did not satisfy Palmerston or Clarendon but, seeing that there was little to be achieved by pursuing the matter further with the Austrian Foreign Minister,

193

they turned to Napoleon who relied upon Britain's support to preserve his crown.

Much depended on the British ambassador in Paris, as far as protocol would allow him in his discussions with the Emperor, to influence opinion in favour of Britain. But, as Napoleon explained, his exchequer was exhausted and his people simply wanted an end to the war. What he did not say was that he had encouraged his government to bear in mind the possibility of developing a closer relationship with Russia in the near future.

Cowley could sympathize with the desire for peace and was realistic enough to write to London on 25 January informing Clarendon that French public opinion would not allow the conclusion of peace to depend upon Britain's particular requirements.

At a dinner the next day for French officers honoured by Queen Victoria, the British ambassador attempted to encourage better relations by ending a toast with the words:

> Before we separate, allow me to propose one toast more. To the establishment of peace! I am not afraid to mention such a toast in the presence of so many soldiers, for they, who know what are the horrors of war, can appreciate, better than others, the blessings of peace. God grant that the negotiations which are about to open, may end in an honourable and lasting peace.

Nevertheless the suspicion persisted in London that Britain had been outmanoeuvred by France and that an unsatisfactory peace would be the likely outcome of any treaty formulated in Paris.

After further talks it was perhaps inevitable that a compromise solution should be reached when the French Foreign Minister contacted his opposite number in St Petersburg to inform him about Britain's special conditions regarding the Aaland Islands. At the same time he assured Britain that France would support her during the forthcoming negotiations.

Russian ministers, who had been well aware of the special conditions attached to clause five, advised the Tsar to accept the proposal and, on 1 February a protocol was signed in Vienna appointing dignitaries to arrange for an armistice and begin final negotiations leading to the acceptance of a peace treaty. The venue for the conference was still to be decided. Vienna had been suggested by Buol, but for obvious reasons it was unacceptable to Britain and Russia. Brussels was proposed by Napoleon III but rejected by Clarendon, who remembered the sympathy extended by the Belgians to the Tsar at the beginning of the war. Eventually, it was the Tsar himself, who entertained hopes of forging closer links with France, who decided the issue when he chose Paris and was supported in his choice by Britain.

There remained several issues to be resolved, the most important being the request by Sardinia and Prussia to be represented. Sardinia's Chief Minister, Count Camillo di Cavour, urged his country's inclusion in the peace talks as a reward for the service it had rendered to the allied cause, and Lord Palmerston had no hesitation in lending his support. But, since Britain had not yet agreed to an armistice, it would be conditional on Sardinia's continued participation in the war. The Austrian Foreign Minister, conscious of the threat it posed to the Austrian Empire, stood alone in his objection to Sardinia's inclusion, putting forward his reason that they were not a great power; but his argument carried little weight and he was quickly overruled by both France and Britain. The inclusion of Prussia however, was a different matter. King Friedrich William's refusal to commit his country during the war, in the opinion of Napoleon, did not merit its presence, and in a later conversation with Cowley, he wondered whether Prussia could be excluded entirely. Eventually, with the agreement of Britain, Prussia was allowed to take part in the final stage of the negotiations.

Meanwhile hostilities in the Crimea continued, although in a less aggressive fashion. 'Seldom is a shot fired now on either side,' commented Ensign Vieth. 'Both Armies seem to have a common idea, viz: that of making preparations for the winter and neither apparently has any intention of attacking or wasting ammunition.'

In the British camp the troops were making the best of a second Russian winter. A rumour that, come the spring, an expedition was to be launched against the Russians in the Caucasus was not received with any great enthusiasm. The first intimation of peace came at the end of January, but in writing to his parents, Lieutenant Henry Clifford could not conceal his scepticism. 'All say we are to have peace,' he wrote. 'I don't believe it yet, but I believe I am the only one out here who does not believe it.' In fact there seemed to be some justification for his pessimism, for the very next day the Russians began an artillery bombardment from their batteries on the north side of Sevastopol which lasted for several days, but no infantry action followed and the next few weeks passed relatively quietly.

The peace conference was convened on 25 February at the Quai d'Orsay with the twelve negotiators sitting at a round table in the Salon des Ambassadeurs. The British were represented by Clarendon and Cowley, the Russians by Counts Orlov and Brunnow, the delegates from the Ottoman Empire were Ali Pasha, and Mohammed Bey, their ambassador in Paris. The Austrian representatives were Buol, and Hubner the ambassador, whilst Sardinia sent Cavour and Villa-Marina. The sessions were held in the afternoon between 1.00 p.m. and 5.00 p.m. with various preliminaries being discussed at the first meeting and, on 28 February a telegram brought the welcome news that an armistice had been signed by the belligerent parties and hostilities in the Crimea were brought to an end.

George Frederick Dallas noted that:

> Today is a rather memorable day to this army as the Armistice was settled and arranged this morning by the various chiefs of staff. I don't quite see the use of it, as it interrupts nothing except active hostilities which in all probability could not take place until April, & all preparations and movements of troops, reinforcements arriving, even the completion of our work of destroying the South Side, go on as usual. On the whole we have somewhat the best of it as they sometimes killed one of us & and we never fired at all at them.

On the day the armistice was signed, Major Ranken tragically met his death whilst supervising the destruction of a large barrack building in the Karabelnaia district of Sevastopol. An explosive charge detonated prematurely, burying him beneath the collapsing masonry. With the period of inactivity which followed the armistice, the senior officers on both sides did their best to impress with ceremonial parades and lavish entertainment. At a review of allied troops, the Russian General Luders expressed his unqualified admiration. 'It was a sight that the many lookers on would never see in their lives again,' confessed Frederick Vieth. 'A line of regiments of infantry, squadrons of cavalry, and batteries of field artillery, that stretched along for eight or nine miles, was certainly an uncommon and imposing spectacle. Of course the Russian General was much pleased, at least he said so in a very complimentary speech.'

'General (*sic*) Pelissier was on the ground in a carriage drawn by four horses,' added Captain Dunscombe, 'the French were delighted with the review and the Sardinians were in ecstasies. Mrs Seacole was there with a cart full of grub, but none of us poor regimental officers could get near it.'

As peace talks continued in Paris, each representative felt himself bound to protect his country's interest. Clarendon and Cowley were united in their distrust of Walewski, the French Foreign Minister, and they were determined not to yield an inch in a stand against Russia, whilst Count Orlov, anxious to avoid a humiliating peace, thought the best way to do that would be by driving a wedge between France and Britain. Orlov had arrived on 22 February and immediately proved to be a tough and able negotiator. He had been instructed to concede the proposal for the Aaland Islands but to remain firm on all others, particularly that concerning the Bessarabian territory. His persuasive manner influenced Napoleon III to the extent that he began to waiver in his support for Britain. Clarendon was not impressed and, although he enjoyed the company of Napoleon, he later admitted to Stratford that he found Napoleon to be, '... so weak that he might just as well be dishonest'.

The first session of the conference dealt with terms for the armistice which were expected to last until the end of March. The next day the real business began with Count Orlov proposing to leave Bomarsund undefended, providing that the demands relating to Bessarabia be dropped in exchange for Kars. Although Russia had abandoned its claim to a general protectorate over the Orthodox population, her religious and cultural ties were as strong as ever and Clarendon was to be proved correct in confiding his suspicions to Lord Palmerston that, 'Russia means to be very troublesome,' and it was the Russian possession of Kars which proved to be Orlov's trump card. Eventually Kars was returned to the Ottomans in exchange for the allies agreeing to a reduction of the territorial demands in Bessarabia.

Additionally, apart from the one concession relating to territory around the mouth of the Danube, Russia's growing power and influence in the Balkans had barely suffered. The situation was fully appreciated by Clarendon but he was quick to recognize that, unless he gave ground, Britain would find itself alone and unsupported. One other controversial point raised was the question of unification of Wallachia and Moldavia into the single state of Romania. France held the view that it would act as a buffer to any future territorial expansion by Russia, but the proposal was opposed by Austria and Turkey, who believed that any such move would be detrimental to regional stability in the Balkans.

It was Clarendon who resolved the issue by arguing in favour of maintaining the integrity of the Ottoman Empire, for that had been the sole reason for the war, and it was finally agreed that the two principalities should have independent administrations while remaining under Ottoman suzerainty.

The third point in the proposals, namely the neutralization of the Black Sea, was also discussed but this proved to be controversial. Russia looked upon the Black Sea as being their territorial waters, and Orlov refused outright to accept any form of naval restriction in the Sea of Azov. Supported by France, he was successful in preserving the naval ship yards at the mouth of the Dniepier and Bug Rivers, but he was forced to accept a demand that the Russian fleet be excluded from the Black Sea.

Following the final meeting on 10 March, Lord Clarendon felt confident enough to confide to the Prime Minister: 'We have made great progress today and peace may almost be looked upon as a *fait accompli*.' Negotiations came to an end and the peace treaty was signed during the afternoon of Sunday, 30 March 1856. The one country which had good reason for feeling resentful that it had achieved very little from the talks, was Sardinia, one of several states who had nurtured hopes of building an Italian nation.

The Foreign Secretary, who fully supported Sardinia, did his best to put its case in his final report to Viscount Palmerston on 17 April. '...the only exception to the general feeling of satisfaction is on the part of Sardinia Piedmontese who lament that no measure should have been taken to remedy the evils under which Italy has so long laboured and who distrust, more perhaps they are quite justified in doing, the policy and intentions of Austria.'

Although Clarendon had drawn attention to Austria's opposition to Italy's desire for unification, there was little interest shown by other delegates and, without the support of Napoleon III, nothing could be done to aid King Victor Emmanuel in obtaining his country's independence. Clarendon left Paris the very next day.

One important measure that did find unanimous agreement, was an amendment to the laws of naval warfare. It had been suggested by Lord Clarendon, who had long been concerned to outlaw privateering, despite the fact that the last incident had occurred more than forty years before and, supported by Count Orlov, the following measures were drawn up.

1. There should be no seizure of enemy goods other than war material, when the ship sailed under a neutral flag.
2. There should be no seizure of neutral goods when sailed under an enemy flag, unless it was contraband of war.
3. In order to be legal, blockades had to be effective and not simply just declared on paper.

The amendment, when it became known, was bitterly opposed by the United States who even went as far as to seek Russian support, but were met with an ignominious rebuff. Faced with the intransigence of Britain and France, America refused to sign the Declaration of Paris. The conference ended on 16 April with a statement that, although governments were to be the sole judge of their own interests, it was the delegates' wish that countries should apply for neutral arbitration before resorting to warfare.

The peace treaty of 30 March was celebrated a fortnight later in the Crimea with a salute of 101 guns from the heights above Balaklava, an occasion not without a few dissenting voices. 'When peace came in 1856,' wrote Lieutenant Wolseley, 'I may truthfully assert that very many in our army regretted it very much, for we felt that whilst at the final assault the French had won – and they well deserved their brilliant success – we had failed.'

On 13 April General Codrington and Marshal Pelissier reviewed a march past of Russian troops on the Mackenzie Heights, which did much to allay fears that the Russian military might not respond favourably to the agreed terms. 'Antagonisms were for the time apparently forgotten, if one might judge from the hospitality extended on both sides,' wrote Frederick Vieth. 'A large Russian band composed of quite 150 or 160 performers played each fine afternoon ... and a pretty compliment was often paid to us, when on the band playing "God Save the Queen", all the Russians present removed their head gear.'

The good relations which now existed between the antagonists were further demonstrated when the Russian General Luders, who had replaced Gorchakoff, reviewed British and French troops on the Balaklava plateau and gave a celebratory lunch for the allied generals and their staff, which so impressed General Codrington that he confessed to Panmure that he had enjoyed a banquet in which caviar, roast beef and two large sturgeon had been served.

The ordinary rank and file, British, French, Turk, Sardinian and Russian, could also now relax and fraternize. In fact, many found that relations were to a remarkable degree, cordial. The Russians, in particular, were pleased to find that they were able to purchase items from the British shops in Balaklava, luxuries which were unobtainable in their own country, and they were constantly amazed by the extent of goods available to their former foes.

Unfortunately, this amiable state of affairs did not last. Before many weeks had passed incidents of drunken brawling became commonplace. Colonel Sterling was convinced that a recent pay award the government had introduced to encourage recruitment, was largely to blame. 'The result of the extra pay given to our soldiers with back pay to the amount of 45s. per man, has been frightful drunkenness,' he wrote. 'They are quite miserable poor fools.'

Captain Earle also widely condemned the award and, in a letter to his father, he pointed out that:

Everything is being done to make the men more comfortable, but the ridiculous amount of pay which they receive only induced them to commit excesses which are unprecedented. The extra 6d a day field allowance and 8d a day whenever they are on fatigue duty increases their pay to nearly 3/-, half a crown too much for any soldier. It only serves to fill the pockets of all the scoundrels who keep canteens in the camp.

Relations between the British and the French quickly deteriorated, the British troops being provoked by the French, boasting of their exploits. Lieutenant Clifford, again in a letter, summed up the situation:

> I'm glad we are not likely to be much longer with the French, for they do not see our improvements in soldiering with pleasure and cannot hide their bitter feelings towards us. With them there is a sort of over bearing manner which their officers will not stand, and on our part we are jealous of their good fortune in the siege and are anxious to have a second try at it and see what we can do now that we are more experienced. I heard lots of fellows say yesterday; 'How I wish those b——-y French would just come out with their sixty thousand men and fight us', and all that sort of thing.

This ill feeling between allies was fortunately short lived for, by the end of April, the task of organizing the return of the troops, stores and equipment to their respective countries, had begun in earnest. The first to go were the Sardinians followed by the French. Writing on 6 June, Captain Dallas told his family:

> You cannot conceive a more utterly desolate scene than a deserted camp, and it's very sad riding past little huts where one has spent a many jolly hour, now emptying and falling to pieces. Two regiments of Guards have gone & the Fusiliers go tomorrow. We shall miss them dreadfully, for I and others spent much of our spare time playing cricket &c at their camps.

Within a few weeks George Frederick Dallas was on his way home, the last British regiment leaving on 12 July 1856.

On 26 July the Royal Fusiliers disembarked at Portsmouth amid scenes of great excitement. Sergeant Gowing was particularly moved by the reception the Fusiliers received. 'They wanted to kill us with kindness,' he wrote, 'for as soon as they got hold of us, it was brandy in front of us, gin in rear of us, rum to the right of us, whisky to the left of us, gin in rear of us, and a crossfire of all kinds of ales and lemonades, to say nothing of the pretty girls, and we got many a broadside from them.'

Diplomatic relations were resumed between Britain and Russia in May, with the British Embassy in St Petersburg being re-established later that summer when it soon became engaged in encouraging the resumption of trade, following the lifting of the blockade in the Baltic.

The Crimean War had been a salutary experience for the British army. Of the 19,500 deaths which had occurred, the greatest majority had resulted from sickness and disease attributed largely to ignorance and poor sanitation. Happily the latter stages of the war were distinguished by marked improvements in the soldiers' living conditions both abroad and at home, although in Britain it was to be 1861 before cesspits were replaced by lavatories in most barracks. The quality of meals improved and better leisure facilities were provided in a bid to curb the drunkenness so common among the lower ranks. These long overdue reforms were brought about largely by an outburst of public indignation, following various journalists' accounts of Crimean mismanagement most notably in the Commissariat.

In the first winter of the Crimean campaign, the troops had been denied an issue of solid fuel since regulations restricted it to home based garrisons. It had not been the fault of Lord Raglan, who had urged the Commissary General, James Filder, to give the men fuel for their fires, but of Filder himself who, in the opinion of many, was totally unfit to manage such a large organization. Now, the absurd ruling over fuel and many other bureaucratic anomalies in the army's system of supply, were no longer to be tolerated. Of more interest to many of the soldiers, who had served in the Crimean campaigns, was the decision to award a clasp for Balaklava to the Crimea medal with its blue and yellow ribbon, in addition to those for Alma, Inkerman and Sevastopol.

But perhaps the greatest innovation introduced by Royal Warrant on 29 January 1856, was a new award for gallantry fashioned from captured Russian cannon to a design by Prince Albert; the Victoria Cross. It was presented personally by Queen Victoria at a specially convened parade held in Hyde Park in June 1856, to no less than sixty-two recipients from a total of 111, among whom was the Hon. Henry Hugh Clifford, for conspicuous gallantry at the Battle of Inkerman.

The ceremony undoubtedly brought back memories of the many campaigns they had fought, by the veterans who witnessed the parade. It certainly did for Sergeant Major Timothy Gowing:

A flood of thoughts came across my mind regarding the different fields I had fought on, and the many hair-breadth escapes I had. I thought of the Alma ... I thought of the wild charge of our handful

202

of cavalry at Balaklava, of our desperate fight at Inkerman, of our terrible work in the trenches ... truly I had much for meditation, verily I had much to be thankful for ...

For a short time, following the ending of hostilities, France enjoyed the best of years. It remained a close ally of Britain and its military reputation had been greatly enhanced by the fall of Sevastopol. But, in little more than three years after the Crimea, Napoleon III had thrown away most of those advantages in a war with Austria over the future of Italy and, in 1870, when France suffered its most humiliating defeat since Waterloo, in a disastrous war with Prussia. Within six months Napoleon III was seeking exile in Britain.

The War of 1870, although of short duration, gave Russia the opportunity of repudiating the clauses of the Paris treaty relating to the neutralizing of the Black Sea and, in October, she began to rebuild the Black Sea Fleet and to restore Sevastopol as a naval base after improving the city's defences. In 1871 at a European Conference held in London, Russia's sovereign rights were restored. As an indirect result, five years later, Russia and Turkey were again brought to the brink of war when the Sultan's forces put down an uprising in the province of Bosnia and Herzegovina. Disraeli refused to intervene in the Balkans following prompting from Russia and Austria, and the controversy dragged on until January 1877 when the new Sultan Abdul Hamid II made it clear that he was no longer interested in pursuing his predecessor's policies. His decision did little to alter Russia's territorial ambitions, for, in April, Russian forces invaded Turkey and in eight months were threatening Constantinople.

It seemed that there was a danger of the Crimean War being repeated when the British public voiced their support for the Sultan. France was too weak militarily to intervene and it was left to the Mediterranean Fleet to steam into the Dardanelles during February 1878. The British fleet remained in those waters until the summer, but with the memory of that previous conflict fresh in the minds of the politicians, good sense prevailed and Lord Salisbury, with Bismarck's approval, summoned a conference in Berlin, at which Serbia, Montenegro and Romania were given their independence. Austria occupied Bosnia Herzegovina, most of Bulgaria was given back to the Sultan and Russia was awarded

Bessarabia. In fact British politicians, conscious of the criticism they had been subjected to from the general public, were only too willing to disregard affairs in Europe as far as possible in favour of the universally held belief that Britain enjoyed a political, moral and economic superiority over the rest of Europe.

The Crimean War had been a conflict governed by the use of black powder and the tactics employed differed little from those of the Napoleonic period. Senior officers led from the front and shared the same risk of death or serious injury as the troops they commanded. It was to be sixty years before Britain found herself involved in another European war; the longest period in British history. Just as Tsar Nicholas had labelled Turkey as 'the sick man of Europe', it was little Serbia, independent of Turkish rule since 1878 who, in June 1914, became the greatest threat to European unity. The war which followed the assassination of Franz Ferdinand and his wife in Sarajevo, quickly resolved itself into a stalemate of trench warfare and massive artillery bombardments, similar to those that took place before Sevastopol. Despite its eventual success, the only real benefit to the British army arising from that campaign, was the rapid transformation of an outdated military system into perhaps one of the most proficient in Europe.

Just as blame for the recent events in Iraq has been laid at the feet of politicians, so the government of Lord Aberdeen, in the opinion of Field Marshal Viscount Wolseley, can be rightfully accused of taking Britain into an unnecessary conflict. 'The Government of the day, plunged stupidly into war with a great European power of whose military strength it was apparently ignorant,' he wrote. 'It had invaded the Crimea with little knowledge of its geography and still less of its rigorous climate.' In a tribute to the men who endured the miseries of the Russian winter without adequate protection, he had this to say: 'Few men now remain to tell the story of that first, that unlucky winter. Many of its incidents have faded from my memory, but if I live for ever I should not forget the manly uncomplaining resignation of our soldiers throughout its appalling miseries.'

No doubt many of the present generation would acknowledge that the soldiers of the Crimea were a breed of men like no other.

SELECT BIBLIOGRAPHY

Alexander, J., *Passages in the life of a soldier*, Hurst & Blackett, London, 1857

Aloysius, M., *Memories of the Crimea*, Burns & Oates, London, 1897

Bell, G., *Rough notes of an old soldier*, Day & Son, London, 1867

Bentley, N. (ed), *Russell's dispatches from the Crimea*, Hill & Wang, London, 1966

Blackwood, Lady Alicia, *A residence in the Bosporus*, Hatchard, London, 1881

Braybrooke, W.L., *Diary*, Edward Stamford, London, 1855

Calthorpe, S.J.G., *Letters from headquarters*, John Murray, London, 1856

Duberly, H., *Journal kept of the Russian War*, Longman Brown Green & Longmans, London, 1855

Gowing, T., *A soldier's experience*, Thomas Forman & Sons, Norwich, 1884

Hamley, F.B., *The campaign of Sebastopol*, Blackwood, Edinburgh, 1855

Hibbert, C., *The destruction of Lord Raglan*, Penguin Books Ltd., London, 1961

Hodasevich, R., *View from within the walls of Sebastopol*, John Murray, London, 1856

Hume, T., *Reminiscences of the Crimea*, Unwin, London, 1894

Kinglake, A.W., *The invasion of the Crimea*, William Blackwood & Sons, London, 1885

Massie, A., *N.A.M. Book of the Crimea War*, Sidgwick & Jackson, London, 2004

Mawson, M.H. (ed), *Eyewitness in the Crimea. The letters of Lt. Col. G.F. Dallas*, Stackpole, London, 2001

Money, A., *Sebastopol*, Richard Bentley, London, 1856

Pack, R., *Sebastopol trenches*, Kerby & Endean, London, 1878

Pennington, W.H., *Left of six hundred*, Waterlow & Sons, London, 1887

Portal, R., *Letters from the Crimea*, Warren & Son (printers),Winchester, 1900

Porter, W., *Life in the trenches*, Longman Brown Green & Longmans, London, 1856

Ranken, G., *Six months at Sebastopol*, publisher unknown, London, 1857

Reilly, E., *Siege of Sebastopol*, Eyre & Spottiswoode, London, 1859

Robins, C. (ed), *Captain Dunscombe's Diary*, Withycut House, Cheshire, 2003

Sterling, A., *The story of the Highland brigade*, John McQueen, London, 1855

Taylor, G.C., *Journal of adventure*, Hurst & Blackett, London, 1856

Tolstoy, L., *Sebastopol*, Walter Scott, London, 1911

Wolseley, Viscount Garnet, *The story of a soldier's life*, Archibald Constable & Co. Ltd., London, 1903

INDEX

Sterling, Colonel Anthony, 15, 16, 31, 32, 36, 87, 90, 92, 153, 156, 185, 188, 200
Strange, Lieutenant Jocelyn, 14, 17, 23, 27, 62, 80, 94, 114, 127, 141
Stratford, Lord de Redcliffe, 62, 94, 164, 166, 167, 185, 186, 187, 197
Sullivan, Bartholomew, 143
Sweaborg, 142, 143, 144, 145, 184

Taylor, George Cavendish, 70, 87, 91, 116, 123, 124, 141, 161
Tchernaya, 73, 145, 147, 149
Telegraph Hill, 21, 22, 23, 25, 28, 29, 35, 146
Thompson, Captain, 166, 168, 169, 170
Todleben, Colonel Franz Eduard, 42, 107, 151
Tolstoy, Count Leo, 13, 99, 112, 113

Tsar Alexander II, 105, 145, 174, 192, 193
Tsar Nicholas, 1, 4, 8, 13, 103, 104, 105, 204

Waleski, Count, 189, 190, 191, 197
Wallachia, 2, 3, 14, 190, 198
Williams, Colonel William Fenwick, 162, 164, 165, 166, 167, 168, 169, 170, 171
Wolseley, Lieutenant later Field Marshal Viscount Garnet Joseph, 5, 93, 105, 126, 130, 134, 159, 199, 204
Wombwell, Captain George, 39, 80, 88

Yenikale, 123, 125

Zouaves, 25, 29, 72, 74, 77, 107, 128, 129, 148, 149, 154, 161, 162